JOHNSON AND BOSWELL

JOHNSON AND BOSWELL

The Transit of Caledonia

PAT ROGERS

CLARENDON PRESS · OXFORD
1995

Oxford University Press, Walton Street, Oxford OX2 6DP

Oxford New York

Athens Auckland Bangkok Bombay
Calcutta Cape Town Dar es Salaam Delhi
Florence Hong Kong Istanbul Karachi
Kuala Lumpur Madras Madrid Melbourne
Mexico City Nairobi Paris Singapore
Taipei Tokyo Toronto

and associated companies in
Berlin Ibadan

Oxford is a trade mark of Oxford University Press

Published in the United States
by Oxford University Press Inc., New York

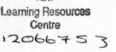

British Library Cataloguing in Publication Data
Data available

Library of Congress Cataloging in Publication Data
Rogers, Pat, 1938–
Johnson and Boswell: The Transit of Caledonia/
Pat Rogers,
Includes bibliographical references (p.   ).
1. Johnson, Samuel, 1709–1784—Journeys—Scotland—Hebrides.
2. Johnson, Samuel, 1709–1784. Journey to the western islands of
Scotland.   3. Boswell, James, 1740–1795. Journal of a tour to the
Hebrides.   4. Boswell, James, 1740–1795—Journeys—Scotland—
Hebrides.   5. Travellers—Scotland—Hebrides—History—18th
century.   6. Authors, Scottish—18th century—Biography.
7. Authors, English—18th century—Biography.   8. Scotland—
Civilization—18th century   I. Title
PR3533.R64 1995   828'.603—dc20   [B]   94–30111
ISBN 0–19–818259–7

1 3 5 7 9 10 8 6 4 2

Typeset by Cambrian Typesetters, Frimley, Surrey
Printed in Great Britain
on acid-free paper by
Bookcraft Ltd.
MidsomerNorton, Avon

FOR
*Sarah, Beth,
Andrew, and Jane*

Je ne connois pas votre Ecosse, sur la carte elle me paroit un peu hors du monde.

(Belle de Zuylen to James Boswell, 16 February 1768)

Acknowledgements

Some chapters of this book have appeared in a slightly different form, as follows: Chapter 3 in Prem Nath (ed.), *Fresh Reflections on Samuel Johnson: Essays in Criticism* (Troy, NY: Whitston, 1987), 328–48; Chapter 4 in P. J. Korshin (ed.), *The Age of Johnson*, 5 (1992), 280–301; Chapter 7 in G. Clingham (ed.), *New Light on Boswell* (Cambridge: Cambridge University Press, 1991), 56–71. Other parts of the book are unpublished. An earlier version of Chapter 2 was given as a plenary lecture at the fifth DeBartolo Conference at the University of South Florida in 1991, and Chapter 4 was given as the Rodney Baine Lecture at the University of Georgia in 1989. I am grateful to publishers and editors for permission to reprint material, and to those who attended the lectures and made valuable suggestions.

I am indebted to Barbara Looney for her active support in bringing the book into being, and to Elizabeth Latshaw for her excellent secretarial work. I should also like to thank the two publishers' readers, who made incisive and constructive criticisms of an earlier draft, and isolated some of its weaknesses with sympathy and tact.

Contents

Abbreviations

The following short forms of reference are used in the text:

IJ   J. W. von Goethe, *Italian Journey*, trans. W. H. Auden and Elizabeth Mayer (n.p.: Pantheon Books, 1962).

JM   *Johnsonian Miscellanies*, ed. G. B. Hill, 2 vols. (Oxford: Clarendon Press, 1897; repr. New York: Barnes and Noble, 1970).

JTC   *Boswell's Correspondence with Hon. Andrew Erskine and Journal of a Tour to Corsica*, ed. G. B. Hill (London: De La Rue, 1879).

JWI   *A Journey to the Western Islands of Scotland*, ed. Mary Lascelles (Yale Edition of *The Works of Samuel Johnson*, ix; New Haven, Conn.: Yale University Press, 1971).

L   *The Letters of Samuel Johnson*, ed. R. W. Chapman, 3 vols. (Oxford: Clarendon Press, 1952).

LSJ   James Boswell, *The Life of Samuel Johnson*, ed. G. B. Hill and L. F. Powell, 6 vols. (Oxford: Clarendon Press, 1934–64). Boswell's *Journal of a Tour to the Hebrides* is cited from vol. v of this edition except where specifically indicated.

Introduction

The chapters which make up this book are grouped around two figures, Samuel Johnson and James Boswell, and in particular around one event. The episode in question was the tour of the Hebrides and Western Islands of Scotland which the two undertook in 1773. Its outcome is to be found principally in the remarkable books which resulted from this undertaking: Johnson's *Journey to the Western Islands of Scotland* (1775), and Boswell's *Journal of a Tour to the Hebrides* (1785). These works do not provide the exclusive focus of the present book, but one or other is present throughout.

The theme of this book could also be defined in terms of Johnson and Boswell's place within the wider world—that is, their relationship to some external developments during their lifetime. These include the transformation of Scottish culture in the years after the second Jacobite rising and the enduring legacy of Jacobitism; the rapid unfolding of the Scottish Enlightenment; the opening-up of the world by means of overseas exploration in the era of Cook and Joseph Banks; the gradual expansion of tourism beyond the traditional aristocratic grand tour, and the quest for new locations (including, after this Scottish jaunt, picturesque Scotland) and the cult of the primitive, where a key role was played by the prose poems of James Macpherson, which turned Ossian into a leading figure within European literature and art for decades to come. There was also the rise of a virulent anti-Scottish feeling around the time of the *North Briton*. All these matters surface, in one way or another, in the text of the two Hebridean narratives, and each enters the argument of this book, although I have not attempted to provide a full account of their multiple manifestations in the thought of the period.

This is not so much a study of the Scottish Enlightenment as such as a series of readings of Johnson and Boswell in their dealings with specific matters which surfaced during their trip to the Hebrides. Again, I do not seek to explore the entire background of travel literature of the age—this has been well covered by earlier scholars. Instead, the book concentrates on those aspects of travel which are relevant to the conception and execution of the tour. These limitations have their consequences for the subject-matter of the chapters which follow. There is nothing about the controversial issue of a Scottish militia, which exercised many minds during the third quarter of the eighteenth century (see *LSJ* ii. 431), and nothing about the science and medicine for which Edinburgh was famous. The concerns of Johnson and Boswell, as they moved from the capital around the perimeter of the nation, lay rather with the science of man, as pioneered by figures like Hume, Kames, Ferguson, Reid, Smith, Monboddo, Hailes, and their contemporaries—and even some of these were largely outside Johnson's ken. What I seek to show is that the central themes uncovered by the *Journey* and the *Tour* were matters widely debated at the time, and not that the two authors were responding to precise contributions to this debate—although in the Conclusion it is argued that Johnson seems to draw on some of the ideas found in Ferguson's *Essay on Civil Society*, and even to foreshadow certain themes of Smith's *Wealth of Nations*.

It scarcely needs to be said that Johnson travelled to Scotland with a full sense of the renown which the Edinburgh school of thinkers and social critics had acquired. He could not have been unaware of the work of David Hume, not just his widely read *History of Great Britain* but also his essays, which frequently address concerns close to Johnson's own. Whatever his dislike for Hume, he was regularly forced to confront the man and his works by Boswell's incessant prompting. There is an instance as adjacent to the Hebridean tour as this exchange reported in *The Life of Samuel Johnson* under the date 30 April 1773: the subject was Goldsmith.

BOSWELL. 'An historian! My dear Sir, you surely will not rank his compilation of the Roman History with the works of other historians of this age?' JOHNSON. 'Why, who are before him?' BOSWELL. 'Hume,— Robertson,—Lord Lyttelton.' JOHNSON. (His antipathy to the Scotch beginning to rise) 'I have not read Hume; but, doubtless, Goldsmith's History is better than the *verbiage* of Robertson, or the foppery of Dalrymple.' (*LSJ* ii. 236–7)

The exchange continues a little longer. The alleged anti-Scottish bias of Johnson will be considered in Chapter 8; we may note here that he is claiming not to have read Hume's *History* specifically, and that his other target was Sir John Dalrymple's *Memoirs of*

Great Britain (1771), which he had criticized, to Boswell's dismay, on 3 April. The better-known Dalrymple, Lord Hailes, had not yet begun to publish his *Annals of Scotland* (1776–9), although his friend Boswell was to transmit sections of the work in progress to Johnson, who made suggestions for their improvement in 1774.

Boswell assembled many notable illuminati to meet Johnson when the great man arrived in Edinburgh. There were two long sessions with William Robertson, Principal of Edinburgh University, and Johnson was also introduced to Adam Ferguson, Lord Hailes, the poet Thomas Blacklock, the physician John Gregory, Sir Alexander Dick, and many others. Several were personal allies of Boswell, and it was part of the younger man's scheme in luring Johnson to Scotland to display his own range of intellectual acquaintances. Further eminent thinkers, including Thomas Reid, were encountered at Aberdeen and Glasgow. Then, when the travellers got back to the capital after their tour, in November, the same array of distinguished persons was wheeled into place, with additional names. Johnson once more came into contact with Lord Monboddo, for instance. The clash of elderly titans which Boswell had engineered during the circuit was one of several such staged confrontations, including the encounter with Lord Auchinleck, Boswell's Whiggish, Presbyterian, and altogether Scottish father— this meeting took place at the family seat near the end of the tour.

Yet of all this there is scarcely a trace in Johnson's narrative. In his second paragraph he dismisses 'Edinburgh, a city too well known to admit description' (*JWI* 3), and launches into the journey northwards. But were the eminent members of the university 'too well known to admit description'? Boswell did not think so. Again, at the end of his peregrination, Johnson passes rapidly over the concluding days, once the travellers have dipped back beyond the Highland line. He makes a hasty excuse for his reticence: 'We now returned to Edinburgh, where I passed some days with men of learning, whose names want no advancement from my commemoration, or with women of elegance, which perhaps disclaims a pedant's praise' (*JWI* 162). All he can find room for is Braidwood's academy for deaf children. Boswell must have been monumentally disappointed. Instead of a resounding tribute to the great Edinburgh names whom he had put on show for Johnson's benefit, a touching little tribute to a small humanitarian enterprise. The great university, pillar of Edinburgh's educational structure, is nowhere

mentioned: instead he notes 'one subject of philosophical curiosity
to be found in Edinburgh, which not other city has to shew'.
Johnson treats the academy as a kind of tourist site for the educated
traveller, and declines to accept Boswell's invitation to hymn the
intellectual achievements of the Athens of the north. (Similarly, late
in the *Journey* he writes: 'to describe a city so much frequented as
Glasgow, is unnecessary': *JWI* 159.)

At some level this must have been a conscious decision. Perhaps
Johnson was issuing a tacit rebuke to the theorists of primitivism
and the students of savage society who had never strayed far from
their metropolis—certainly none had ventured to Skye. The
structure of the *Journey* makes an implicit comment on the nature
of the Scottish enquiry into the state of man. The book, I shall
argue, tests many of the ideas adumbrated in the works of
Enlightenment authors, but it does so by means of fieldwork and
first-hand observation. The theorists are left to sit at their desks in
Edinburgh, and the text of the *Journey* consigns them to a
peripheral role. Nor does Johnson show any desire to hymn the
burgeoning glories of the New Town, erected to create a city fit for
intellectual heroes to live in—the North Bridge had been completed
in 1772.

The method of Johnson's book is part narrative, part discursive.
Whereas the great productions of the Scottish Enlightenment (as,
broadly, with its French equivalent) had been works of pure
analysis, Johnson provides a study of manners and morals,
conducted within that society—on the hoof, so to speak. Emigration is no longer an abstract issue, to be debated at a safe distance,
but an urgent practical affair, brought to the attention of the
travellers by the sight of a ship loaded with emigrants on the point
of setting sail from Skye (see below, p. 216). When writers like
Adam Ferguson mention the Americans, that is native or Indian
Americans, they do so as if they had encountered warring Scythian
tribes in the pages of Herodotus. Johnson, by contrast, writes of
America as a real place, an understandable destination for people
living in extreme deprivation at home; whilst he argues strongly
that emigration is not the answer for the Highlands, his sense of the
human conditions experienced in the wilder regions of Scotland
enables him to attain some fellow-feeling for the plight of these men
and women. His book does not refuse to pass judgement, but it
judges on the basis of empirical evidence.

Naturally, this was not what Boswell wanted at all. His own *Tour* is in part a means of supplying the deficiencies of the *Journey*—deficiencies, that is, in displaying Scottish culture as a whole. Boswell shared many of his friend's views about the Highlands and Islands, where of course he was as much a stranger as the Englishman. But he wanted the story of their trip to include the renown of Edinburgh intellectual life, perversely left out of Johnson's account, and so his own narrative spends pages at the beginning and end on this slighted portion of the tour. Moreover, Boswell devotes careful attention to exchanges with Monboddo, Lord Auchinleck, Lady Macleod, and the Duchess of Argyll, which Johnson had primly concealed—although even he was unwilling to 'exhibit [his] honoured father, and [his] respected friend, as intellectual gladiators, for the entertainment of the publick' (*LSJ* v. 382), so the record here is censored.

By way of prologue to these issues, Chapter 1 addresses a question which appears never to have been directly confronted: why Johnson finally acceded to Boswell's promptings and fulfilled his lifelong dream of a visit to the Hebrides in 1773. The answer suggested is that Johnson, who had just passed his 'climacteric' or sixty-third birthday, was using this traditional marker of the onset of old age to perform a *rite de passage* into his own final stage of life. Scotland was chosen because it represented a flight from the classical ethos of the south in which Johnson had been educated and had spent his writing career. It was, I contend, an autumn journey which was meant to prepare Johnson for the winter of his days. It was, aptly, a key figure in the Scottish Enlightenment, and a member of the Club, Adam Smith, who called the climacteric a 'dangerous promontory of Human life', after rounding which he hoped 'to sail in smooth water for the remainder of [his] days' (see below, p. 15). The Club had been founded in 1764 by Joshua Reynolds and other friends of Johnson; by 1773 it numbered seventeen members, including Boswell (elected that year).

Johnson rounded a promontory of his own during the tour—his sixty-fourth birthday. His departure from Skye, where this event had occurred, was not on smooth water, but in the teeth of a gale. The travellers had been detained on the island for several days because of bad weather—a matter of enough public interest to reach the newspapers. There was a curious parallel here with the opening of *Rasselas*, which Johnson had composed fifteen years before. In that work the leading characters live in a fruitful valley, surrounded by gardens of fragrance amid 'verdure and fertility'. But it is a prison to them, and they feel the need to escape to a wider world of sensations through a cavity in the mountains. On Skye Johnson had seen a barren and harsh landscape, where it was a struggle simply to keep alive. None the less, 'At Dunvegan', he tells us, 'I had tasted lotus, and was in danger of forgetting that I was ever to depart, till Mr Boswell sagely reproached me with my sluggishness and softness' (*JWI* 71). There could be no escape into a primitivist day-dream. Johnson had to re-enter his own life, and that meant entry into old age.

Chapter 2, the longest chapter, argues that Johnson performed directly the opposite of a traditional grand tour when he set out for the northern fastnesses with Boswell. Here I discuss his frustrated hopes of a trip with the Thrales and Baretti to mild southern climes, a frustration which was the more painful since many of his fellow members of the Club had been able to visit the classic ground of Italy. But the journey that he did make can be seen not as second best, but rather as a radical alternative, a wilful reversal of grand-tour norms. The comparison is enforced by looking at the *Italienische Reise* of Goethe, based on a sojourn in Italy which took place only fifteen years after the tour of the Hebrides. In many respects, what Goethe experienced was the ultimate consummation of grand tourism, and we can make the fullest sense of what Johnson undertook if we place his narrative squarely alongside that of Goethe.

Chapter 3 approaches both travel narratives in the context of the excitement generated by overseas discoveries, and especially by the voyages of exploration in the 1760s and early 1770s. Both Johnson and Boswell had many personal contacts with central figures in this activity, including Cook, Banks, Solander, and Phipps. It was not only the Pacific expeditions which aroused the intense curiosity of educated Europeans, though these were the most dramatic examples of the tendency at work, and had the most obvious literary sequel in Diderot's *Supplément au voyage de Bougainville*. I argue further that the European travels of Baretti and Burney left an obvious mark on the Hebridean narratives.

There is a direct link to Chapter 4, which endeavours to forge the unlikely pairing of Johnson and Omai, the Tahitian brought to England by Cook's party. Omai set out on his long journey to

Europe whilst Johnson and Boswell were actually in the midst of their journey, and he became a familiar figure to the Club and what might be termed the extended Johnsonian circle, including Hester Thrale and Fanny Burney. Underlying this chapter is the debate about the nature of such concepts as the primitive, the savage, and the barbarian. This was an area of intellectual concern which had become the particular property of Scottish Enlightenment figures, among them David Hume, Adam Smith, and Adam Ferguson. And again the currency of Ossian looms behind the debate.

Hester Thrale appears once more in Chapter 5. This may appear to be the most circumscribed and technical portion of the book, but it has a relevant function. Its main concern is to establish the relation between the printed narrative of Johnson's *Journey* and the series of newsletters that he sent to the Thrales at Southwark describing the progress of his trip. However, in order to understand why Johnson decided to add or exclude materials when he came to write his *Journey* in 1774, we need to consider such matters as his possible anxieties over the Scottish response to his narrative. Surprisingly, no detailed attention has ever been given to this comparative exercise, and the analysis may reasonably claim to offer some insights into the process of composition of the *Journey*.

In Chapter 6 the focus shifts to Boswell, and particularly to his motives for undertaking the tour. Here I contend that Boswell was actuated in large part by his desire to re-enact the flight of the Pretender after the battle of Culloden in 1746. His desire to identify with Charles Edward was based firstly on his lingering affection for a semi-mythical feudal Scotland, which in turn proceeded from a desire to acknowledge the Scot in himself. Rather than express his para-Jacobite sympathies directly, he projected attributes of the Pretender on to his companion Johnson. But he also wanted to identify with the hardiness of the Prince, and to replicate some of the arduous experiences the latter had undergone. Just as he had tried to model himself on the brave and independent Corsican freedom fighter Pasquale Paoli, so he wished to take on the role of an adventurous partisan in the Scottish Highlands. The itinerary of the tour was devised so as to make sustained contact with the Prince's flight through the heather; and matters were contrived so that one hero, Johnson, should sleep in the bed which the other hero, Charles Edward, had occupied at Kingsburgh. The argument of this chapter seeks to show that the interpolated narrative of 'the

Wanderer' connects in very concrete and explicit ways with the surrounding narrative of 'the Rambler'.

Boswell's private anxieties receive more attention in Chapter 7. This deals with the Scotticism, which is a markedly idiomatic use of the language by Scots, either in writing or in speech. Boswell was not alone in his worries over the Scotticism; it plagued authors as distinguished as Hume, and it arrogated the attention of an august body of Edinburgh illuminati known as the Select Society. Nevertheless, Boswell's linguistic worries were compounded by his mixed feeling about his own nationality, as Hume's, for instance, were not. The tour he made with Johnson was, *inter alia*, a way of testing his own Scottish identity, and only a short step separates issues of linguistic uncertainty from issues of political and cultural nationhood in the aftermath of Culloden.

The final chapter concerns an issue hovering behind the *Journey*: that is, the moral panic which grew up in England in the third quarter of the eighteenth century on the subject of Scottish influence. This phase of anti-Scottish feeling is a familiar datum in histories of the period, since it finds expression in such diverse fields as politics, literature, painting, and architecture. But there is no connected treatment of the issue in its most specific aspects—again a surprising omission, when one considers that figures such as Hume, John Wilkes, the Earl of Bute, Smollett, and others of comparable stature are involved in the story. More pertinently, there is a direct link here with the content and reception of Johnson's own *Journey*, and again with Boswell's own anxieties.

The Conclusion attempts briefly to draw together various threads of argument and to make whatever general deductions seem feasible. In particular, I seek to locate the findings regarding the two books based on the 1773 trip within the more general Enlightenment debates already mentioned.

In an appendix, Lord Monboddo is brought together with the travellers in order to show how complex issues underlie a single famous episode, and to illustrate the interconnections between such themes as Ossian and the state of primitive society.

Most recent discussion of Johnson and Boswell has concentrated on the inner man. Emphasis generally lies on their private psychological struggles and, indeed, on the pathology of their behaviour. There are good reasons for such an approach, but it does not tell the whole truth. Johnson's was a reactive personality.

Boswell's was deeply insecure. They both felt the impress of their age, and their literary achievement can be fully understood only if we contemplate their work as it was composed, amid the storm and stress of the times. This is particularly so with regard to the books they wrote about the Hebridean journey. They made the trip at a fraught moment in Scottish history, and they came into physical proximity with the primitive at the very moment when this concept floated on the air of every soirée in Edinburgh, London, and Paris. At the precise juncture when the idea of progress in human civilization became a serious talking-point, almost for the first time in recorded history, the two men visited a scene where the theses of the philosophic community were being tested in real life. To read these texts without an awareness of the battles of ideas which were being fought out in the 1760s and 1770s would be like reading *Paradise Lost* with no sense of the political and theological struggles of the seventeenth century, or reading *Childe Harold* in total detachment from the Napoleonic wars. The chapters that follow are an effort to recover the immediate context of the journey and to define some of the external forces which bore upon the travellers. This book seeks to show that even figures as individual, as self-tormented, and as inwardly complex as Johnson and Boswell did, after all, live in a wider world.

I

'Trembling on the Brink of his own Climacterick': Johnson's *Journey to the Western Islands* and the Onset of Old Age

> Lord! what a degree of strenth and stability, you have given to the Crutches of an Old man, who last week, climd to the very top of the grand Climaterial hill, which had three score and three small hills, to pass, before we arrive at its summit. In passing some of these, my journey has been very much chequerd with a variety of uncommon adventures. And I now consider myself at liberty to smoak the pipe of Old age, alongst with some Veterans . . .
>
> (Sir Alexander Dick to Boswell, 1 November 1766)

Samuel Johnson celebrated his sixty-fourth birthday on the island of Skye. He had arrived with James Boswell on 2 September 1773, and was detained on the island by bad weather until 3 October. The birthday itself fell on 18 September (this was the New Style date that he observed after 1752; at the time of his birth in 1709 the day was 7 September). As we shall see, Johnson was not anxious to make much of the occasion; but his own text in the published account of his journey reveals a hidden consciousness of this especially significant date.

In the centre of his *Journey*, Johnson devotes several pages to a general review of the manners and mores of Skye. This is headed 'Ostig in Skye', referring to the tiny settlement in the south of the island where the travellers were awaiting a fair wind: they had reached this spot on 28 September. At one point the discussion of life in 'primitive' surroundings turns to the question of longevity:

It is generally supposed, that life is longer in places where there are fewer opportunities of luxury; but I found no instance here of extraordinary longevity. A cottager grows old over his oaten cakes, like a citizen at a turtle feast. He is indeed seldom incommoded by corpulence. Poverty preserves him from sinking under the burden of himself, but he escapes no other injury of time. Instances of long life are often related, which those who hear them are more willing to credit than examine. To be told that any man has attained a hundred years, gives hope and comfort to him who stands trembling on the brink of his own climacterick. (*JWI* 84)

As often in the text, a submerged personal meaning seems to underlie the confident human generalities. Johnson is alluding to a venerable and distinct body of thought concerning the process of human ageing; but he calls up a particular current of ideas in his final phrase. I intend to look first at the wider background of these ideas and then to consider their possible application to Johnson himself.

I

Take, for instance, the Life of Man, which is the Difficulty of Birth, the Difficulty of Death, and the Difficulty of the Grand Climacteric.

LECTOR. What is the Grand Climacteric?

AUCTOR. I have no time to tell you, for it would lead us into a discussion on Astrology . . .

(Hilaire Belloc, *The Path to Rome*)

The entry for the noun *climacteric* in *OED* (1st edn.) contains the following:

A critical stage in human life; a point at which the person was supposed to be specially liable to a change in health or fortune. According to some, all the years denoted by the multiples of 7 . . . were climacterics; others admitted only the odd climacterics (7, 21, 35, etc.); some also included the multiples of 9. *Grand* (*great*) *climacteric* (sometimes simply *the climacteric*): the 63rd year of life (63 = 7 × 9), supposed to be specially critical. (According to some, the 81st year (81 = 9 × 9) was also a grand climacteric.) The phrase appears to have been taken immediately from the Spanish.

The citations under this entry date from 1634, and include passages from Dryden's translation of the *Aeneid*, Addison, *Joseph Andrews*, and *Don Juan*. A second transferred sense was that of 'a critical period, point, or epoch in any career or course': the citations include a letter from Pope to John Arbuthnot. We may also note the adjectival form of the word, defined by *OED* as 'critical, fatal'. The secondary sense recorded here is 'phys[ical] and med[ical]': 'Applied to that period of life (usually between the ages of 45 and 60) at which the vital forces begin to decline (in women coinciding with the "change of life")'. A nineteenth-century usage evolved, with 'climacteric disease' applied to a loss of strength in middle and later years. The other form, *climacterical*, is recorded from 1590 to 1839, the last from De Quincey. This is synonymous with the simple adjective *climacteric*, but can mean 'critical, dangerous'.

It is natural to fill in the lexicographic picture by consulting Johnson's own *Dictionary of the English Language*. Unsurprisingly, we find the definition corresponds closely with what we have found in *OED*. For the noun, Johnson provides similar information, in a slightly more discursive form: 'Certain observable years are supposed to be attended with some considerable changes in the body . . . [the ages of 7, 21, 49, 63, and 81 are cited] which last two are called the grand *climacteric*.'[1] Citations are made from Browne's *Pseudodoxia Epidemica* (*Vulgar Errors*; perhaps Johnson's way of indicating his own scepticism) and from one of Pope's letters, amongst other sources. Pope writes of his elderly mother, for whom every day is a *climacteric* at her great age. Johnson has an additional noun, *climacter*, defined as 'A certain space of time, or progression of years, which is supposed to end in a critical and dangerous time'. There is nothing especially noteworthy about the entries supplied by Johnson, although we may note a slightly stronger emphasis on purely corporeal effects than emerges from *OED*: the stress is on changes 'supposed to befall the body' (*climacteric*, adj.).

Medical writers had long recognized the climacteric as a useful notion, if not always a physical reality.[2] A characteristic entry in

[1] Samuel Johnson, *A Dictionary of the English Language* (London, 1755), sig. 4R 1r.

[2] Sources cited in the text are: Ephraim Chambers, *Cyclopaedia: Or, An Universal Dictionary of Arts and Sciences* (London: J. and J. Knapton, 1728), i. 237 (subsequent editions, from the second of 1738, reproduce virtually the same material with only minor changes); John Harris, *Lexicon Technicum: Or, An Universal Dictionary of Arts and Sciences* (London: D. Browne, 1708), sig. Tv; John Quincy, *Lexicon Physico-Medicum: A Dictionary of Physics Physiology and Chemistry as related to Medicine and Biology*, 4th ed. (London: J. Osborn and T. Longman, 1730), 84. I am extremely grateful to Dr Paul Baines for help and advice in tracking down this material.

Ephraim Chambers's *Cyclopaedia* (1728) lays out not just the astrological base for the beliefs involved, but also provides a potted history of the notion.

CLIMACTERIC, *Annus Climacterius*, a critical Year, wherein, according to the Astrologers, there is some very notable Alteration in the Body to arise; and a Person stands in great danger of Death. See CRITICAL [the cross-reference is to 'critical days' in illnesses, observed to tåke place on the 7th, 14th and 20th [*sic*] days].

The first *Climacteric* is the seventh Year of a Man's Life; the rest are Multiples of the first, as 21, 49, 56, 63, and 81; which two last are called the *Grand Climacterics*, and the Dangers here suppos'd more imminent.

The Opinion has a great deal of Antiquity on its side. *Aulus Gellius* says, it was borrow'd from the *Chaldeans*; who might probably have received it from *Pythagoras*, whose Philosophy turn'd much on Numbers; and who imagin'd an extraordinary Virtue in the Number 7.

Marc. Ficinus gives us the Foundation of the Opinion: He tells us, there is a Year assign'd for each Planet to rule over the Body of Man, each in his turn; now, *Saturn* being the most malific Planet of all, every seventh Year, which falls to his Lot, becomes very dangerous; especially those of 63 and 81, when the Person is already advanc'd in Years.

Some hold, according to this Doctrine, every seventh Year an establish'd *Climacteric*; but others only allow the Title to those produc'd by the Multiplication of the *climacterical* Space by an odd Number 3, 5, 7, 9, &c. Others observe every ninth Year as a *Climacteric*.

Chambers goes on to cite classical treatments of the topic:

Hevelius has a Volume under the Title of *Annus Climacterius*; describing the Loss he sustain'd in the burning of his Observatory, &c. which it seems happen'd in his first *grand Climacteric*.

Suetonius says, *Augustus* congratulated his Nephew upon his having pass'd his first *grand Climacteric*, whereof he was very apprehensive.

Authors on the Subject, are *Plato, Cicero, Macrobius, Aulus Gellius*, among the Antients; *Argol, Maginus*, and *Salmasius* among the Moderns. *S. Augustin, S. Ambrose, Beda*, and *Boetius* countenance the Opinion.

The word *Climacteric* comes from the Greek κλιμαξ, κλιμαχος, *Scala*; q. d. by a Scale, or Degrees.

Among works of a more narrowly technical bent, a typical description is found in John Harris's *Lexicon Technicum* (1704), cited here from the second edition of 1708:

CLIMACTERICAL Years, are certain observable Years, which are supposed to be attended with some grand Mutation of Life or Fortune; as the 7th Year, the 21st, (made up of three times seven) the 49th, (made of 7 times 7) and the 63d (being 9 times 7) and the 81st, (which is 9 times 9) which two last are called the *Grand Climactericks*. *Aulus Gellius* saith, This Whim came from the *Chaldeans* first, and tis probable *Pythagoras* had it from them, who used to talk much of the Efficacy of the Number 7, with which he was mightily in love.

This treatment seems to have been borrowed wholesale by John Quincy in his *Lexicon Physico-Medicum* (1719), where exactly the same facts and allusions are simply repeated in slightly different words.

  A more sustained discussion than that found in the technical works is that of Sir Thomas Browne, who devotes a long section of *Pseudodoxia Epidemica* (1646) to a dismissive chapter (IV. xii) 'Of the great Climacterical year, that is Sixty three'. Browne, of course, was a major source of quotations for the *Dictionary* and the subject of one of the most interesting of Johnson's shorter biographies. He mentions the superstitious associations of the numbers 7 and 9, and proceeds:

And so perhaps hath it happened unto the numbers 7 and 9, which multiplied into themselves do make up Sixty three, commonly esteemed the greater Climacterical of our lives. For the daies of men are usually cast up by Septenaries, and every seventh year conceived to carry some altering character with it, either in the temper of body, mind or both. But among all other, three are most remarkable, that is, 7 times 7 or fourty nine, 9 times 9 or eighty one, and 7 times 9 or the year of Sixty three; which is conceived to carry with it the most considerable fatality; and consisting of both the other numbers was apprehended to comprise the vertue of either: is therefore expected and entertained with fear, and esteemed a favour of fate to pass it over. Which notwithstanding many suspect to be but a Panick terrour, and men to fear they justly know not what: and to speak indifferently, I find no satisfaction, nor any sufficiency in the received grounds to establish a rational fear.

The author immediately launches into a series of refutations of this doctrine, exploring the inaccuracies, illogicalities, and fallacies of the astrological and pseudo-scientific justifications for the belief. He explodes the biblical sources claimed for the notion, and points out that 'The Psalms of Moses hath mentioned a year of danger differing from all these: and that is ten times 7 or seventy; for so it is said, *The daies of Man are three-score and ten.*' A host of arguments is brought to bear, many of them relating to mistaken chronology, and all tending to show the unreliability of the entire doctrine.

Vulgar errors only get to be so because enough people accept them as the truth. It is clear that many of the beliefs Browne was attacking, including his very next instance, 'Of the Canicular or Dog-daies', preserved and even increased their hold on the popular imagination in the period following Browne's death. Astrology, as we have often been reminded, did not vanish in the floodlight of Newtonian science. Even educated people still clung to vestiges of the old faith well into the supposed age of reason.[3]

It would not be difficult to show that the usage we are examining here survived as a familiar locution into Johnson's time, as it was employed by his friends and contemporaries. For example, Adam Smith wrote to a fellow member of the Club, Bishop John Douglas, in March 1787: 'This year I am in my grand Climacteric; and the state of my health has been a good deal worse than usual.'[4] Smith seems to feel not just that he is undergoing a normal ageing process, but that the advent of his sixty-fourth year (as we should reckon it, since he was born in 1723) heralded a distinct decline, as it were, of itself. More facetiously, William Cowper wrote to his cousin in May 1767: 'I dare say you condole with me upon poor A——'s publication. Surely the wrong Side of the grand Climacteric is no Season for rhyming'—the poet's uncle, Ashley Cowper, had produced a book of verse.[5] And as we shall see presently, Mrs Piozzi was to take note of her own climacteric in *Thraliana*.

None the less, Johnson seems to have preserved an especially acute awareness of this traditional notion. Ageing bore in on his imagination with particular force because of his horror of death—a topic too well documented to need rehearsal here. Again, his habit

---

[3] *The Works of Sir Thomas Browne*, ed. G. Keynes, 4 vols. (Chicago: University of Chicago Press, 1964), ii. 306–23 (here pp. 307, 315). For the survival of folk beliefs, see the classic study by Keith Thomas, *Religion and the Decline of Magic* (London: Weidenfeld and Nicholson, 1971). Thomas devotes a few sentences specifically to the climacteric (pp. 616–17). Even when the idea weakened that the sixty-third year was likely to be fatal, the belief that it marked the beginning of physical decline may have lasted.

[4] *The Correspondence of Adam Smith*, ed. E. C. Mossner and I. S. Ross (Oxford: Clarendon Press, 1977), 301. Smith proceeds: 'I begin to flatter myself that, with good pilotage, I shall be able to weather this dangerous promontory of Human life; after which I hope to sail in smooth water for the remainder of my days.'

[5] *The Letters and Writings of William Cowper*, ed. J. King and C. Ryskamp, 5 vols. (Oxford: Clarendon Press, 1979–86), i. 165.

of minute self-scrutiny in his private journal drew attention to dates and anniversaries, with particular prayers regularly set out to commemorate events such as his wife's death. More widely, Johnson harboured an almost obsessive concern with using time wisely: not for nothing was the parable of the talents one of his favourite biblical texts. It follows that he observed the progress of passing years with a peculiarly intense anxiety.

One of the clearest signs of the impress of the idea on Johnson's mind comes in the *Rambler*, 151 (27 August 1751), which he devoted to the successive stages of mental life. He showed how particular passions predominate in the human breast during different phases of human existence. But underlying the paper is a parallel with bodily changes, set out at the start:

The writers of medicine and physiology have traced with great appearance of accuracy, the effects of time upon the human body, by marking the various periods of the constitution, and the several stages by which animal life makes its progress from infancy to decrepitude. Though their observations have not enabled them to discover how manhood may be accelerated, or old age retarded, yet surely if they be considered only as the amusements of curiosity, they are of equal importance with conjectures on things more remote, with catalogues of the fixed stars, and calculations of the bulk of planets.

It had been a task worthy of the moral philosophers to have considered with equal care the climactericks of the mind; to have pointed out the time at which every passion begins and ceases to predominate, and noted the regular variations of desire, and the succession of one appetite to another.

The *Rambler* essay conducts a fairly orthodox review of the concerns of various age-groups, ending with a picture of avarice in old age:

The man whose vigour and alacrity begin to foresake him, by degrees contracts his designs, remits his former multiplicity of persuits, and extends no longer his regard to any other honour than the reputation of wealth, or any other influence than its power. Avarice is generally the last passion of those lives on which the first part had been squandered in pleasure, and the second devoted to ambition. He that sinks under the fatigue of getting wealth, lulls his age with the milder business of saving it.[6]

---

[6] *The Rambler*, ed. W. J. Bate and A. B. Strauss, Yale ed. of *The Works of Samuel Johnson*, in progress: vols. i–x, xiv–xvi published (New Haven, Conn.: Yale University Press, 1969), v. 37–8, 41–2.

Johnson wrote this at the age of 41; he might conceivably have thought that his middle years were marked by ambition, but he cannot have supposed that his youth had been squandered in pleasure. None the less, the idea of time squandered unmistakably points at one of his recurrent modes of self-criticism.

In another sense, the essay falls into line with the tendency of the Hanoverians to demarcate separate stages of life and to attribute almost reified qualities to the successive periods of human existence. The habit went back to classical and medieval thinkers, of course, but in the eighteenth century it acquired a certain precision and finality appropriate to the era which saw the invention of the ethical calculus. Thus in 1774, just one year after the Hebridean jaunt, Sir William Jones—soon to be a member of the Club, and a close acquaintance of Johnson—wrote to his pupil Lord Althorp of a scheme that he had invented, that is the 'andrometer', involving 'a mathematical scale of achievements proper to man, divided in quinquennial periods over the life span'.[7] The extreme and absurd strictness of this scale is revealing, even though most educational theorists set out expectations for intellectual progress in a less mechanical way (and one might recall that Hester Thrale was able to grade her friends on a scale of one to twenty for qualities ranging from morality to person and voice.)[8]

It is true that on one occasion when Boswell brought up the standard 'divisions' of life for debate, Johnson bad-temperedly dismissed the topic; but as the famous encounter with Oliver Edwards reminds us, he had a particular dislike of any talk about senility. The conversation took place at Bolt Court in April 1778, prompted by a dinner which the painter Allan Ramsay had given the previous evening and which had been attended by Johnson and Boswell:

BOSWELL. 'What I admire in Ramsay, is his continuing to be so young.' JOHNSON. 'Why, yes, Sir, it is to be admired. I value myself upon this, that there is nothing of the old man in my conversation. I am now sixty-eight, and I have no more of it than at twenty-eight.' BOSWELL. 'But, Sir, would

---

[7] *The Letters of Sir William Jones*, ed. G. Cannon, 2 vols. (Oxford: Clarendon Press, 1970), i. 175.

[8] *Thraliana: The Diary of Mrs Hester Lynch Thrale (later Mrs Piozzi) 1776–1809*, ed. K. C. Balderston, 2nd edn., 2 vols. (Oxford: Clarendon Press, 1951), i. 329–31.

not you wish to know old age? He who is never an old man, does not know
the whole of human life; for old age is one of the divisions of it.'
JOHNSON. 'Nay, Sir, what talk is this?' BOSWELL. 'I mean, Sir, the
Sphinx's description of it;—morning, noon, and night. I would know
night, as well as morning and noon.' JOHNSON. 'What, Sir, would you
know what it is to feel the evils of old age? Would you have the gout?
Would you have decrepitude?'—Seeing him heated, I would not argue any
farther; but I was confident that I was in the right. I would, in due time, be
a Nestor, an elder of the people; and there *should* be some difference
between the conversation of twenty-eight and sixty-eight. A grave picture
should not be gay. There is a serene, solemn, placid old age. (*LSJ* iii. 336–7)

It is a supplementary irony that Boswell, the would-be Nestor, the
perpetual *laudator temporis acti*, was never to attain the status of
venerable sage: he barely passed the age Johnson had reached when
the two men first met. But it would be difficult to claim that
Johnson ever came to know the 'serene, solemn, placid old age' of
Boswell's gushing hopes. Most typologies that were devised to set
out the 'ages of man' in order attributed a cooling of passion to the
later years—indeed, quite specifically to the post-climacteric years:
the allocation of avarice to old age (as in the *Rambler* paper) was
originally born of the belief that colder and drier humours
predominated with advancing age. As Byron says at the end of the
first canto of *Don Juan*: 'So for a good old-gentlemanly vice, | I
think I must take up with avarice.'[9]

As it happens, avarice is almost the last quality that one would
impute to Johnson, at any period of his life. Nevertheless, he moved
into his later years altogether aware of received views on the likely
concomitants of senility, both physical and mental. His obvious
determination not to decline into the lean and slippered pantaloon,
expressed in the conversation about Ramsay but apparent everywhere, represents a conscious bid to defeat general expectations.
And it is surely obvious that his resolution to undertake the
arduous and possibly dangerous Hebridean trip at the age of 63 can
be aligned with this fixed intention of not growing old, or at least
old in the conventional sense. It may be that some of his

---

[9] *Don Juan*, ed. T. G. Steffan, E. Steffan, and W. W. Pratt (Harmondsworth:
Penguin, 1973), 100. Byron actually uses the key term of this chapter when writing of
Catherine the Great in canto X, stanza 46: 'Though her years were waning, | Her
climacteric teased her like her teens' (p. 386).

acquaintances tried to persuade him not to go, as Hannah More certainly stood out against the planned trip to Italy three years later: 'I lament his undertaking such a journey at his time of life with beginning infirmities; I hope he will not leave his bones on classic ground' (*JM* ii. 188). The conditions to be experienced in the north of Scotland in the autumn were more severe in many ways than anything to be anticipated on a Mediterranean voyage. For Johnson to undertake the Scottish journey 'at his time of life' was a transgression of the ageist dogmas of the period, and fully characteristic of the man for that very reason.

Among birthday entries in his spiritual diary, we might note one for the year 1764: 'This is my fifty sixth birthday, the day on which I have concluded fifty five of my years.' The last clause here is in consonance with modern usage, but the former statement is not (we should term it the 'fifty-fifth birthday', since we omit the actual day of birth in calculating the ordinal number). Two years before the Hebridean trip, Johnson entered in his journal under 18 September 1771: 'I am now come to my sixty-third year,' again in line with present-day usage. This could have been an ominous juncture; as usual, Johnson goes on to meditate on the use he has made of the past year. He reflects: 'Perhaps Providence has yet some use for the remnant of my life.' But we do not have an entry for the following year, when Johnson actually attained the age of 63. We have to move forward to an entry he made in his diary whilst on Skye, dated 24 September 1773: 'On Sunday last was my sixty fourth birthday. I might perhaps have forgotten it, had not Boswel told me of it'—and, to his greater distress, told the people who were entertaining him as well.[10] The matter is mentioned briefly in Boswell's *Journal of a Tour to the Hebrides*: 'Before breakfast, Dr Johnson came up to my room, to forbid me to mention that this was his birth-day; but I told him I had done it already; at which he was displeased; I suppose from wishing to have nothing particular

---

[10] *Diaries, Prayers, Annals*, ed. E. L. McAdam, jun., D. Hyde, and M. Hyde, Yale ed. of *The Works of Samuel Johnson*, i. (New Haven, Conn.: Yale University Press, 1958), 81, 142, 160. The last entry reads: 'But when I consider my age, and the broken state of my body, I have great reason to fear lest Death should lay hold upon me, while I am only yet designing to live.' He notes that 'The last [sixty-fourth] year is added to those of which little use has been made', and that exercise and change of air have failed to strengthen his body.

done on his account' (*LSJ* v. 222). In the *Journey* Johnson maintained a dignified silence in his account of this portion of the tour, stating that 'At Dunvegan I had tasted lotus' (*JWI* 71) and praising the hospitality of the Macleod family. However, in private he was not so reticent: writing to Hester Thrale in Southwark on 21 September, he particularized Boswell's offence:

I cannot forbear to interrupt my Narrative. Boswel, with some of his troublesome kindness, has informed this family, and reminded me that the eighteenth of September is my birthday. The return of my Birthday, if I remember it, fills me with thoughts which it seems to be the general care of humanity to escape. I can now look back upon threescore and four years, in which little has been done, and little has been enjoyed, a life diversified by misery, spent part in the sluggishness of penury, and part under the violence of pain, in gloomy discontent, or importunate distress. But perhaps I am better than I should have been, if I had been less afflicted. With this I will try to be content. (*L* i. 356)

In drawing attention to the birthday, Boswell causes Johnson to 'interrupt' his narrative to Hester Thrale; but he also interrupts the chosen narrative of Johnson's progress through Scotland—the willed sequence of impressions and experiences. The older man is obliged now to 'look back upon threescore and four years', when his ostensible desire is to concentrate upon the present, and to regale Mrs Thrale with his current adventures in the Hebrides. The impatience expressed is only partly directed at Boswell. It is also a recognition of how illusory any pretence of 'getting away from it all' must be for any one with Johnson's degree of introspection and active moral censorship of his own behaviour. There may be something disingenuous in the phrase 'if I remember it', for his diary suggests that he regularly commemorated the event, and that he wrote some searching passages of self-examination on the anniversary.

Why, then, did he wish to suppress his birthday in 1773? Perhaps, as Boswell surmised, he wished to have 'nothing particular done on his account'. But he was ready enough to be fêted at other times during the journey, to march through the streets of Aberdeen with his 'burgess-ticket' in his hat, and to accept the recognition of dukes, judges, lairds, and ministers. For some reason, the need for privacy was to grow much more urgent as the date of his birthday came round.

II

It has seldom, if ever, been observed that the opening sentences of the two narratives of the Hebridean expedition fix on exactly the same point. In his *Journey* Johnson writes: 'I had desired to visit the *Hebrides*, or Western Islands of Scotland, so long, that I scarcely remember how the wish was originally excited; and was in the Autumn of 1773 induced to undertake the journey, by finding in Mr Boswell a companion, whose acuteness would help my inquiry . . .' (*JWI* 3). Boswell starts his *Tour* with the same circumstances, viewed from a different angle:

Dr Johnson had for many years given me hopes that we should go together, and visit the Hebrides. Martin's Account of those islands had impressed us with a notion that we might there contemplate a system of life almost totally different from what we had been accustomed to see; and, to find simplicity and wildness, and all the circumstances of remote time or place, so near to our great native island, was an object within the reach of reasonable curiosity. (*LSJ* v. 13)

Here Boswell goes on to gloss Johnson's opening observation with the statement that the latter had told him in 1763 that 'his father put [Martin] Martin's account [*A Description of the Western Isles of Scotland*, 1703] into his hands when he was very young'. This pushes the germ of the idea back at least fifty years. The conversation to which Boswell alludes can be identified as having taken place on 21 July 1763, duly reported in *The Life of Samuel Johnson*:

The mention of this gentleman led us to talk of the Western Islands of Scotland, to visit which he expressed a wish that then appeared to me a very romantick fancy, which I little thought would be afterwards realized. He told me, that his father had put Martin's account of those islands into his hands when he was very young, and that he was highly pleased with it. . . . He said he would go to the Hebrides with me, when I returned from my travels, unless some very good companion should offer when I was absent, which he did not think probable; adding, 'There are few people to whom I take so much to as you.' (*LSJ* i. 450)

In other words, the project of such a visit had been in contemplation from almost the very beginning of their friendship. We do not know if the prospect of the journey was ever canvassed in the intervening years, although discussion of matters connected with the Highlands (such as the link between Scottish and Irish forms of the Gaelic language) certainly did crop up in conversation—and this was just the kind of thing that Johnson hoped to settle when he did embark on the tour. Boswell recalled the long gestation of the project at Col (Coll) on 5 October: 'I said, it was curious to look back ten years, to the time when we first thought of visiting the Hebrides. How distant and improbable the scheme then appeared!' (*LSJ* v. 286). Something had changed, and it had changed in Johnson.

A natural question arises, though again it does not seem to have been put very often. Why did Johnson finally accede to Boswell's pressure and bring to realization what seems to have been a lifelong ambition—why, that is, did the plan reach fruition suddenly in 1773, and not earlier or later? It is possible, of course, that Johnson vaguely felt that he did not have much time left, a consideration which certainly weighed in his mind and that of others when the abortive Italian trip was planned a few years later. But even this presupposes that he had come to look on himself as approaching old age. In any case, it does not explain why this sense of his own situation came to a head at this precise juncture.

It would be unrealistic to look for a single all-embracing answer to this puzzle. Nevertheless, I think there are grounds for identifying one powerful and predominant reason for Johnson's new resolution. This proposed explanation has the additional merit, I hope, of making more sense of the *Journey*, by giving its ideological components a firm root in Johnson's own personal needs and aspirations.

My suggestion is that Johnson felt the time had come to make his long-planned survey of the Highlands and Islands because he had arrived at an *acceptance* of his own ageing condition; and that this was brought home to him by the fact that he had just passed his own climacteric. It is highly improbable that the man who had written the *Dictionary* definition of this concept, and who disported himself in idle moments with arithmetical problems, would have failed to notice that the dread epoch had inescapably arrived. If so, it is almost equally improbable that the habit of moral self-scrutiny would desert him at this juncture, and that he would fail to contemplate the long-accredited attributes of life after the climacteric. The combined effect, if these assumptions have any validity, would be to impress on him the need to conduct a major revaluation of his life, and to prepare himself for the new status of an old man. This was not the mere social recognition we now accord to 'senior citizens', a matter of subsidized travel or special bank accounts. It meant a new existential order of things, a new choice of life.

As already noted, Johnson disliked reminders of his advancing years, and 'did not relish [it] at all' when his distant acquaintance from youth, Oliver Edwards, insisted on reverting to the topic (*LSJ* iii. 307). He happily went along with the idea that he was a 'young buck' in Skye, after Flora Macdonald had reported that she had heard of the imminent arrival of such a person (*LSJ* v. 184–5). (This was on 12 September, less than a week prior to the disturbed sensations brought about by Johnson's birthday.) Plainly, as we have seen, the tour was a prolonged effort to defeat the expectations of age, and a heroic demonstration of the adventurous and youthful spirit which survived in Johnson's corporeal frame. But that frame was starting to decay. Boswell does not make too much of this fact: he states at the outset of the *Tour* that Johnson 'was now in his sixty-fourth year, and was becoming a little dull of hearing'. There are also references to his poor sight and his convulsions, as well as to the scars left on his face by scrofula. But, if anything, the effort is to play down signs of physical ageing. 'During the whole of our Tour he shewed uncommon spirit, could not bear to be treated like an old or infirm man, and was very unwilling to accept of any assistance'—at Icolmkill, he even waded out from the boat to the shore, while his companions were hoisted on men's shoulders (*LSJ* v. 368). It is only in the course of the narrative that Boswell lets slips such information as the following: 'Ever since his last illness in 1766, he has had a weakness in his knees, and has not been able to walk easily' (*LSJ* v. 318). From time to time we learn of Johnson's fatigue, or his inability 'to take so hardy a walk' (*LSJ* v. 168) as his friend, or his having to stand by while Boswell shins up a wall to read an inscription. The buoyancy of the narrative cannot altogether conceal the underlying truth: Boswell was shepherding an elderly man round a difficult and sometimes dangerous itinerary. Much more than in London (the usual meeting-place of the two men), Boswell was obliged to take account of Johnson's growing infirmities.

It is well known that Johnson did not generally stray far, or for long, from the capital. By the 1770s his regular trips out of town had settled into a pattern, involving visits to Oxford or to Lichfield and Ashbourne: the two were combined in the 'jaunt' in 1776, when he was accompanied by Boswell. There were no other *regular* ports of call. I exclude Brighton, since Johnson only went there with the Thrales, in Henry Thrale's lifetime, and seems to have regarded the resort as merely Streatham by the sea. There were single journeys with the Thrales after the Hebridean venture, notably the tour of North Wales in 1774 and the brief trip to Paris in 1775. But the only fixed and unshepherded forays out of London were those to the haunts of Johnson's youth, in Staffordshire and Derbyshire, and to Oxford. These could fairly be seen as attempts to recover lost youth, to revisit the mood as well as the scene of childhood, to expiate the sins of the past (most notably with the penitential return to Uttoxeter). They were pilgrimages as much as pleasure-trips, and it has often been observed that the journeys home to Lichfield could only begin once Johnson's mother had died.

It is altogether different with the sojourn in the Hebrides. As Boswell's opening statement to the *Tour* makes clear, the idea was to 'contemplate a system of life almost totally different from what we had been accustomed to see; and, to find simplicity and wildness, and all the circumstances of remote time or place, so near to our great native island . . .' To that degree it was a voyage *abroad*. Moreover, it sought ways of life remote in 'time or place', so that the travellers were reaching out both beyond their own literal experience and also beyond the reach of mainstream European civilization, under whose auspices they had received their education. For Johnson, the effort was to penetrate the recesses of a 'primitive' society, even though he discovered in the event that 'We came thither too late to see what we expected, a people of peculiar appearance, and a system of antiquated life.' Johnson's objective is graphically stated when he admits to the partial failure of his undertaking: 'Such is the effect of the late regulations, that a longer journey than to the Highlands must be taken by him whose curiosity pants for savage virtues and barbarous grandeur' (*JWI* 57–8). The suppression of the clan system after Culloden had foiled Johnson's efforts to test the theories of the Scottish literati concerning the 'childhood' of mankind. There was a conscious *belatedness* here, which again reflects an awareness that Johnson had come to Scotland late in his own career—when he was already entering 'antiquated life' himself.

But there is a paradox here. The simpler forms of social organization, as described by Adam Smith or Adam Ferguson, were generally seen as representing the infancy of human development. Yet they were, in the backward perspective which all history must involuntarily adopt, the 'oldest' forms of society. In the event, the travellers could not find the true state of nature as the philosophers had described it, and, according to Boswell, they were glad enough to find themselves back on the mainland, in a comfortable carriage, after the rigours of the Hebrides: 'We had a pleasing conviction of the commodiousness of civilization, and heartily laughed at the ravings of those absurd visionaries who have attempted to persuade us of the superior advantages of a *state of nature*' (*LSJ* v. 365). None the less, the two men made the journey deliberately in order to dispense with 'the commodiousness of civilization', and this meant a reversal of the values of their classically based education.

This fact underlies an observation Boswell offered when the two men arrived on Mull on 20 October. There they encountered a minister named Neal Macleod: 'He told us, he had lived for some time in St Kilda . . . and had there first read Horace and Virgil. The scenes which they describe must have been a strong contrast to the dreary waste around him' (*LSJ* v. 338). The aim is to go behind Horace and Virgil to a preliterate world. Moreover, the standard typologies of the time, inherited from medieval and Renaissance sources, identified wintry chill and desolation—to be found in St Kilda, but equally experienced by the travellers when confined to the Inner Hebrides—with old age. The standard set of correspondences ranged the various attributes along a scale which, most relevantly to our purposes, can be read off along the line of winter. It ran through old age (as against spring for childhood etc.); night (as against dawn); water (as against air); the west (as against the south); phlegm (as against blood); the phlegmatic temperament (as against the sanguine); and so on.[11] Thus the bleak inhospitable landscape of the Highlands corresponds to the wintry climate of old age, as this hallowed taxonomy defines the matter. In that sense Johnson was purposefully seeking out a terrain appropriate to senility, where a more conventional itinerary on the grand tour

[11] See e.g. Jean Seznec, *Survival of the Pagan Gods* (Princeton, NJ: Princeton University Press, 1972), 47.

model would have carried him to the warm and sanguine climes of the Mediterranean—the cradle of European civilization, rather than the chilly midnight of social living (see Chapter 2, below.)

Johnson, in fact, was in flight from his upbringing and education. The tour was not a quest to 'find' himself, in the modern sense, certainly not a serious attempt to regain a lost childhood: the literary outcome of such a quest, if it were successful, would be an idyll, and the *Journey*, with its stark realism and sober language, belongs to a very different area of the generic map. It is better considered as a sort of fugue, an act of wilful self-withdrawal, which allows Johnson to meditate on large issues of history and culture. Some of his most profound enquiries were concerned with the nature of a preliterate civilization, where Erse can be seen as 'the rude speech of a barbarous people, who had few thoughts to express, and were content, as they conceived grossly, to be grossly understood' (*JWI* 114). Johnson had many thoughts to express, and conceived far from grossly; but his time was running out, and he needed space to reconsider the meaning of that civilization which had shaped his mind and pervaded his life. Yet the sparseness and remoteness of the landscape forced him to confront his own physical (as opposed to moral or intellectual) inadequacies, as London seldom did. So the journey involved a belated act of self-recognition, in the role of a man approaching his end, 'on the brink' of old age, in his climacteric year.

III

Johnson never went to Scotland again. He was invited to go back by Margaret Boswell in 1782; but he had spent 'almost this whole year in a succession of disorders', and had to refuse the invitation in a letter written on 7 September: 'The journey thither [to Auchinleck] and back is, indeed, too great for the latter part of the year; but if my health were fully recovered, I would suffer no little heat and cold, nor a wet or a rough road to keep me from you' (*L* ii. 517). But his health was never to be fully restored, and he subsided amid a complex array of disorders before he could travel north again. He writes, perhaps with a grim awareness, that it was what Boswell called the 'transit . . . over the Caledonian Hemisphere' (*LSJ* v. 382) which had revealed to him the limits of his physical powers.

The assumption I have made throughout is that Johnson was finally impelled to make his long-planned excursion by some previously unsuspected factor. Boswell remarks at the start of the *Tour*: 'He had disappointed my expectations so long, that I began to despair; but in spring, 1773, he talked of coming to Scotland that year with so much firmness, that I hoped he was at last in earnest' (*LSJ* v. 14). Why should he suddenly begin to think of 'coming to Scotland that year'? Nothing very much had changed in his external circumstances. He had not been involved in any major literary undertaking since the publication of his edition of Shakespeare in 1765—and he would not be so involved, barring the revision of the *Dictionary* and the writing of the *Journey* itself, for many more years. His planned companion had been back in Britain and available for further jaunts since 1766. Something triggered Johnson into action, and it was in force by the summer of 1773. Boswell wrote to him again on 29 May, and he replied on 5 July, apparently full of enthusiasm for the trip. He had been troubled by an eye inflammation, but this was getting better, and he hoped to be 'able to take some delight in the survey of a Caledonian loch' (*LSJ* ii. 264; *L* ii. 41). There was no going back on the plan.

My suggestion, already noted, is that the advent of Johnson's climacteric acted as the required catalyst. In other words, that he was spurred into action by the passing of his sixty-third birthday in September 1772, and by the kind of seven-year check-up which every climacteric would promote—but especially the grand climacteric. Musing on his condition at the age of 63, he was brought to consider a journey away from his familiar surroundings, far beyond the frontiers of his childhood and youth, where he could reposition himself existentially. The trip would not be to recover his health (as the Italian trip would have been), but to test his stamina and to push his body to the limits. This would show how far the bodily decay to be ushered in by the climacteric—expected but fiercely resisted—had set in. Thus the journey would serve as a rite of passage to old age.

One further possibility deserves brief consideration. It is well known that the eighteenth-century nomenclature for ages differed from contemporary practice, and many people seem to have had difficulties in keeping an exact tally of their own age. Thus Hester Thrale regularly misstated her age by a year, and even celebrated her eightieth birthday one year early, in 1820. Since we know that

Johnson called his 1764 anniversary his 'fifty-sixth birthday' (see above, p. 19), the chances of confusion are high. Is it conceivable that he thought that it was in September 1773, on completing what we could call his sixty-fourth year, that he had achieved the end of his sixty-third year (a usage sometimes found)? In other words, could he have considered 18 September 1773, the birthday he celebrated in Skye, as marking the onset of his climacteric? I think this is most unlikely, though not impossible. For one thing, Hester Piozzi actually managed to get the date right. On 27 January 1804 she wrote in *Thraliana*, 'My Birthday—*Grand Climacteric*, kept very chearfully thank God.'[12] And one might suspect that when writing to Hester Thrale, thirty years earlier, Johnson would have alluded to the climacteric if this had been the case. On balance, it seems more probable that he saw the anniversary in 1773 as marking the end of the year of his climacteric, and his gloom regarding its passing was made the more intense because, in coming to the Hebrides, he had hoped to diminish his own sense of idleness.

'I can now look back upon threescore and four years, in which little has been done, and little has been enjoyed . . .' The reminder of his birthday confronted him 'with thoughts which it seems to be the general care of humanity to escape'. But Johnson could never escape thoughts about the use he had made of the time allotted to him, and he cannot have expected that his encounter with the very different 'scheme of life' in the Hebrides would offer any easy escape routes. In fact, he himself stood 'on the brink of his own climacterick', though now—especially as his sixty-fourth birthday went by—on the far side of the chasm. His reference in the *Journey* to the 'hope and comfort' of long life afforded to those 'trembling' on this brink has a terrible personal application, for Johnson had recently crossed that bridge into old age. and knew he could never again stand on the near side of it. 'At sixty-four,' he wrote gloomily to Mrs Thrale, 'what promises, however liberal of imaginary good, can Futurity venture to make' (*L* i. 357). That perhaps is exactly why, at long last, he went to Scotland. Like Adam Smith, he knew that he had to 'weather this dangerous promontory of Human life',

---

[12] *Thraliana*, ii. 1048. Hester celebrated her twentieth wedding aniversary on what we should call the nineteenth; but then George III's jubilee was celebrated on the forty-ninth anniversary.

and he hoped to sail into smooth waters for the 'remnant' of his own years on earth.

Little wonder, then, that Johnson saw no need to repeat his experience in the Western Isles. The matter came up in 1783:

> The tour which Johnson and I had made to the Hebrides was mentioned. JOHNSON. 'I got an acquisition of more ideas by it than by anything that I remember. I saw a quite different system of life.' BOSWELL. 'You would not like to make the same journey again?' JOHNSON. 'Why no, Sir; not the same: it is a tale told . . . Description only excites curiosity: seeing satisfies it. Other people may go and see the Hebrides.' (*LSJ* iv. 199)

Not only had Johnson seen all that he wished to see. He had made his once-for-all entry into a new state, and he could not go back to his pre-Hebridean condition of life.

As Chapter 5 attempts to show, a large part of Johnson's narrative was based on the series of journal-style letters he sent to Hester Thrale. It was thus an autumn journal, based on a voyage into the autumn of Johnson's own life. One could describe the idea of the climacteric as a sort of equinox in human existence, corresponding to the vernal marker of 21[13] (anyone who reached the later climacteric of 81 could be seen to have survived into the winter solstice). More generally, the 'critical period, point, or epoch in any career or course' (*OED*) increasingly meant not the sudden blow of death, but the beginnings of a gradual descent into senility. It was an appropriate juncture at which to take stock of life, and to accept the role of a Nestor. Johnson found this last difficult, and perhaps it gave him more psychological ease to experience his painful change of life at a safe distance from his usual haunts in London, Oxford, and Lichfield. The nature of this removal—that is, the implications of the particular mode of travel he undertook—will be the subject of the next three chapters. Our attention will shift from time to place—from 'Why 1773?' to 'Why Scotland?'

---

[13] Cf. Hester Piozzi writing on the eve of her fifty-eighth birthday: 'Such Tricks did [me] no Mischief Seven Years ago,—but It does not suit the *Autumnal* Equinox': *The Piozzi Letters*, in progress: vols. i–iii published, ed. E. A. Bloom and L. D. Bloom (Newark, Del.: University of Delaware Press, 1988–), iii. 49.

2

The Grand Detour: Johnson's
Un-Italian Journey

Two of the great classics of eighteenth-century travel literature are
Johnson's *Journey* (1775) and Goethe's *Italienische Reise* (1815–
16).[1] Goethe describes his stay in Rome between 1786 and 1788,
whilst Johnson's book is devoted, of course, to the tour of Scotland
that he made with Boswell in 1773. Some immediate discrepancies
appear: the destination of the voyage, the delay in the publication
of Goethe's account, the length of the travellers' stay, and the
contrast of a solitary voyage as against a joint expedition. What the
books have most obviously in common is their literary distinction.
Each man relates a crucial encounter with a hitherto unfamiliar
world and makes his personal experience the occasion for a broader
survey of culture and the environment.

The argument I have to propose here is that a more fundamental
difference underlies the discrepancies, and serves at the same time
to throw their element of congruence into a sharper light. In brief, I
shall contend that Johnson's trip constituted a kind of anti-grand
tour, reversing the usual expectations of the literature surrounding
this familiar *rite de passage*. By contrast, Goethe, though he did not
exactly perform a grand tour in the usual sense, replicated many of
the experiences of those who did, and the text of his *Italian Journey*
reflects this. The emphasis here will be on Johnson, with Goethe in
the role of a control rather than an object of primary attention. This
involves some simplification and possible distortion of this work,
but a book so famous and so thoroughly studied can reasonably be
left to look after itself, whatever academic indignities it may be
forced to endure.

Johnson's book describes an expedition for which he prepared
himself mentally (as the young tourist was advised to prepare

---

[1] References are to J. W. von Goethe, *Italian Journey*, trans. W. H. Auden and
Elizabeth Mayer (n.p.: Pantheon Books, 1962), abbreviated for clarity, where
necessary, as *IJ*.

himself) and which proved to be deeply educative for the elderly Englishman, as the last paragraph of his narrative is enough to make clear:

Such are the things which this journey has given me an opportunity of seeing, and such are the reflections which that sight has raised. Having passed my time almost wholly in cities, I may have been surprised by modes of life and appearances of nature, that are familiar to men of wider survey and more varied conversation. Novelty and ignorance must always be reciprocal, and I cannot but be conscious that my thoughts on national manners, are the thoughts of one who has seen but little. (*JWI* 164)

Nevertheless, it was an undertaking running clean contrary to the norms of the grand tour. Johnson made his journey not in youth, but 'on the brink of his own climacterick' (see Ch. 1); it was also made in the wrong company, for the wrong duration, in the wrong climate, by the wrong mode of conveyance—and, crucially, to omit other inappropriate features for the present, it was made in the wrong geographical direction. The contrast would have been even starker for Johnson than it is for us. Thus, in the earlier parts of the discussion I shall provide evidence of the usual substance and appurtenances of a grand tour, drawing particularly on the testimony of friends and colleagues of Johnson who did make a more or less orthodox visit to continental Europe.[2] This is then placed against the inverse evidence drawn from the *Journey*, to illustrate the contrary nature of Johnson's experience. Subsequently, Goethe's account of his Roman sojourn will be explored in order to make a more particular comparison of two outstanding and emblematic narratives which point in opposite directions, both in a literal or geographic sense and in historical terms.

---

[2] Standard sources on the subject are: William Edward Mead, *The Grand Tour in the Eighteenth Century* (1914; repr. New York: Benjamin Blom, 1972), still the fullest survey; and Jeremy Black, *The British and the Grand Tour* (London: Croom Helm, 1985), more selective but useful for manuscript diaries and narratives. Also informative is Christopher Hibbert, *The Grand Tour* (London: Thames Methuen, 1987), which is a popular account, based on existing sources, and gives no references, but which does provide a well-written and comprehensive overview of the subject. These works are cited only in the case of localized facts or specific quotation in the text. Other general comments (e.g. the statement that travellers commonly took a given route) are extensively documented in these three sources, and a reference is not routinely supplied in the notes.

I

The three sisters never made it to Moscow; Scott Fitzgerald's narrator did not get across to the war in Europe; and Des Esseintes's planned journey to London was arrested at the Gare Saint-Lazare. In the same way, Samuel Johnson failed in his lifelong ambition to visit the Mediterranean. A familiar statement by Johnson is recorded by Boswell under the date 11 April 1776:

A journey to Italy was still in his thoughts. He said, 'A man who has not seen Italy, is always conscious of an inferiority, from his not having seen what it is expected a man should see. The grand object of travelling is to see the shores of the Mediterranean. On those shores were the four great Empires of the world; the Assyrian, the Persian, the Grecian, and the Roman.—All our religion, almost all our law, almost all our arts, almost all that sets us above savages, has come to us from the shores of the Mediterranean.' The General observed, that THE MEDITERRANEAN would be a noble subject for a poem. (*LSJ* iii. 36)

The General here is Pasquale Paoli, the hero of Corsican independence, one of the many members of Johnson's circle with a deep firsthand knowledge of this cradle of civilization. (Paoli's influence on Boswell's aims for the tour is discussed in Chapter 6, below.)

In the preceding weeks Johnson had been eagerly planning a trip to Italy in the company of the Thrales, along with Giuseppe Baretti.[3] It was only on the previous day that he had learnt that the journey would not now take place, owing to the death of the Thrales' only surviving son Henry. Johnson had told Boswell that he was 'disappointed, to be sure; but it is not a great disappointment'. At this stage it seems to have been assumed that this was merely a postponement and that the long-expected visit would take place another year; but this never happened.[4] Of course, Johnson had been with the Thrales to Paris in 1775, 'the only time in his life that he went upon the Continent', as Boswell points out (*LSJ* ii.

[3] For the full history of various projects, see E. S. De Beer, 'Johnson's Italian Tour', in *Johnson, Boswell and their Circle* (Oxford, Clarendon Press, 1965), 159–69.
[4] There was a scheme to revive the journey in 1781, but this too came to nothing: see De Beer, 'Johnson's Italian Tour', 162. I exclude from the discussion a later plan to have Johnson pass the winter of 1784 in Italy for the sake of his health: for this, see *LSJ* iv. 326–8, 336–8.

385). Such prospects still beckoned in 1773, at the time of the visit to Scotland and the Hebrides; but Johnson must have been conscious then that the Highland jaunt constituted the nearest thing he had ever experienced to the grander tour he still hoped to make.

Not everyone thought the planned Italian journey a wise enterprise. As previously noted, Hannah More had referred to Johnson's embarking on a farewell circuit of his acquaintances prior to 'his great expedition across the Alps. I lament his undertaking such a journey at his time of life, with beginning infirmities; I hope he will not leave his bones on classic ground.'[5] Such an objection would have applied equally to the northern trip less than three years earlier, and the likelihood of obtaining prompt and efficient medical aid would have been considerably less on that occasion. However, it is clear that Johnson and Mrs Thrale continued to regard the plan for continental travel as a live option for the future. Less than a month after the collapse of the original scheme, Hester Thrale mused upon the literary outcome of such a trip (she dates the letter 3 May 1776 in her collection of correspondence with Johnson): 'Should you write about Streatham and Croydon, the book would be as good to me as a journey to Rome, exactly . . . The sight of Rome might have excited more reflections indeed than the sight of the Hebrides, and so the book might be bigger, but it would not be a better a jot.'[6] Boswell too had expressed 'an earnest wish' for his 'remarks on Italy'; Johnson had prevaricated, at first saying that he could not undertake such a book, but then leaving the way open for Boswell to conclude that 'a journal of his Tour upon the Continent was not wholly out of his contemplation' (*LSJ* iii. 19).[7]

Mrs Thrale took up the more general issue in what we know is an authentic letter, dated two months later, around 13 July:

Why what an uncomfortable Reflection it is at last that those who are best qualified to travel, & tell what they have seen at their Return should be almost always obliged for one Reason or another to stay at home.

---

[5] Quoted from William Roberts's *Memoirs of Hannah More*, in *LSJ* iii. 457.

[6] Hester Lynch Piozzi, *Letters to and from the Late Samuel Johnson*, 2 vols. (London: Cadell, 1787), i. 319. This is one of the letters without manuscript authority that is excluded by R. W. Chapman in his edition of *The Letters of Samuel Johnson* (Oxford: Clarendon Press, 1952), but Chapman is far from claiming that the 'inauthentic' letters were a pure fabrication.

[7] In his private journal Boswell expressed his strong desire that 'Dr Johnson should see Italy and give us his grand remarks': *Boswell: The Ominous Years*, ed. C. Ryskamp and F. A. Pottle (London: Heinemann, 1963), 317.

My great delight like yours would be to see how Life is carried on in other Countries, how various Climates produce various Effects, and how different Notions of Religion & Government operate upon the human Manners & the human Mind: for 'tis they at last which cause all the distinction between National Characters, as the Method in which our Bones & Fibers are disposed creates all the Variety observed in the human Figure: yet I do not commend those Voyagers who teize one with too much of such Stuff to shew their own Profundity, any more than I like a Painter who exhibits none but Anatomical Figures. I think however we have had little to lament of on that Side lately, as counting Pictures & describing Ruins seems to have been the sole Business of modern Travellers—but when *we* go to *Cairo* one shall take one Department, another shall take another, and so a pretty book may be made out amongst us that shall be commended, and censured, and cuffed about the Town for a Twelve Month, if no new Tub takes the Whale's Attention. (*L* ii. 66)

The dream remained potent for Hester Thrale; after her marriage to Piozzi, of course, she was to undertake a prolonged period of residence on the Continent, following more or less the regular grand-tour itinerary. The result was her volume of *Observations and Reflections* on the countries she had visited. This is a remarkable book which deals with both 'human Manners & the human Mind' along with a certain amount of 'counting Pictures & describing Ruins'. It is not quite what Johnson would have made of such a tour, but it is more than a mere 'pretty book'. Once again we find Johnson cast in the 'near miss' role. He might, despite everything, have been able to take the projected excursion; after all, his intended companion did so within a decade, and she was a middle-aged woman who had been cruelly ostracized by society. It would not have been so very absurd for Johnson, even at his advanced age, to attempt as much. But he never had the opportunity.

We know precisely what form the visit to Italy would have taken if Baretti's hopes had been realized. E. S. De Beer has summarized his intentions as follows: the party was to proceed in three four-wheeled chaises, of which two would be occupied by the Thrales, Johnson, and Baretti, and the third by a maid and a manservant. A German courier would ride at the head of the procession, with yet another servant on horseback as an outrider. They would also hire additional servants in those cities where they passed a long period of time. They were to travel as comfortably and luxuriously as possible, 'for with money one can do everything'—a far cry from the basic conditions endured by Johnson and Boswell in Scotland. The planned route was entirely predictable: from Paris via Lyons and Chambéry and the Mont Cenis pass to Turin; then via Genoa, Milan, some of the northern cities, including Bologna, and finally to Rome. On their return they would pass time in Tuscany and then make their way home through Switzerland or the Tyrol. There was even some talk of venturing into Sicily, something that Goethe was actually to undertake, although it was not part of the regular route. Much of the progress would be conducted in zigzags across country, 'for we do not mind whether the road is straight or crooked, so long as we see everything and quench our thirst in this matter'. There were diversions to visit Baretti's own family, and Samuel Johnson's young friend Topham Beauclerk suggested that Baretti would keep the party so long 'in the little towns of his own country that they would not have time to see Rome'. Alarmed by this prospect, Johnson had declared that he would not allow Baretti to be sole manager of the operation. In the event, of course, no such tour ever took place. If it had done, it is likely from this evidence that it would have been leisurely, genteel, orthodox, with Rome as a clear destination—everything that the northern journey was not.[8]

One of those 'best qualified to travel', then, was obliged to stay at home; one of the most eloquent communicators on the issues which Mrs Thrale outlined was forced to remain silent. In fact, his only comparable experience (we can discount the short and limited visit to Paris, of which he left no detailed account) was the earlier journey to the Highlands, which corresponded to the traditional tour in the distances covered, the remoteness of the destinations from London, and the close observation of men and manners. It is almost as though Johnson foresaw the ultimate futility of his yearnings for a sojourn in Mediterranean climes. He anticipated his disappointment by creating a grand detour, a journey which

---

[8] This paragraph is based on material quoted from Baretti's *Epistolario* by De Beer, 'Johnson's Italian Tour', 160–5. Relevant letters are translated in Lacy Collison-Morley, *Giuseppe Baretti* (London: John Murray, 1909), 285–91. When the plan was revived in 1781, Mrs Thrale was prepared for Baretti to accompany the party, despite her dislike of him—'somebody we must have; Croza would court our Daughter, & Piozzi: could not talk to Johnson, nor I suppose do one any Good, but sing to one:—& how should we sing *Songs in a strange Land*?' (*Thraliana*, ed. K. C. Balderston, 2nd edn., 2 vols. (Oxford: Clarendon Press, 1951), 487).

swerved away from the usual tourists' route and from the accustomed tourists' lore. Thousands of less competent observers had enjoyed the chance to tread on classic ground; Johnson was denied this possibility, but he showed how confrontation with a very different culture could yield equally profound reflections on civilization, history, and literature. Mrs Thrale had perceived as much. Streatham and Croydon, villages in the hinterland of the capital, would not really have done, though. The crucial fact is that, imaginatively, Johnson went as far from London as any visitor to Rome or even Cairo.

II

Within his own circle, Johnson was part of a minority who had not made an extensive stay on the continent of Europe. This assertion could be supported in several ways, but the simplest method may be to consider the position with regard to fellow members of the Club. In order to do this, I have isolated what might be termed the active Club, that is those who had not died (like Samuel Dyer) or withdrawn (like Hawkins) from the Club prior to 1770, and who were elected during Johnson's lifetime. This gives a total of forty individuals who were eligible to attend the Club in the last fifteen years of Johnson's life (in all such counts, naturally, I excluded Johnson himself). Among this group, at least twenty-two had spent a prolonged period on the mainland of Europe. This figure excludes marginal cases, such as Sheridan's brief elopement to France, but it covers any substantial travel on the Continent.

It is true that a grand tour in the strictest sense was more usual among the full-blown aristocrats of the Club, such as Lord Palmerston and Lord Charlemont. But even within Johnson's inner circle of intimate friends, his own biographer, Boswell, had conducted what was outwardly a quite orthodox tour after leaving Utrecht in 1764 (his itinerary thenceforth had nothing peculiar about it, apart from the diversion to Corsica). In any case, the more fundamental fact is that, one way or another, the central figures in the group, those with the most regular contacts with Johnson, had managed to undertake the equivalent of a tour.

The divergences from the standard pattern take different directions. Gibbon's was a familiar quest for art and antiquity in

Italy, unrepresentative only in the seriousness of the traveller and the delay in its accomplishment—Gibbon was in his twenty-eighth year at the time (1763–4). Reynolds passed three years abroad, engaged on his studies as a painter, but most of this was taken up by his sojourn in Rome, where his extracurricular activities brought him into the sphere of more orthodox tourists and visiting milords. Adam Smith undertook a familiar version of the tour, but in the capacity of the leader rather than the led—he acted as tutor to the young Duke of Buccleuch. Also on this trip was Sir Alexander Macdonald, whom Johnson met (and disliked) on Skye (*JWI* 49–50; *LSJ* v. 147–56). Most of the time was spent in France, with extensive periods in Paris, but side-trips included a journey to Geneva, with the far from unusual meeting with Voltaire (Boswell and Palmerston also enjoyed this opportunity). Goldsmith's wanderings through Europe are normally looked on as representing something at the opposite end of the scale from grand tourism, and they were certainly conducted under less favourable auspices. But the route—from the University of Leiden through Paris to Switzerland and Italy—was a customary one, and he too may have met Voltaire. Burke's early visits to France are thinly documented; on the other hand, Garrick's overseas travels, especially the prolonged spell he passed in France, Italy, and Bavaria (1763–4), were well known to the world in general and to Johnson in particular. Charles Burney's musical tours had a highly specialized purpose, but they took him to the usual venues in 1770 and 1772.[9]

Quite apart from Club members, a number of those well known to Johnson, with whom he maintained good relations over a period of time, were experienced tourists. These included—to list names more or less at random—figures such as Sir William Chambers, the architect, who had studied in Rome after visiting Paris and Florence; the Earl of Carlisle (who travelled with Charles James Fox); and Joseph Cradock.[10] Even the lowly Robert Levet had passed a period in Italy and France. It is true that the tour had also been undertaken by people who could be described as enemies, or at least as targets of Johnson's dislike and scorn: Wilkes (who met

---

[9] See Ch. 3, below.

[10] There is little firm documentation of Johnson's firsthand dealings with Carlisle, but they can legitimately be deduced from circumstantial evidence. Carlisle's close friend Reynolds proposed him for membership of the Club in 1790, but he was rejected.

up with Boswell in Italy); the group centred on Gray and Walpole; not to mention Lord Chesterfield. In general, the ritual was one for males, but several women made extensive trips to the Continent, including Elizabeth Montagu, who took Elizabeth Carter with her; Lady Knight, who lived for many years in Italy with her daughter Cornelia; and, some time after Johnson's death, Fanny d'Arblay, as she then was.

However, the most influential figures outside the ranks of the Club were Paoli, with his European history of both action and reflection, and Giuseppe Baretti. Johnson did not want the projected Italian voyage to be 'directed' by Baretti, by which he seems to have meant planned in advance, rather than superintended along the route. Perhaps the ministrations of Baretti in France during the visit of 1775 had been over-officious, although Johnson described him in a letter home as 'a fine fellow' (*LSJ* ii. 386).[11] Nevertheless, Johnson was perfectly well aware that Baretti had written a popular book on the *Manners and Customs of Italy* (1768), which was widely used as a tourist guide. Wherever Johnson looked around him, in polite society, he would encounter such persons. We think of him as someone who was in touch with the great ideas of his time and the main sources of European civilization; but in some respect, of course, he was underprivileged, an outsider who was unable to take a full part in the higher conversation of the age, because of his lack of firsthand experience of Italy. Unlike most of his main allies, he was (in the area which then counted) an untravelled man.

It is inconceivable that Johnson was not fully aware of these themes and variations on the grand tour, especially those undertaken by his own closest associates, when he conducted his own travels, actual and projected. He would inevitably have been conscious, even after the brief adventure which took him to Paris in 1775, that all the Club members mentioned had spent as long as he had done in Paris, and most of them considerably longer. And all except Smith had penetrated deep into Italy for a protracted stay. The author of the most compendious history of the subject remarks

---

[11] For Baretti's notions of the form that the Italian tour should take, see p. 35 above, as well as De Beer, 'Johnson's Italian Tour', 159–67. For Baretti's management of the French expedition, see Collison-Morley, *Baretti*, 280–4. The influence on the *Journey* of an earlier tour made by Baretti is discussed in Ch. 3, below.

that on one matter 'eighteenth-century tourists were practically all agreed, and that was that a grand tour on the continent without a visit to Italy was no grand tour at all'.[12] And Johnson clearly envisaged very much the ordinary kind of thing: 'Mr Thrale is to go, by my advice, to Mr Jackson, (the all-knowing) and get from him a plan for seeing the most that can be seen in the time that we have to travel. We must, to be sure, see Rome, Naples, Florence, and Venice, and as much more as we can' (*LSJ* iii. 19). These words were spoken 'with a tone of animation', as Boswell informs us; we can hardly doubt that Johnson had amended his early plan, whilst still a student at Oxford, to visit the universities of France and Italy (specifically naming Padua), in favour of a more orthodox journey which would include sightseeing and socializing with the Thrales in addition to contact with the learned. Baretti's projected itinerary certainly indicated as much.

All these plans were hatched after the return from the short Parisian expedition—that is, within two and a half years of the longer trail through the Scottish mountains. That journey, however, had also been pondered. Everyone at the time was familiar with the standard justification for the tour, as set out in the most influential guide to the subject by Thomas Nugent: 'That noble and ancient custom of travelling, a custom so visibly tending to enrich the mind with knowledge, to rectify the judgment, to remove the prejudices of education, to compose the outward manners, and in a word to form the complete gentleman.'[13] Johnson might not have paid much more than lip-service to the formation of manners; and he had his own version of the benefits of travel. There is no need to quote his famous pronouncements on the topic, including those he sent to Mrs Thrale from the Hebrides; an excellent book by Thomas Curley provides all the background we need.[14] But it is worth underlining one expression in Nugent, the ambition 'to rectify the judgment', as a peculiarly Johnsonian task, and one that points to the self-educative purpose of the Scottish adventure. We must look again at the very last phrases of the *Journey*: 'Novelty and ignorance must always be reciprocal, and I cannot but be conscious

---

[12] Mead, *The Grand Tour*, 207.

[13] Thomas Nugent, *The Grand Tour*, 2nd edn. (London, 1756), p. xi, cited by Mead, *The Grand Tour*, 4.

[14] See Thomas M. Curley, *Samuel Johnson and the Age of Travel* (Athens, Ga: University of Georgia Press, 1976).

that my thoughts on national manners, are the thoughts of one who
has seen but little' (*JWI* 164). It would not be perverse or excessive
to paraphrase the final words as 'one who has not yet seen Italy'.
For Johnson knew that the archetypal survey of 'national manners'
was based on firsthand experience of Europe, and generally
involved explicit analysis of France and/or Italy. His own friend
Goldsmith had sketched out a 'prospect of society' in *The Traveller*
(1764), organized around parallel characterizations of these
countries together with the Low Countries and Switzerland. The
guilty hint of 'ignorance' creeps into the text of the *Journey* at its
culminating point. 'Surprised by modes of life and appearances of
nature' in Scotland, Johnson can only guess at the response which
would be elicited by the noble and historic vistas of the south.

III

What, then, had Johnson missed? Or, to put it slightly differently,
what had his friends expected and taken from their *giro d'Italia*? It
would be possible to spend many pages debating this question, but
a more cursory answer will emerge from selective quotations.
Representative items of evidence are furnished by Gibbon, Boswell,
Lord Palmerston, and Mrs Piozzi.

In his autobiography Gibbon gives an account of his arrival in
Rome in 1764—around the time when several of the Johnson circle
happened to be abroad. Their collective testimony would have
reached Johnson in the following decade, and it is here, rather than
in the better-publicized travel narratives of Smollett and Sterne,
that we should look for an impress on Johnson's own mind.
Gibbon provides, in summary form, the central ideological message
of tourism:

By the road of Bologna and the Apennine I at last reached Florence, where I
reposed from June to September, during the heat of the summer months. In
the gallery, and especially in the TRIBUNE, I first acknowledged, at the feet
of the Venus of Medicis, that the chissel may dispute the pre-eminence with
the pencil—a truth in the fine arts which cannot, on this side of the Alps be
felt or understood. At home I had taken some lessons of Italian; on the spot
I read with a learned native the Classics of the Tuscan idiom; but the
shortness of my time, and the use of the French language, prevented my
acquiring any facility of speaking; and I was a silent spectator in the

conversations of our envoy, Sir Horace Mann, whose most serious business was that of entertaining the English at his hospitable table. After leaving Florence I compared the solitude of Pisa with the industry of Lucca and Leghorn, and continued my journey through Sienna to Rome, where I arrived in the beginning of October. My temper is not very susceptible of enthusiasm, and the enthusiasm which I do not feel I have ever scorned to affect. But at the distance of twenty-five years I can neither forget nor express the strong emotions which agitated my mind as I first approached and entered the *eternal City*. After a sleepless night, I trod with a lofty step the ruins of the Forum; each memorable spot where Romulus *stood*, or Tully spoke, or Caesar fell, was at once present to my eye; and several days of intoxication were lost or enjoyed before I could descend to a cool and minute investigation.[15]

No single passage in Boswell's journals renders quite so perfectly the dream of learning embodied in eighteenth-century *gran turismo*. But scattered through his account are numerous brief hints, which together bear on the theme: 'I have felt many a change of sentiment since I crossed the Alps,' he tells W. J. Temple on 22 April 1765, continuing later in the same letter:

I am now wrapped up in the study of antiquities and fine arts. I have already surveyed most of the monuments of ancient grandeur, and have felt the true, venerable enthusiasm. What would I not give when we used to Climb Arthur Seat, when our minds were fresh to all the charms of Roman poetry, and our bosoms glowed with a desire to visit the sacred shades. I have had many hours of rich enjoyment. But you must be sensible that a letter can give you but very imperfect accounts. My journal will be pretty well. But my conversation will be great. How I anticipate our mutual satisfaction.

Basking in the 'delicious' weather at Frascati, he 'felt' the genius of the place and wrote a Tusculan disputation on happiness. His present study of pictures had given him hopes of forming 'a true taste'.[16] The aesthetic impulse may be stronger than in Johnson

---

[15] *The Autobiographies of Edward Gibbon*, ed. John Murray (London: John Murray, 1897), 267. Mann, Horace Walpole's friend and the long-serving British minister in Florence, welcomed generations of tourists, especially those who shared his interest in *virtù*. See also n. 29, below. In his French journal Gibbon noted on 20 Oct. 1766: 'J'ai etè dans un songe d'antiquitè qui n'a etè interrompu que par les Commis de la Douane' (*Gibbon's Journey from Geneva to Rome*, ed. G. A. Bonnard (London: Nelson, 1961), 235).

[16] *Boswell on the Grand Tour: Italy, Corsica and France, 1765–1766*, ed. F. Brady and F. A. Pottle (London: Heinemann, 1956), 71–2. Cf. what Boswell wrote

himself, but there is an underlying philosophical and moral aim which many travellers shared and which spoke directly to Johnson's preoccupations.

Viscount Palmerston made his tour in 1763–4 at the age of 25, several years prior to his admission to the Johnson circle.[17] (He was proposed for the Club in 1783, with Johnson's support, but only gained entry just before Johnson's death. However, he was a close friend of several members of the group.) Like many, he was struck by what he encountered in Italy: 'I never saw a statue worth looking at till I crossed the Alps, or which gave me the least idea of the powers of the art,' he wrote home in 1765. It was this quest for 'ideas', rather than mere sights or trophies, which distinguished the more philosophical tourist, such as Johnson would unquestionably have been. When such individuals crossed the Alps (the phrase recurs, marking the sense of passage and exploration of novelty), they saw with different eyes. And the more thoughtful investigators considered this to involve a cognitive leap, requiring a Johnsonian rigour of mind rather than merely sensuous apprehension. As Palmerston writes: 'The great remains of antiquity [at Rome] . . . are what naturally attracts one's admiration first, and their effect depends upon the disposition of the mind and not upon any particular skill or practice in the arts.' Even a collector, a virtuoso, or a dilettante—Palmerston was something of all three—could make this recognition. On his return home, Palmerston was elected to the Society of Dilettanti in 1766, one year after Reynolds; he attended its Sunday dinners at the Star and Garter along with Garrick, Beauclerk, Joseph Banks, and others. Like most well-heeled tourists, he had sat for his portrait in Rome—not by Batoni this time, but by Angelica Kauffmann, who was to spend several years in London as a friend of Reynolds and a member of the Royal Academy, which was actively supported by its honorary professor,

to Jean-Jacques Rousseau three weeks later (ibid. 85): 'I have almost finished my tour of Italy. I have viewed with enthusiasm classical sites, and the remains of the grandeur of the ancient Romans. I have made a thorough study of architecture, statues, and paintings; and I believe I have acquired taste to a certain degree.'

[17] Information in this paragraph is derived from Brian Connell, *Portrait of a Whig Peer* (London: André Deutsch, 1957), 35–69. Palmerston was unusual in making another extended tour through Europe in the wake of the French Revolution, between 1792 and 1794, with another protracted stay in Italy: ibid. 261–305.

Samuel Johnson. These scattered items of evidence could be extended to show how Palmerston's Italian journey supplied a kind of template for his later intellectual interests, a possibility once again closed to Johnson.

Finally, in what must be a rapid and selective survey, there is Hester Piozzi. Of course, she did not make her long stay on the Continent until after her second marriage and the death of Johnson. It is, however, legitimate to invoke her testimony on three grounds. First, her eventual voyage was in some measure a fulfilment of the trip that she had planned to take a decade earlier with Johnson and Henry Thrale. Second, she still had her former mentor strongly in mind, as is revealed in references both in the text of her *Observations and Reflections* and, more especially, in the private letters that she wrote home.[18] Third, she brought to her sojourn abroad some of the feelings of release and enjoyment which the conventional tourist (a young man let loose from parental restraint for the first time) experienced, a product of her delighted escape from English decorum in the wake of her joyous new marriage.

Early in the *Observations* Mrs Piozzi remarks that 'one comes to Italy to look at buildings, statues, pictures, people!'[19] She did her share in respect of all four categories—and, indeed, contemplated works of art with more intelligence and judgement than most who had preceded her. But her special interest in people, what the age called 'manners', is a characteristic which links her with Johnson, and probably reflects the impact on her mind of Johnson's conversation. So, along with the customary visit to Herculaneum and Pompeii, the constant recollections of Virgil, and the standard round of the galleries, there are small human observations which suggest Johnson:

---

[18] See e.g. *The Piozzi Letters: Correspondence of Hester Lynch Piozzi* i. *1784–1791*, ed. E. A. Bloom and L. D. Bloom (Newark, Del.: University of Delaware Press, 1989), 120, 123. Occasionally Mrs Piozzi was glad to be free of Johnson's presence, as when she decided to 'let loose' a fondness for painting which she was forced to suppress while Johnson was alive (p. 385).

[19] Hester Lynch Piozzi, *Observations and Reflections Made in the Course of a Journey through France, Italy, and Germany*, ed H. Burrows (Ann Arbor: University of Michigan Press, 1967), 86 (henceforth cited as *Observations*). In view of Goethe's close friendship with Kauffmann, it is worth noting that Hester Piozzi decided to delay her enquiries as to the present state of painting in Italy until she reached Rome, for 'Angelica Kauffmann being settled there, seems a proof of their taste for living merit' (p. 91).

The University of Padua is a noble institution; and those who have excelled among the students are recorded on tablets, for the most part brass, hung round the walls, made venerable by their arms and characters. It was pleasing to see so many British names among them—Scotchmen for the most part, though I enquired in vain for the admirable Crichton. Sir Richard Blackmore was there, but not one native of France. We are spiteful enough to fancy, that was the reason that Abbe Richard says nothing of the establishment.[20]

She is perhaps most rhapsodic about Naples; and when she leaves the city to return to Rome, she gives vent to a heartfelt passage of rich and resourceful prose:

My stay has been always much shorter than I wished it, in every great town of Italy; but *here* where numberless wonders strike the sense without fatiguing it, I do feel double pleasure; and among all the new ideas I have acquired since England lessened to my sight upon the sea, those gained at Naples will be the last to quit me. The works of art may be found great and lovely, but the drunken Faun and the dying Gladiator will fade from one's remembrance, and leave the glow of Solfaterra and the gloom of Posilippo indelibly impressed. Vesuvius too! that terrified me so when first we drove into this amazing town, what future images can ever obliterate the thrilling sensations it at first occasioned? Surely the sight of old friends after a tedious absence can alone supply the vacancy that a mind must feel which quits such sublime, such animated scenery, and experiences a sudden deprivation of delight, finding the bosom all at once unfurnished of what has yielded it for three swiftly-flown months, perpetual change of undecaying pleasures.[21]

Again one sees the stress on 'ideas' rather than souvenirs, and here too the phrase concerning 'the vacancy that a mind must feel' is drawn straight from Johnson's moral vocabulary. Throughout her journey Piozzi testifies to the profound impact which Italy has made on someone who had dreamed of these sights since childhood, and who had long anticipated in her imagination the hallowed prospects of the ancient world. So also, it does not need saying, Johnson had dreamed and anticipated. The difference was that he was never able to redeem the loss caused by the death of

---

[20] Hester Lynch Piozzi, *Observations*, 73.

[21] Ibid. 265. Piozzi often regrets leaving the cities she has visited—something that was true of many tourists, but seldom, if ever, of Johnson, when he moved on from one part of the Highlands to another.

little Henry Thrale, as Henry's mother was, to her great benefit and, ultimately, to ours as well. There is a brief hint of pathos even for Piozzi herself, as she looks back on her return to Rome:

We have left these scenes of fabulous wonder and real pleasure however; left the warm vestiges of classic story, and places which have produced the noblest efforts of the human mind; places which have served as no ignoble themes for truly immortal song; all quitted now! all left for recollection to muse on, and for fancy to combine: but these eyes I fear will never more survey them. Well! no matter—[22]

It does not require much in the way of sympathetic imagination to read into such a passage the added pathos which comes from the realization that Johnson was never once to survey these 'scenes of fabulous wonder'.

IV

No one in the era could have failed to be aware that the 'grand tourist' dream commonly fell far short of the actuality of a real tour. A series of satires published in Johnson's lifetime, from the *New Dunciad* of 1743 to Cowper's 'Progress of Error' in 1782, presented a jaundiced view of idle and raffish young men wasting their opportunities. To bring the matter close to Johnson's own experience again, it may be true that the 20-year-old Earl of Carlisle was busy studying Roman antiquities for 'seven or eight hours a day' in 1768—it may equally well not be true.[23] In any case, Carlisle and his boon companion Charles James Fox squandered thousands of pounds on gambling, drinking, clothes, aimless travel, and the rest. Fox joined the Club in 1774, and maintained his expensive and sometimes dissolute life even as he advanced towards political power. Such evidence of the possible anti-educative effects of tourism would not greatly have disturbed Johnson, who had many more favourable cases to contemplate, particularly among

[22] Ibid. 269.
[23] Quoted by Hibbert, *The Tour*, 165. For the more characteristic activities of Fox and Carlisle, see ibid. 32, 153, 214. It is, however, true that amid their junketings both men made more successful efforts than most to learn the Italian language: see Mead, *The Grand Tour*, 116–17.

serious-minded Club members who had deferred their sojourn on the Continent.[24]

Johnson could not have replicated the standard tour, even if he had wished to: his age alone forbade that. Nevertheless, it might have been possible to undertake a smaller version, something along the lines of the Paris visit, but in the Low Countries instead (where his friend Reynolds went twice, to Flanders and the United Provinces, in order to study art, and where Boswell had been a student at the University of Utrecht). Such an expedition would have lacked the central humanist purposes of a journey to Italy, but it would have been a replacement of sorts.

What Johnson actually did was to reverse the entire thrust of the experience. He went north, when all the ideological coils of the grand tour were wound around the south. He went not to a recognized cradle of civilization, but to an area widely regarded as a home of savages. Even though his journey began and ended at the Athens of the north, he spent only a short time in Edinburgh and gave it a cursory line at the start of his account ('we left Edinburgh, a city too well known to admit description') and a page at the end, concentrating exclusively on a school for deaf and dumb children (see above, pp. 3–4.) There is no mention of the far from deaf and dumb Enlightenment figures who crowded to meet Johnson and whom Boswell particularized with such relish in his version of the jaunt. Johnson's journey, as a text and, seemingly, as an experience, was designed to shun the familiar, and thus it rewrites the rules of tourist travel, which served to remind the voyager of ideas and sensations already transmitted via classical culture. It is largely an accident that Scotland had suffered unprecedented unpopularity in

---

[24] It would be useful to know more of the less-documented trips which took place around these years, including Malone's visit to Paris with Lord Spencer (another Club member), in 1776. This also applies to Topham Beauclerk's visit to Italy, starting in 1762. This was designed chiefly for reasons of health, but again it was partly 'directed' by Baretti. Johnson wrote to Beauclerk in the expectation that he would have reached Italy, but in fact he had got as far as Paris, in company with Bennet Langton (see *L* i. 138–40, 145–7). In July 1764 Beauclerk had reached Venice, where he had £10,000 stolen: see Baretti's letters to Garrick, cited by Collison-Morley, *Baretti*, 143–9. Boswell seems to have met Baretti in Venice (Collison-Morley, *Baretti*, 149). Proof can be found that Johnson was aware of the touring experiences of his fellow Club members, even those with whom he was less intimate and who joined the circle comparatively late. See his questioning of Lord Eliot and his knowledge of Eliot's tutor (Walter Harte), in *LSJ* iv. 333, under 27 June 1784.

England during the 1760s, after the ascendancy of Lord Bute—
though there may have been a scintilla of Johnsonian perversity in
choosing to visit this despised nation at such a juncture.[25] But once
more this circumstance underlies the oddity of Johnson's decision
when set in the context of general touring expectations.

Some of these departures from the norm were heightened by his
choice of Boswell as his mentor. In the opening paragraph of his
Journey Johnson draws conspicuous attention to this decision,
speaking of him as 'a companion, whose acuteness would help my
inquiry, and whose gaiety of conversation and civility of manners
are sufficent to counteract the inconveniences of travel, in countries
less hospitable than we have passed' (*JWI* 3). Few among the
Johnson circle thought Boswell a suitable companion for the great
man at any time, and none of them would have entrusted
themselves to a long trek in the almost unrelieved company of this
pushy little man. Boswell was, again, almost the opposite of a
conventional travel companion. He was much younger than
Johnson—the tutor was always a man of mature years employed to
keep the youthful energies of a tourist under restraint—and he was
a native of Scotland—and it was not usual for the tutor to be a
representative of the visited people.[26] Mrs Boswell's famous quip to
the effect that she had seen many a bear being led by a man, but
never the reverse, catches this topsy-turvy quality with perfect
precision. Boswell is on one level the cicerone, the knowledgeable
guide who can mediate between Johnson and the unfamiliar world
he has entered, but it is also Boswell who dances and flirts and
scrambles up rocks, sulks and drinks, longs for home, and generally
behaves like a callow young tourist. As with so many features of the
trip, the company Johnson kept marked his tour as an inversion of
routine protocol.

As we have seen in Chapter 1, the opening sentence of Johnson's
Journey refers to his long-standing desire to visit the Hebrides. It is
well established that this claim is true, but Boswell had also been
planning for a number of years to get his revered master to see his
homeland. Paoli had made a short trip in Boswell's company in
1771. Thus, there were competing pressures on Johnson, and
collaborative energies were utilized in the undertaking. It may, for

[25] See Ch. 8, below.
[26] For the ordinary role of the tutor, see Mead, *The Grand Tour*, 103–39, and
Hibbert, *The Tour*, 20–3.

instance, have been in Boswell's mind to extract Johnson from the influence of the Thrale household for a while. This is relevant to our present argument in so far as the desire to leave the beaten track was common to both men. Johnson wrote to Mrs Thrale from Skye: 'I have now the pleasure of going where nobody goes, and seeing what nobody sees' (L I. 348). To be able to achieve this, he went along with the plans of his unrespectable friend, and instead of merely diverging a small way from the hallowed route, he swerved one hundred and eighty degrees in the opposite direction. Boswell had apprised Voltaire of his hopes of a Hebridean journey, in company with Johnson, as far back as 1764, and Voltaire had drily given his approval, so long as he was not obliged to make the trip as well.[27] What all this shows is that an already eccentric choice of itinerary was made irredeemably so by the readiness with which Johnson allowed himself to fall in with Boswell's own peculiar plans. The whole trip became a sort of counter-culture gesture, a flight from the polite, and in some ways even an attack on the ratified. It was a deliberate search for the *extreme*—a point underlined in a remark Boswell made to Johnson in 1776: 'You and I, Sir, have . . . seen together the extremes of what can be seen in Britain:—the wild rough island of Mull, and Blenheim Park' (*LSJ* ii. 451). The Hebrides were, morally and physically, the *ultima Thule*.

There are a number of considerations here. One is that grand tourists generally met each other: they hung around together in Rome, they attended the same soirées in Florence, they employed the same guides in Naples, they were presented to the same noblemen in Venice. This did not only apply to grand aristocrats; it corresponded with Boswell's experiences in Italy. By contrast, the travellers in Scotland, once they had passed the university cities and embarked on the main part of their journey, met nobody they knew (with very few exceptions), nobody similarly engaged on such a tour, hardly anybody of their own social position, scarcely anyone with an English background (the Italian tourists often clung to one another in a national group).[28] There were welcoming hosts in the Highlands and Islands, but no figure such as Horace Mann who, year after year, welcomed similar parties of visitors to Florence.

[27] *Boswell on the Grand Tour: Germany and Switzerland, 1764*, ed. F. A. Pottle (London: Heinemann, 1953), 273.
[28] On British tourists sticking together, see Dr John Moore, quoted by Mead, *The Grand Tour*, 134–5.

There were no group portraits or conversation pieces by Thomas Patch; no feeling of solidarity induced by the sense that thousands of one's compeers had made the same bows to the same grandee in the same drawing-room for decades.[29]

Underlying this difference is a more fundamental fact. The grand tour was in essence an urban experience; though the traveller had to get from one place to another, this was regarded as a disagreeable necessity—the real point of the exercise lay in the sojourn at towns and courts. As W. E. Mead remarked after an extensive trawl of Italian narratives: 'As a rule the tourist wasted little time upon country districts, which in general were thinly inhabited and destitute of the comforts of life. Italy was in a peculiar sense a land of cities.'[30] By stark contrast, Johnson sought out a region destitute of comforts, moving into 'northern regions . . . now so thinly peopled' (*JWI* 97). It could also be said that the Scottish Highlands was in a very particular sense, a country without cities. After leaving Edinburgh, St Andrews, and Aberdeen, the travellers entered no settlement of any size until they reached Glasgow near the end of their journey—even Inverness was scarcely more than a village. As Johnson himself observed: 'There is not in the Western Islands any collection of buildings that can make pretensions to be called a town' (*JWI* 131). Consequently, only the first thirteen pages of his narrative, along with the last four, contain anything resembling a description of urban life. This is a precise inversion of the usual proportions.

The discrepancy is exaggerated by the fact that 'for the most part tourists manifested little desire to visit places off the beaten track'.[31] In the words of Johnson's friend Baretti: 'No English traveller that ever I heard ever went a step out of those roads, which from the foot of the Alps lead straight to our most famous cities.'[32] This is not a distortion of the reality, though it does exaggerate a little. Even Goethe, arriving at a different angle from the English

---

[29] Mann's extensive activity in greeting British visitors to Florence can be traced in his correspondence with Horace Walpole, much of which relevant to the theme is collected in Dr [John] Doran, *'Mann' and Manners at the Court of Florence 1740–1786* (London: Bentley, 1876), *passim*; and in Lesley Lewis, *Connoisseurs and Secret Agents in Eighteenth-Century Rome* (London: Chatto, 1961). For Patch, see Lewis, *Connoisseurs and Secret Agents*, 172–3. Mann often introduced the British to Cardinal Albani, their most prominent sponsor in Rome: Lewis gives a full account of Albani's career.　　　　　　　　　　　[30] Mead, *The Grand Tour*, 272.
[31] Ibid. 208.　　　　　　　　　　　　　　　　　　　　　　[32] Ibid. 273.

visitors as it were, reversed their most common mode of departure in his progress from Munich to Rome via Innsbruck, Trentino, and Venice. There were practical reasons behind this conservative choice of route. As Mead observes: 'To see any town that involved even a slight detour was, for one who had a fixed agreement with a *vetturino*, commonly impracticable.'[33] (Goethe still managed to get out and walk by himself to Assisi.) Still, at a deeper level this lack of imagination must be ascribed primarily to a somewhat rigid pattern of expectations and cultural assumptions; the tour was a set menu rather than a series of unlimited options, table d'hôte and not à la carte. Johnson, of course, makes his entire journey into one long detour, skimming round the edge of the known British mainland almost into *ultima Thule*.

Another disincentive to the orthodox tourist was the poor state of the roads off the main highways: all the historians of the subject include a section which covers the lamentations of voyagers concerning mud, dust, upset coaches, and swollen ditches. Johnson only had good roads for a very small portion of his trip in the opening segment. He notes on his second page, after leaving Edinburgh and entering Fife: 'The roads are neither rough nor dirty; and it affords a southern stranger a new kind of pleasure to travel so commodiously without the interruption of toll-gates' (*JWI* 4). But this easy and pleasant progress was short-lived, and by the time the pair reached Inverness they were obliged to 'bid farewel to the luxury of travelling' (*JWI* 29), exchanging their carriage for horseback. Johnson had known what was coming, and could not have embarked on his venture without anticipating the situation he found in Skye: 'In the Islands there are no roads, nor any marks by which a stranger may find his way' (*JWI* 53). Consequently, there are no petulant complaints: unlike the cosseted grand tourist, Johnson regarded the hard slogging from one place to another as a normal feature of his expedition.[34]

---

[33] Mead, *The Grand Tour*, 273.

[34] Johnson refers in a letter to Hester Thrale of the need for 'scrambling' on occasions: *L* i. 387. Even on the mainland, there had been virtually no permanent roads until General Wade was sent to establish a system of routes linking the military garrisons, after the first Jacobite rising. There were scarcely any charts of the waters around the Hebrides until the work of Murdoch Mackenzie, published in the 1770s. At the time of the first rising, General Hawley, is said to have had access only to one hand-drawn map of the Highlands. See further Elizabeth Bray, *The Discovery of the Hebrides* (London and Glasgow: Collins, 1986), 58–69.

A related issue is called up shortly afterwards, when Johnson writes: 'It need not, I suppose, be mentioned, that in countries so little frequented as the Islands, there are no houses where travellers are entertained for money' (*JWI* 54). Once more, this is precisely the opposite of what the Italian tourist could expect. Not all the inns were felt to be good ones, and petty cavils about the beds, the food, and the service were a wearisome litany absent from few travel narratives, but there was certainly a wide range of hostelries catering for the visitor. In fact, a tourist industry had already grown up in the main cities of Italy and along the high roads which linked them.[35] This circumstance reflects the contrast already noted: between a set itinerary with known stopping-points and a journey virtually into the unknown; a difference in physical conditions, but also, ultimately, in metaphysical outlook, since Johnson sought essentially the new, the tourists essentially the familiar (even if it was familiar only by reputation or from literary allusion: Goethe was not the only tourist to feel that he was revisiting sites rather than seeing them for the first time).

Under the heading of the mode of travel, one further point needs to be stressed. The grand tour was overwhelmingly a land-based event; apart from the unavoidable need to cross the Channel, British visitors seldom left terra firma. Some made the crossing from Nice to Genoa or Leghorn by felucca, to avoid the horrors of an Alpine passage, but apart from brief journeys by river or canal (especially in Holland), it was rare to take to the water again. Scarcely anybody then attempted pleasure-parties on the lakes of Lombardy: Mrs Piozzi was a rare exception. And, whilst it may not be precisely true, as Colette once observed, that 'La Méditerranée, ce n'est pas la mer,'[36] it could be claimed with total conviction that no tourist would deliberately have exposed himself or herself to the oceanic perils endured by Johnson and Boswell as they made their frightening passages between tiny islands amid heaving Atlantic billows, in pervasively damp, chilling weather. The risks they ran were emphasized by the drowning of their friend Coll, only one year later, in the very Sound of Ulva which the travellers had lately crossed—a fact noted by Boswell (*LSJ* v. 331).[37] In general, Johnson

[35] See Black, *The British and the Grand Tour*, 60–7.

[36] Colette, *Bella-Vista* (n.p.: Ferenczi, 1937), 35.

[37] Pennant and Banks had both braved the treacherous waters around the Hebrides in 1772, but they were at the start of a trend which was only just establishing itself when Johnson and Boswell travelled the following year.

was not an aquatic animal; his willingness to brave these dangerous seas testifies once more to something beyond physical hardihood— it points also to a desire to escape from the known. In principle, the grand tour might have embodied such a yearning; in practice, it largely catered to the opposite set of human urges.

V

Johnson soon contrived to assimilate his journey to traditional expectations by writing of Forres as 'the town to which Macbeth was travelling, when he met the weird sisters in his way. This to an Englishman is classic ground' (*JWI* 25). At least Shakespeare could be seen as an adequate substitute for Virgil, whom Goethe, like many others, hymned, or Horace, the particular lodestar of Boswell. In May 1765 Boswell had visited Tivoli with Lord Mountstuart, the son of Lord Bute; there, 'upon seeing the famous *Fons Bandusiae* he spouted Horace's ode on the spot . . . Boswell expressed his "classical enthusiasm" at seeing the countryside described by Horace in a letter to John Johnston.'[38] There were, however, constant obstacles to reconstructing a classical pantheon in the Highlands, and these are worth exploring in more detail.

First of all, the climate which so transformed Goethe's sense of reality was, in Johnson's case, distinctly un-Mediterranean. The text of the *Journey* is sprinkled with allusions to 'the violence of the weather' (*JWI* 69) confining the travellers; or to regions where 'the climate is unkind and the ground penurious' (*JWI* 138). 'The winter of the Hebrides', we are told, 'consists of little more than rain and wind' (*JWI* 52). More extensively, a little later on: 'Their weather is not pleasing. Half the year is deluged with rain. . . . Their winter overtakes their summer, and their harvest lies upon the ground drenched with rain. The autumn struggles hard to produce some of our early fruits' (*JWI* 78). Johnson even anticipates the potential for tourist attraction in Loch Lomond, 'had [it] been in a happier climate' (*JWI* 159). A perpetual chill hangs over the narrative. Voltaire had perhaps not been far wrong in 1764, when he

---

[38] *Boswell on the Grand Tour: Italy, Corsica and France*, 87–8.

explained to Boswell that the Academy of Painting in Glasgow had proved a failure because 'to paint well it is necessary to have warm feet'.[39]

Allied to the harsh climate is the barren terrain. Notoriously Johnson made much of the treeless landscape: 'I had now travelled two hundred miles, and seen only one tree not younger than myself' (*JWI* 21). Similiarly: 'The country about Dunvegan is rough and barren' (*JWI* 70). Such scenery prompts many philosophical asides: 'It is natural, in traversing this gloom of desolation, to inquire, whether something may be done to give nature a more cheerful face' (*JWI* 139). The very adjective 'cheerful' suggests the Virgilian epithet *laetens*, and one could paraphrase the urge here as that of making Ceres reassume the land. Italian tourists commented on the heavy vegetation under a southern sky; they drew for the reader a world of myrtle groves and vine-strewn hillsides. British visitors to Florence, inspired by Milton, flocked to the chestnut forests of the abbey of Vallombrosa. Thus, by contrast, the 'uniformity of barrenness [which] can afford very little amusement to the traveller' (*JWI* 40) also defeats the authorial urge, since literary materials had been made up, for the educated British male, by the elements of an Italian landscape. What Johnson encountered in the north was a scenery that resisted the imagination. 'In the penury of these malignant regions' (*JWI* 82), not only was agriculture primitive (though 'perhaps rather feeble than unskilful': *JWI* 79) but there were 'few opportunities of luxury' (*JWI* 84). Thus manners, too, tended to be gross, until the Union brought 'progress in useful knowledge' (*JWI* 28). It is true that the pacification of the Highlands meant that Johnson now thought that 'a longer journey must be taken by him whose curiosity pants for savage virtues and barbarous grandeur' (*JWI* 58). But though the anthropological purity of noble savagery is not available, the *Journey* leaves us in no doubt that primitive living, in the shape of poverty and subsistence farming, still survived. There was plenty of poverty in Italy, of course, but tourists could see it as picturesque in Naples; and as for the most backward regions in Calabria and Sicily, they remained quite off the map and outside most travellers' experience.

If we move from the physical circumstances of the Highland people to their cultural expression, two main issues stand out. The

---

[39] *Boswell on the Grand Tour: Germany and Switzerland*, 280.

first is the relative absence of historical monuments, at least in terms of intelligible and decipherable relics. As early on in the journey as St Andrews, before crossing the Highland line, Johnson deplores the treatment of the ancient city: '[We] surveyed the ruins of ancient magnificence, of which even the ruins cannot long be visible, unless some care be taken to preserve them; and where is the pleasure of preserving such mournful memorials? They have been till very lately so much neglected, that every man carried away the stones who fancied that he wanted them' (*JWI* 5). Again, it is true that the ruins of Rome had been similarly despoiled for centuries, but by this date the ancient sites were more often being looted by antiquarian collectors than turned over by house-builders. Several times Johnson makes harsh reference to the depredations of the Reformation, often in a tone of mirthless irony: 'Two chapels were erected by their ancestors, of which I saw the skeletons, which now stand faithful witnesses of the triumph of Reformation' (*JWI* 122). A characteristic turn of phrase links the Reformation, a form of carnage Rome had not known, with the destruction which the city had suffered from the barbarian hordes: 'We read with as little emotion the violence of Knox and his followers, as the irruptions of Alaric and the Goths' (*JWI* 9).

The absence of well-preserved monuments makes it impossible to read the culture in its historical aspect. For, as Johnson remarks on Skye: 'Edifices, either standing or ruined, are the chief records of an illiterate nation' (*JWI* 73). Ignorance leads to speculative and unreliable archeology; thus the local minister, with all the enthusiasm of a Jonathan Oldbuck, believes a ruined enclosure at Ulinish (Ullinish) to be a Danish fort. Others 'suppose it the original seat of the chief of the Macleods' (*JWI* 72). Sceptically, Johnson wonders whether it may not be of more recent origin, and used by cattle-rustlers, enjoying his role of Edie Ochiltree as he corrects the fantasizing natives. However, the most serious point at issue here is the lack of certainty in the absence of records, research, and good upkeep. The few scraps of information which the local people do preserve are greedily received, though not always treated as reliable. Johnson's profound native scepticism is consolidated here by the dearth of authentic monuments and the limitations of a basically illiterate culture. Grand tourists were advised to study 'the ancient inscriptions and ruins and antiquities, which are very curious and instructive to one that takes delight in such things',[40] but his impulses were baulked at every turn. Instead of the 152 churches to inspect in Florence, or the 107 'notable palaces' on view in Rome,[41] duly registered in the guidebooks, there were very few buildings of any character or aesthetic appeal, let alone antiquity. Johnson dutifully sets out to examine a squalid hut not far from Loch Ness, not as a locus of *virtù* or connoisseur interest, but simply as a piece of contemporary social observation. Tourists did not generally concern themselves unduly with the modern; even the finest architectural achievements of the baroque era in Rome were disdainfully swept aside in the quest for remnants of a noble past. Johnson has no such choice available to him. In the towns much of the medieval heritage had been destroyed by the reformers. In the countryside there was scarcely anything meaningful left to relate the history of the savage community; Raasay 'has little that can detain a traveller' (*JWI* 66). Hence the thankfulness with which Johnson grasps the opportunity to align Iona with Marathon as a site of abiding historical interest (see p. 167).

This blankness is directly related to the second aspect of Highland culture which requires some discussion. This is a matter on which Johnson expressed views which were controversial in his own day and remain so—that is, on the nature of a preliterate, or illiterate, or non-literate society. Johnson devotes several paragraphs to this theme, including an interesting reflection in his general section on 'The Highlands' on the relation between distinct languages, in isolated mountainous country, and distinct 'manners' or ways of life (*JWI* 43–4). When he reaches the Gaelic-speaking districts, 'our guides now became doubly necessary as interpreters' (*JWI* 42). Tourists were frequently just as baffled, though more often in Germany than in Italy. Johnson was to speak Latin when he visited Paris, and no doubt could have got away with this in Rome—it was only a minority of visitors who made serious efforts to learn the native language, although Johnson's friend Charles

---

[40] Lord Carpenter, quoted by Black *The British and the Grand Tour*, 238. Ruins in Italy were educative; they prompted 'melancholy thoughts of the imperfection and instability of every work of man' (Thomas Pelham, ibid. 237). Ruins in the Highlands were unexpressive, prompting mere speculations and baffled conjectures ('It might once have been a dwelling . . . I imagine them to have been places of only occasional use . . . [we] went away without knowing how far it [a cave] was carried': *JWI* 72–3). [41] Hibbert, *The Tour*, 149, 170.

James Fox was one of the exceptions.[42] Almost all the travellers flocked to the opera, which gives added point to Johnson's little joke about listening to Erse songs like 'an English audience to an Italian opera, delighted with the sound of words which I did not understand' (*JWI* 59).

Despite this, Johnson's major concern lies not in language as such, but in linguistic transmission through the written word, as this affects the possibilities of preserving racial memory. His general position is bleak, by the standards of modern anthropological theory:

> In nations, where there is hardly the use of letters, what is once out of sight is lost for ever. They think but little, and of their few thoughts, none are wasted on the past, in which they are interested neither by fear nor hope. Their only registers are stated observances and practical representations. For this reason an age of ignorance is an age of ceremony. Pageants, and processions, and commemorations, gradually shrink away, as better methods come into use of recording events. (*JWI* 65).

One wonders what Johnson would have made of papal ceremonies and the semiology of carnival time.

He returns to the theme in more detail when concluding his general survey of Highland life. Starting from the premiss that 'The nation was wholly illiterate. Neither bards nor Senachies could read or write,' he goes on to weigh the consequences of this: 'Where the Chiefs of the Highlands have found the histories of their descent is difficult to tell,' he complains, 'for no Earse genealogy was ever written.' And, in a final burst of despair: 'Thus hopeless are all attempts to find any trace of Highland learning' (*JWI* 112). The point of citing these familiar passages is not to assess their adequacy, which is a task for a different branch of enquiry; what matters here is that Johnson describes the unavailability of Highland culture for serious human investigation. In that sense, he has only met with what he might have expected, in reversing the normal tourist perspective on the past. If Erse is 'the rude speech of a barbarous people, [with] . . . few thoughts to express' (*JWI* 114), then that is as it should be within Johnson's mental map. Quasi-

---

[42] The best discussion of this point remains that of Mead, *The Grand Tour*, 115–18. It should be added that the best-known Italian–English dictionary of this era was that produced by Baretti in 1760: Johnson, as is well known, wrote the dedication to this work.

technical terms such as 'rude', 'barbarous', 'savage', 'civility', and so on may or may not have the precise denotations which they would have in the philosophical history of Adam Smith and Adam Ferguson (see also pp. 218–22 below). But even if they do not, they certainly adumbrate an attitude towards history, and they show that Johnson recognized the authentically primitive, in his terms, in its proper setting. Tourists went south to see the home of civilization in its pristine purity. Johnson went north to see savage culture in its clearest expression, and though he believed that he had arrived too late to see ancient 'manners' in spontaneous action, he did encounter what he thought was the inevitable cultural legacy of preliterate societies (*JWI* 57).

As everyone knows, Johnson is really gunning for the bards here, and particularly for the author of Ossian. His conclusion is stark: 'I believe there cannot be recovered, in the whole Earse language, five hundred lines of which there is any evidence to prove them a hundred years old. Yet I hear that the father of Ossian [James Macpherson] boasts of two chests more of ancient poetry, which he suppresses, because they are too good for the *English*' (*JWI* 116–17). It is not necessary to go into the broader *Kulturkampf* at this point. For our present purposes, the key aspect is the dubiety surrounding Ossian, the lack of historic canon, a corpus of literature long worked over by scholars, the vagueness of the claims, and the air of topical scandal. Instead of the 'cool and minute investigation' which was to follow Gibbon's first impulse of intoxicated joy in Rome, performed under the tutelage of 'a sober Scotch antiquary of experience and taste',[43] we are presented with the impudent demagoguery of a charlatan, where no hard facts have been established. Virgil is the literary embodiment of a society whose works have been preserved, by will or by chance (Johnson was writing in the aftermath of the rediscovery of Pompeii and Herculaneum, but he does not hold out much hope for a parallel revitalization of Scottish archeology). Ossian, on the other hand, is the poet of inauthentic history, a vatic figure created in the absence of a genuine folk memory.

Most of the *Journey* is more positive in its outlook than this section on the bards. Nevertheless, Johnson is consistent through-out in viewing the places he visits through the wrong end of a

---

[43] Gibbon, *Autobiographies*, 267–8.

tourist's telescope—or perhaps it would be more apt to say, through an inverted Claude glass. Everything he encounters has a ghostly obverse in the experience of the travellers whose accounts he had read and the many recent tourists with whom he had conversed. Some of the differences are of a superficial or 'social' kind: most tourists took a full retinue of servants, this pair had only Boswell's Bohemian valet; many took or hired a fine carriage, where Johnson and Boswell were forced first on to horseback (Johnson once on to a small Highland pony) and then sometimes on to their hands and knees as they scrabbled over the rocks. (By contrast, the comfortable grand tourist was wafted across the Alpine passes in a litter carried by up to eight porters.) Most tourists, especially the younger ones, spent a good deal of money; Johnson used very little indeed. They often bought fine clothes, *objets d'art*, luxury goods of all kinds; Johnson bought nothing and gave away instructive books instead. They womanized, they sought the headier night-life of the cities; whereas 'the Islands afford few pleasures, except to the hardy sportsman' (*JWI* 102), adumbrating the very kind of country pursuit which even country gentleman forswore when they embarked on their quest for taste and elegant living. They hobnobbed with internationally famous statesmen, scholars, and artists, whereas Johnson himself was the known figure at the party, if anyone was.[44] And so one could go on at wearisome length. One has only to think of a standard component of the grand tour, and one is likely to be able to discover its antithesis in the northern journey made by Boswell and Johnson.

VI

Goethe's sojourn in Italy may be regarded as the supreme consummation of grand-tour experience. He was, needless to say, much better equipped to absorb impressions; he was older than the standard tourist (37 when he embarked on the trip); he had a much deeper knowledge of the fine arts; and, finally, he was incomparably more gifted as a writer when he came to compose his *Italian*

---

[44] Hibbert, *The Tour*, 72, lists the many notabilities whom Gibbon encountered in Paris (see Gibbon, *Autobiographies*, 200–3). Boswell does stress the illuminati of Edinburgh (see *LSJ* v. 24–51), but Johnson himself suppresses this information. He evidently regarded the stay in Edinburgh as a mere prologue to the tour proper.

Journey. With all these individual qualities, he managed to express in its highest abstract form what I have called the ideology of the grand tour.

The comparison with Johnson's Hebridean adventures is not as artificial as one might initially suppose. Goethe set out from Carlsbad in September 1786, little more than a decade after the earlier journey, and at almost exactly the same moment as Boswell published his *Journal of a Tour to the Hebrides*. Johnson had died less than two years before. Moreover, one of the most intimate friendships that Goethe developed in Rome was with Angelica Kauffmann, the Swiss-born painter who had spent some years in England and had become a close ally of Joshua Reynolds. Kauffmann is not mentioned in Boswell's *Life*, but both the biographer and his subject must have known her quite well. She was, after all, a founder-member of the Royal Academy, in which Johnson had a direct interest.[45] A further connection lies in Goethe's meeting in Naples with Sir William Hamilton, already linked with his future second wife Emma. Hamilton was elected to the Club shortly before Johnson's death: more significantly, he had acted as host in Naples to a series of visitors, including, most relevantly, Boswell, Gibbon, Burney, Palmerston, and Fox. Hamilton was also on good terms with Reynolds.

In outline, Goethe's trip possessed many of the features of a routine tour, however special the identity of the tourist. As already noted he entered Italy via Innsbruck and Trentino, usually the departure route for British visitors heading (as so many did) for the Austrian and German courts. He then spent some time in Verona, Vicenza, and Padua: his comments on the University of Padua concentrate on the cramped lecture-halls, but this was one early stopping-place which Johnson, we know, would have wished to visit for himself (for Hester Piozzi's views on this, see p. 44 above). Goethe then made his way to Venice, another of Johnson's chosen localities, where he spent just over two weeks. He then passed through Ferrara, Bologna, Florence, and Perugia en route to the

---

[45] As noted above, Palmerston had sat for his portrait to Kauffmann in Rome: see Connell, *Portrait of a Peer*, 46. Garrick also sat in 1764, and inscribed verses to her. Boswell met her in the same city on 16 Feb. 1765: 'Then Mlle Kauffmann: paintress, singer; modest, amiable. Quite in love' (*Boswell on the Grand Tour: Italy, Corsica and France*, 50.) On Reynolds and Kauffmann, see Derek Hudson, *Sir Joshua Reynolds: A Personal Study* (London: Bles, 1958), 138–41.

Eternal City. The itinerary is less than orthodox only in excluding the cities of western Lombardy and the Ligurian coast: however, none of these was a truly central feature of the standard tour, on a par with Rome, Naples, Florence, and Venice.

It was at the start of November 1786 that Goethe finally came to the place at the heart of his imaginative journey: 'Now, at last, I have arrived in the First city of the world' (*IJ*, 115), he wrote. His first period of residence lasted until 21 February 1787. He then set out for Naples, where he passed the next five weeks. On 29 March he embarked on a curious additional loop, that is a mini-tour of Sicily. He sailed from Naples to Palermo, then went across country to Messina, and returned by sea from Messina to Naples. His second spell in Naples occupied the period from 14 May to 3 June. After this he made his way back to Rome, for his second and longer visit, which did not come to an end until April 1788. This was not an unduly long sojourn for those on the grand tour; indeed, the only feature of the itinerary which calls for special comment is the Sicilian excursion, to which we shall return. Otherwise, Goethe's protracted residence in Rome, and his shorter periods in Naples, reflect a normal allocation of time and attention.

From an emotional and intellectual standpoint, too, the dreams and aspirations that Goethe carried with him are identifiable as the traditional tourist hopes, heightened by the intensity of his own nature. This is true even in respect of the weather. Leaving behind cold, fog, and damp in Munich, he admitted early on that he had 'undertaken this journey in order to escape the inclemencies I had suffered on the fifty-first parallel' (*IJ* 14). He took careful note of the portents with the zeal of an amateur meteorologist, realizing that 'latitude by itself does not make a climate' (*IJ* 14). As he moved south into warmer sunshine, he reflected that 'we Cimmerians hardly know the real meaning of the day' (*IJ* 42). This gives vent to reflections on the way in which life was lived in Italy, involving a different arrangement of hours around the clock. By the time he reached Venice, he was extending his comparative exercise to light: 'We northerners who spend our lives in a drab and . . . an uglier country where even reflected light is subdued . . . cannot instinctively develop an eye which looks with such delight at the world [as the Venetian painters]' (*IJ* 79). For the remainder of his journey he basked in warmth and light, which opened his eyes to new beauty, but also expanded his imagination. The new conditions of physical living had brought about a new sense of possibility: 'I have seen the sea twice, first the Adriatic, then the Mediterranean, but both, as it were, only in passing. In Naples we shall get better acquainted. Everything in me is suddenly beginning to emerge clearly' (*IJ* 162).

The ultimate key to this self-realization was something more inward than merely sun and sea. It lay in the cultural meaning of Rome, the true destination of Goethe's quest, as it was for so many tourists. Like Gibbon, Goethe felt that the great drama of history had revolved around Rome, and that it embodied the spiritual centre of European civilization. There is a sharp contrast here with Johnson, whose journey hinged on no particular locality, although he passed the longest period on Skye. There was no single focus in the Highlands, geographically or spiritually.[46]

Against this, Goethe headed for Rome as for a lost home. In numerous passages he makes clear the special quality that the great city had for him: 'Now I have arrived,' he writes as early as 3 November, 'I have calmed down and feel as if I had found a peace that will last for my whole life . . . All the dreams of my youth have come to life' (*IJ* 116). A few days later: 'As I rush about Rome looking at the major monuments, the immensity of the place has a quietening effect' (*IJ* 120). Some weeks later: 'What I want to see is the Everlasting Rome, not the Rome which is replaced by another every decade' (*IJ* 142). 'There is only one Rome in the world,' he wrote upon his second visit, 'here I feel like a fish in the water' (*IJ* 345). His Roman sojourn was 'the most important period in my life . . . I am living on the spiritual riches of all that is especially precious to me . . . Now everything lies clear before me, and, as Minerva was born from the head of Jupiter, so art has become my second nature, born from the heads of great men' (*IJ* 371–2). The visual impressions remain strong: the landscape in autumn 'is so full of colour that, in any reproduction, it must look like a confused motley. . . . The clear blue shadows stand out delightfully against anything green, yellow, red or brown, and merge into the bluish haze distance' (*IJ* 415). The best weather to date occurred on a visit to Frascati, Albana, and Castel Gandolfo, when Goethe witnessed 'tones in the landscape of very great beauty' (*IJ* 424). But the underlying cause of his well-being lay in a new inner harmony. 'In

[46] To the ancients, the Hebrides had been known as 'the edge of the world', a label which presumes the centrality of the Mediterranean and, above all, of Rome.

Rome I have found myself for the first time,' he writes with enviable simplicity when about to leave (*IJ* 482).

The generalized tour ideology hoped to fashion a gentleman, a scholar, a man of affairs, and a connoisseur. What happened to Goethe is that these educative aims were subsumed in a greater process of personal transformation, of which Italy and, above all, Rome constituted the agent. Lady Hertford had hoped that her son, who, sadly, died on his tour, would return 'a knowing experienced man, a brave and honest patriot, an entertaining and agreeable companion, a genteel and graceful figure, a grateful and faithful friend, a nobleman worthy of the rank and fortune he is born to'.[47] This is the ideal of a Renaissance humanist education, one which Johnson could have admired, stripped perhaps of some of its aristocratic hauteur. Goethe had gone down much the same road, but his course of moral instruction had been filtered through a romantic sensibility. Warmth, light, colour, art, antiquity—all are focused on the unique city, the very fulcrum of Goethe's voyage into the unknown south.

Of course, he came well prepared, in a way that Johnson could not match in Scotland, for all his assiduous reading of Martin's book.[48] For years, Goethe tells us, he had been forced to avert his eyes from Latin texts, in case he was too powerfully affected by the aura they had acquired during his youth—instead he had turned to the safety of the 'abstractions of Spinoza'. His 'passionate desire to see [the world of Rome] with my own eyes' was now realized, and he now felt able to return to the classics he had once loved. 'Now I feel, not that I am seeing them for the first time, but that I am seeing them again' (*IJ* 89–90). Whilst recognizing in the same passage that 'the climate alone would lead me to prefer these regions to all others', and that 'Climate, truly, makes all the

---

[47] See Helen Sard Hughes, *The Gentle Hertford: Her Life and Letters* (New York: Macmillan, 1940), 221, 318.

[48] There was indeed virtually nothing outside Martin for Johnson to read, as Pennant's second Scottish tour, *A Tour in Scotland and Voyage to the Hebrides*, was published only in May 1774. A recent discussion is to be found in Thomas Jemielity, 'Thomas Pennant's Scottish *Tours* and *A Journey to the Western Islands of Scotland*', in P. Nath (ed), *Fresh Reflections on Samuel Johnson* (Troy, NY: Whitston, 1987), 321–27. This situation contrasts with the large library of guides, memoirs, and travellers' vade-mecum volumes available to Goethe, quite apart from ancient texts, such as Vitruvius, which he was able to buy on the spot in Venice (*IJ* 89).

difference to one's life' (*IJ* 89–91), he emphasizes that the architecture of Palladio in Vicenza is especially potent because it revives memories long enshrined in his heart from childhood exposure to books and prints. The appeal of 'classic soil' (*IJ* p. xx) derives from this reanimation of buried sensations. The tour thus stirs a complex series of associations. While crossing the Alps, Goethe had quoted a line of Virgil and observed: 'This is the first line of Latin verse the subject of which I have seen with my own eyes' (*IJ* 25). Later, in Naples, he writes that 'the scales have fallen' from his eyes regarding Homer: his descriptions and similes are in fact 'utterly natural', drawn from life: 'Even when the events he narrates are fabulous and fictitious, they have a naturalness about them which I have never felt so strongly as in the presence of the settings he describes' (*IJ* 305). There are obvious similarities here to Johnson's views about the realistic element in feudal romances, inspired by his sight of wild nature on Skye (*JWI* 77). There is a larger difference concealed, however. The literature and art being revived for Goethe's imaginative contemplation embody the central texts of his civilization, whereas the 'Gothick romances' which Johnson can reclaim are only the primitive fictions of a dark age. The fundamental contrast underlies everything in the two narratives: Goethe sets up his base in the nerve-centre of classical culture; Johnson perpetrates a kind of fugue into *Caledonia Deserta*, the region where civilization (as understood in classical terms) fades off the map.

It is natural to put the main stress on what was distinctive in Goethe's experience of Italy—the inward growth of which, as we have seen, he became conscious. But there is a more orthodox element in his journey, which corresponds to the external benefits accruing to educated tourists of every description. For example, whilst in Venice Goethe was able to enjoy opera, oratorio, Venetian comedy by Goldoni and others (in fact 'one of the few plays by Goldoni which is still performed': *IJ* 85), an improvised harlequinade, and tragedy. He studied the buildings of Palladio with a published guide to hand. When he left, he could feel that 'Venice is no longer a mere word, an empty name' (*IJ* 58), after a round of social occasions not very different from that of casual trippers. Similarly, he did many of the usual things in Naples; he climbed Vesuvius, made an excursion to Pompeii and Herculaneum, and enjoyed the hospitality of Sir William Hamilton. He came late enough to witness the soon-to-be-famous 'attitudes' of Emma Hart, subsequently the Ambassador's second wife. 'This much is certain,' wrote Goethe ambiguously, 'as a performance it's like nothing you ever saw before in your life. We enjoyed it on two evenings' (*IJ* 200). Goethe was among the smaller group which ventured out on 'an excursion to Paestum' (*IJ* 208), and he enjoyed the spectacular views across the Bay of Naples with the painter Kniep.

Goethe was not alone in finding that 'Naples is a paradise; everyone lives in a state of self-forgetfulness, myself included' (*IJ* 198). On his second visit he noted that 'One of the greatest delights of Naples is the universal gaiety' (*IJ* 318). Here he echoes Hester Piozzi, who thought that 'The truth is, the jolly Neapolitans lead a coarse life, but it is an unoppressed one.' Boswell, too, found that the warmth and relaxed atmosphere enlivened his spirits: 'If a man's mind never failed to catch the spirit of the climate in which he breathes, I ought now to write you a most delicious letter, for Naples is indeed a delicious spot: *praeter omnes ridet*.'[49] Much of Goethe's time was spent in ways which match items in the travel diaries of Johnson's friends: Boswell, Gibbon, and Palmerston were amongst those to mix with Hamilton and his set; and Palmerston, as we have seen, had his portrait painted in Rome by Goethe's intimate friend Angelica Kauffmann. It requires no stretching of the evidence, and no illicit play of idle speculation, to suppose that Johnson's planned trip to Italy would have consisted of much the same activities. Perhaps he might have been admitted to an *accademia*, as Goethe was to the most famous, the Arcadia *(IJ* 441–5), and as Boswell had been, no doubt to his great self-satisfaction.[50]

Even in Rome, where Goethe devoted himself to a private course of self-improvement through the medium of art, he led far from an isolated existence. During his second visit he wrote: 'Really I must be becoming a Roman, for the Romans are always accused of thinking and talking about *cose grande*. The idea struck me the other day that in the wide circle of a great city even the poorest and the humblest person feels himself to be somebody, whereas in a

---

[49] Piozzi, *Observations*, 235; *Boswell on the Grand Tour: Italy, Corsica and France*, 59.

[50] F. A. Pottle, 'Boswell as Icarus', in C. Camden (ed.), *Restoration and Eighteenth-Century Literature* (Chicago: University of Chicago Press, 1963), 389–406.

small town even the best and the richest is not himself and cannot breathe' (*IJ* 396). Here is the rationale of the urban emphasis of the historic grand tour: the traveller grew through social relationships as well as by contact with the loci of ancient civilization. Once more Johnson is seen to be in flight from the ideology of the tour. He deliberately abstracts himself from the great metropolis in which he lives, and pursues the 'poorest and humblest' in their narrow provincial circle—conceivably a delayed reassumption of his own Lichfield inheritance, but taken to a far greater extreme in the untracked Highlands. It is notable, too, that Goethe was able to make progress on his own most serious literary projects, including *Egmont* and *Tasso*. It would not be true to say that Johnson suspended operations as a writer, since he was laying the foundations for his own *Journey*, one of the greatest works he ever produced; but there was no time or leisure to embark on other major works of literature, and seemingly no desire to do so. The onset of carnival time briefly interrupted Goethe's work, but in general he was able to maintain a high level of productivity.

All this belongs to the same syndrome. For Goethe, Rome was a place to develop what was already latent in his own nature, to build on his earlier dreams and revitalize his memories, to evolve along predetermined lines. It was an act of confirmation and of rededication, and in this it expressed the ideology of the grand tour in a heightened form. The epigraph to the *Italian Journey* is 'Auch ich in Arkadia!' For Johnson, the Highlands and Islands were an ordeal of testing by the unfamiliar. It was for this reason that his text made so little of the periods spent in Edinburgh, Aberdeen, and Glasgow, where he met the illuminati just as Goethe and the tourists encountered them in Rome. Equally, Johnson almost totally suppressed his passages of arms with Monboddo and Lord Auchinleck.[51] The rhetoric of his *Journey* is designed to play down contact with educated society and with 'civilized' values. Johnson's literary strategies, as much as his existential aims, were thus diametrically opposed to those of Goethe, whose book displays his relish in being absorbed into the main current of European culture.[52]

---

[51] Again Boswell repairs the omission in his narrative, see *LSJ* v. 22–54, 76–83, 379–85.

[52] There is a parallel here with Peter Conrad's findings with regard to British travellers in America: 'Objects in America aren't determined by history or enmeshed

In fairness, some account should be taken of the apparently
Johnsonian addendum which Goethe made to his spell in Italy—his
expedition to Sicily. It is true that this involved comparative
physical hardship, travelling by mule along steep paths and
scrabbling about in wild countryside. It is also true that Goethe
encountered trees and bushes unknown to him, at which he 'took
this blessed strangeness to [his] heart'. His comment is significant:
'There could be no better commentary on the *Odyssey*' (*IJ* 283).
But against this one has to set the fact that Goethe asserted that his
short 'journey across Sicily was quick and easy' (*IJ* 304). It is also
important to note that even in the most remote country, he came
across ancient temples, which were not a feature of the bare
landscape Johnson had traversed. The word we used earlier for this
trip, a 'loop', is perhaps defensible; for the heart of Italy was Rome,
and this was the heart of the journey for Goethe.

The approach adopted here is, of course, only one of many
possible perspectives on the *Italian Journey*. To do full justice to the
book, one would need to consider other aspects of Goethe's mind
and sensibility, particularly those deriving from his German
inheritance. But it may be useful to consider the work in this way
for the light that it throws on Johnson. In the case of his *Journey*,
the insight which results from viewing matters in this context may
be more centrally relevant, even though it is a kind of oppositional
context. Johnson sought the culturally empty wilds of Scotland
when they were still at the limits of known civilization. He was
drawn to bleak, bare, primitive and impoverished states of society,
and he chose a cold, uncomfortable, and sometimes dangerous
mode of travel. He did this in the company of one who had made an
authentic grand tour, and in the full knowledge of what he was, in
one sense, missing. Yet, just as much as Goethe, he was able at the
end of his journey to reflect on man and his nature. The route he
took involved a quest for the unfamiliar, so that he would be
instructed as he was 'surprised by modes of life and appearances of
nature' (*JWI* 149).[53] It was a daring, unorthodox, and character-

by association like those in Europe. Each observer sees them as if for the first time
. . . increasingly, the reason for going to America is not to see America but to
contrive a change in yourself which detaches you from your physical surroundings'
(*Imagining America* (New York: Oxford University Press, 1980), 28). Johnson
similarly sees the Highlands 'for the first time'.

[53] Johnson's comment in 1783, when the Hebridean trip came up in conversation, has already been cited: 'I got acquisition of more ideas by it than by anything

istically independent line of sight, which derived from the initial decision to perform a grand detour from the usual places of pilgrimage, by travelling north rather than south.

that I remember. I saw quite a different system of life', but the sequel (see above, p. 29) is not often remembered. When asked by Boswell if he would like to make the same journey again, Johnson replied: 'Why no, Sir; not the same: it is a tale told. Gravina, an Italian critick, observes, that every man desires to see that of which he has read; but no man desires to read an acount of what he has seen . . . Other people may go and see the Hebrides' (*LSJ* iv. 199). Seeing the things that one had read about expresses the grand-tour ideology, followed by Goethe; but Johnson, seeing the Hebrides for the first time, was writing an account of a region that others had neither seen nor read about.

For a full reading of the 'symbolic journey' of Goethe, and its complex effect on his mind, see Nicholas Boyle, *Goethe: The Poet and the Age*, i: *The Poetry of Desire (1749–1790)* (Oxford: Clarendon Press, 1991), 415–530.

3

'The Transit of the Caledonian Hemisphere': Johnson and Boswell in an Age of Discovery

If the Hebridean trip was not, then, a grand tour—indeed, was more like the antithesis of such a thing—we need to consider what kind of undertaking it was. The first answer I shall suggest, in this chapter, is that it partook in some measure of a European voyage of discovery.

Towards the end of Boswell's *Tour* when the travellers have reached Auchinleck, the author makes an ostentatious gesture of his refusal to show his father and Dr Johnson as 'intellectual gladiators'. 'Therefore,' continues the entry for 6 November 1773, 'I suppress what would, I dare say, make an interesting scene in this dramatick sketch,—this account of the transit of Johnson over the Caledonian Hemisphere' (*LSJ* v. 382). The aim of this chapter is to gloss Boswell's phrase and to supply a context for the Hebridean trip in the accounts of travel, exploration, and discovery which were so conspicuous in the public mind at this very moment.

Recent books have provided us with a wider perspective on travel literature in the eighteenth century, and Thomas M. Curley's valuable study, *Samuel Johnson and the Age of Travel*, has pointed to a pervasive tradition and model. But Professor Curley dwells more on *Rasselas* than on the *Journey* and he sees the work as one shaped to 'a travel book format influenced by previous accounts of Scotland' such as those by Martin Martin and Thomas Pennant.[1]

---

[1] Thomas M. Curley, *Samuel Johnson and the Age of Travel* (Athens, Ga.: University of Georgia Press, 1976), 203; see generally pp. 183–219. Curley acutely notes that the *Journey* states: 'The Highlanders are treated as if they were Eskimos, Siberian nomads, American Indians, and Pacific savages', but he does not develop the point. Other relevant works include Charles L. Batten, jun., *Pleasurable Instruction: Form and Convention in Eighteenth-Century Travel Literature* (Berkeley, Calif., and Los Angeles: University of California Press, 1978); and Percy G. Adams, *Travel Literature and the Evolution of the Novel* (Lexington, Ky.: University Press of Kentucky, 1983).

Neither Curley nor any of the other scholars I have indicated attempts to locate the book within the *immediate* context of travel books in the 1770s, which (Pennant aside) has little to do with Scotland and almost everything to do with overseas voyages, particularly the opening-up of the Pacific regions. Moreover, Johnson's possible debt to close friends who had recently published works of travel (Burney and, especially, Baretti) has not been closely examined. Finally, Boswell's extensive and prolonged contact with travel literature has been almost entirely ignored in assessments of his *Tour*. In what follows, I shall seek first to give a rapid summary of what was just termed the 'immediate' context of the two Hebridean narratives, and then to apply some of these considerations to the text of Johnson and Boswell.

I

Boswell's piquant phrase regarding Johnson's progress through the Highlands has one overwhelming and unavoidable connotation. The first voyage of Captain James Cook (1768–71) had as its ostensible purpose the observation of the transit of Venus, which was indeed carried out, following the Royal Society's specifications, on 3 June 1769. According to Cook's journal: 'The day proved as favourable to our purpose as we could wish; not a cloud was to be seen the whole day, and the air was perfectly clear: so that we had every advantage in observing the whole of the passage of the planet Venus over the sun's disk.'[2] The observers at Tahiti included Joseph Banks, later President of the Royal Society, a member of the Club from 1778, and a central figure in the British culture of his day. After Cook's return in July 1771, there was intense public interest in his various achievements, and by September of that year a contract had been drawn up for what might be termed the 'authorized' account of his travels. Thanks to the influence of Dr Burney and, to a lesser extent, David Garrick, this major contract went to John Hawkesworth, the former editor of the *Adventurer* and a long-time acquaintance of Johnson's.[3] Hawkesworth's

[2] Cited from *Captain Cook: Voyages of Discovery* (Gloucester: A. Sutton, 1984), 30.
[3] For the contract, and Hawkesworth's subsequent misfortunes as a result of his edn., see John Lawrence Abbott, *John Hawkesworth: Eighteenth-Century Man of Letters* (Madison, Wis.: University of Wisconsin Press, 1982), 142–86.

remuneration was the staggering figure of £6,000 a testimony to the eagerness with which the *Voyages* were awaited prior to their appearance in June 1773. No literary work of any description was more vibrantly alive in the public consciousness when Johnson took a coach for Edinburgh on 6 August. Even if Boswell had not drawn attention to the shadow of Cook lying across the travellers' path, it would have been there.

As is often the case, the aptness of the Boswellian phraseology carries with it a certain comic potential. We are invited to contemplate Johnson as a veritable planet, large and titanic; moving, to all appearances (however misleading, in astronomical fact), slowly and with invariable majesty across the northern sky, processing through the zodiac with immemorial calm. The *Tour* shows us that it was not really like that, but Boswell cannot resist the hint of epic, together with the hint of something a little ridiculous—the rolling gait of Johnson faintly suggesting the precession of the planet as it spins through space. I do not mean, of course, that Boswell is ridiculing Johnson in any simple way. But his sense of their joint trip as a kind of astronomical event, to be looked up as a fixed datum in the calendar, wonderfully enshrines the personal meaning which this epochal journey had in his own life, a topic explored later (see Chapters 6 and 7, below).

Joseph Banks, after a minor contretemps, declined to take part in Cook's second expedition, which lasted from July 1772 to July 1775; but he had certainly not lost interest in exploration. Together with the Swedish botanist Daniel Solander, another veteran of the first expedition, he embarked on a more modest but equally significant journey, to Iceland via the Hebrides. This was in the summer of 1772: by that time Johnson was acquainted with both men, as appears from his letter of 27 February in that year (*L* i. 275). On his way north, Banks had visited Staffa, and had given the first detailed description of what was to become known as Fingal's Cave (one cannot keep Ossian out of any Scottish theme in this period). This description was printed by Thomas Pennant in the text of his second Scottish tour (1774–6), and gave the cave its earliest pre-Mendelssohnian renown. Pennant's book was dedicated to Banks, as one who, with Cook, had carried out 'a circumnavigation, founded on the most liberal and scientific principles'.[4] One

---

[4] Cited from A. J. Youngson, *Beyond the Highland Line: Three Journals of Travel in Eighteenth-Century Scotland* (London: Collins, 1974), 13.

misses much in both Johnson's and Boswell's travels if one cannot perceive the vestiges of such a 'circumnavigation' in their progress through the Highlands.

As an inveterate journalist, Boswell had seen the opportunity for good copy when Banks and Solander returned from Iceland and turned up in Edinburgh in November 1772, a few weeks after Pennant had passed through. Boswell had met both Banks and Solander the previous March, on one of his London jaunts, and he had discussed with Johnson the degree of credit which they should receive for the scientific side of the first Cook expedition.[5] He now decided to write up their Icelandic adventures, and 'anecdotes' from their trips duly appeared in the *London Magazine* late in the year.[6] In fact, by this stage Boswell had evidently resolved to become something of an expert on travel and its literature. This may be in part because it was popular and newsworthy; in part because he had scored his only great success to date with a modified travel book, the *Account of Corsica* in 1768. His Corsican adventures had, of course, brought him the friendship of Pasquale Paoli, and in September 1771 he had stage-managed a kind of dress rehearsal for the Hebridean trip two years later. Paoli arrived in Edinburgh together with the Polish Ambassador on 3 September: though incognito, he was soon recognized (*how* disappointing for Boswell!), and in the next two weeks Boswell guided the visitors round Glasgow, the Carron ironworks, Auchinleck, Loch Lomond, and Dumbarton. In this brief walkabout Boswell was already perfecting some of the techniques that he would use when he managed to persuade Johnson to step on Scottish soil.[7]

Not surprisingly, Cook himself was also on Boswell's list. He met Cook on 2 April 1776, at the home of Sir John Pringle: next day he

---

[5] *Boswell for the Defence, 1769–1774*, ed. W. K. Wimsatt, jun., and F. A. Pottle (London: Heinemann, 1960), 43–6, 56. The earlier conversation (also reported in *LSJ* ii. 147–9) shows Johnson as having had a desire to go on a South Sea voyage at one stage. Other topics raised include the merits of a rich young man like Banks going on 'so dangerous an expedition from a thirst for knowledge' (Boswell thinks this a glorious act); Hawkesworth's employment to write the account of Cook's first voyage; and Boswell's fantasy of buying St Kilda ('Pray do', replies Johnson).

[6] Frank Brady, *James Boswell: The Later Years 1769–1795* (London: Heinemann, 1984), 41; *Boswell for the Defence*, 146. The latter source reveals that it was through Banks and Solander that Boswell came into contact with Lord Monboddo, and raised the matter of tailed creatures, which was to figure so conspicuously in a famous part of the Highland jaunt a year later.

[7] *Boswell for the Defence*, 22–4; *Boswell: The Later Years*, 22–4.

gave Johnson an account of the seaman, adding that 'while I was with the Captain [he felt] an inclination to make the voyage'. The response was characteristic: 'Why, so one does,' said the Doctor, 'till one considers how very little one learns.' Boswell, equally in character, persists, and observes that one is 'carried away with the thing in general, a voyage round the world'. Johnson is not to be hoodwinked: 'Yes,' said he, 'but one is to guard against taking a thing in general.'[8] By then the new sensation of London society was the Tahitian Omai, who had been brought back to England in 1774. Johnson was struck with the 'elegance of his behaviour', and thought that there was 'so little of the savage' in Omai that he was afraid of mistaking the Polynesian visitor for Lord Mulgrave one day at Streatham.[9] A fortnight later Boswell dined at the Mitre with Paoli, Pringle, and members of the Royal Society. Unblushingly, he placed himself next to Captain Cook, and had a great deal of conversation with him. In the following weeks he once went out to Mile End, where he had tea in a garden with the Captain. It was against such a background that Boswell eventually pieced together his own expeditionary narrative.[10]

However, his most significant encounter was perhaps not that with Cook, but with an almost equally famous, if less impressive, traveller, James Bruce. Indeed, Boswell conducted one of his full-scale investigative interviews with Bruce in August 1774, when the Scottish traveller returned to Edinburgh from his remarkable Abyssinian journeys. Many people were sceptical about Bruce's claims to have discovered the source of the Nile (albeit the Blue, rather than the White, Nile), and Boswell decided to 'throw

---

[8] *Boswell: The Ominous Years 1774–1776*, ed. C. Ryskamp and F. A. Pottle (London: Heinemann, 1984), 308–10; cf. *LSJ* iii. 7–8.

[9] *LSJ* iii. 8. The best account is E. H. McCormick, *Omai: Pacific Envoy* (Auckland: Oxford University Press, 1977); Michael Alexander, *Omai: 'Noble Savage'* (London: Collins and Harvill, 1977) is sensible but often inaccurate in detail. See further Ch. 4 below.

[10] *Boswell: The Ominous Years*, 341–4. Again we learn of a 'stirring' in Boswell's mind to go on an overseas expedition, here stimulated by an idea to leave 'some men of inquiry' for three years at a time successively in Otaheité, New Zealand, and Nova Caledonia. Boswell reports that he would have been further encouraged to such an undertaking if the government would pay afterwards 'a handsome pension for life'. Plainly he felt the more qualified as he and Johnson had been, as 'men of inquiry', to the remote Highlands. Boswell quoted from his conversation with Cook at Pringle's house, in his journal *The Hypochondriack*, no. 9 (June 1778): see the edn. by M. Bailey, 2 vols. (Stanford, Calif., 1928), i. 165.

together' a piece for the *London Magazine*, although the information had to be dug from Bruce 'as from a flinty rock with pickaxes'. He could not resist appending in this journal a comparison between Bruce and Banks, as a tiger and an elephant respectively. It may be worth noting that when Johnson met Bruce in 1775, he was unable to discern 'any superior sense' in the traveller. Bruce, as Pringle comments, 'was not fully believed', and although he disapproved of Boswell's treatment of him in the *London Magazine*, he did not bring out his own version of his adventures until 1790, and then not very effectively. Boswell says simply that he had seen Bruce 'as a curiosity and extracted from him a good essay for *The London Magazine*; and there was enough'.[11] Nevertheless, for a time Bruce shared some of the limelight with Cook; Fanny Burney wrote a famous account of her meeting with 'the great man-mountain, Mr Bruce', who she also terms 'the great Ethiopian' and 'his Abyssinian Majesty'.[12] Dr Burney was a member of the Johnson circle who most regularly sought out travellers, partly because they might furnish him with material for his *History of Music* (as Bruce did); and again it is right to hold such facts in our consciousness when we read the Hebridean voyages.

Burney's own travels were a possible model for Johnson's *Journey*, as we shall see in a moment. But first we should note a reference in the *Tour* to 'Phipps's voyage to the North Pole' (*LSJ* v. 236). This was *A Voyage towards the North Pole* (1774), reporting a journey to the Arctic Ocean in the summer of 1773; Johnson must somehow have obtained some news of Phipps's progress, though his diary was not yet available. His awareness of the subject is established by a letter to Mrs Thrale when the Hebridean travellers got back to Edinburgh in November 1773: 'They congratulate our return as if we had been with Phipps or Banks: I am ashamed of their salutations.' This is generalized by Boswell in the *Tour*, which reports Dr Johnson as saying: 'I am really ashamed of the congratulations which we receive. We are addressed as if we had made a voyage to Nova Zembla, and suffered five persecutions in Japan' (*L*

[11] *Boswell: The Ominous Years*, 45–6, 98, 114: *Boswell for the Defence*, 271–5, 279. See also *LSJ* ii. 333–4.
[12] *The Early Diary of Frances Burney 1768–1778*, ed. Annie Raine Ellis, 2 vols. (London: Bell, 1913), ii. 13–46: *Memoirs of Doctor Burney*, 3 vols. (London: Moxon, 1832) i. 296–329.

i. 390; *LSJ* v. 392).[13] Yet it had been a journey of much potential, and some real, danger. That the travellers should be greeted on their return as though they had crossed continents does correspond to a genuine truth, and to a sense of cultural displacement which the form and language of both Hebridean accounts reflect more than once.

II

In her *Memoirs of Dr Burney*, his daughter Fanny reports a conversation at the Thrales' home: 'The tour to the Hebrides being then in hand, Dr Burney inquired of what size and form the book would be. "Sir," [Johnson] replied, with a low bow, "you are my model!" ' We should note, too, the immediately following passage: 'Impelled by the same kindness, when the Doctor lamented the disappointment in books of travels;—except your's!' And Johnson even admitted to having read Burney's travels right through, 'except, perhaps, the description of the great pipes in the organs of Germany and the Netherland!—'[14]

It is not self-evident how serious this commendation was. In the first place, we tend not to think of Burney's books as 'travel literature' in the full sense: though they are still read, and were reprinted as recently as 1979, they are more commonly consulted for reasons better indicated by their original titles: *The Present State of Music in France and Italy* [*Germany*, etc.] They survive as pendants to the *History of Music*, as troves of information and documents of research. Their 'travel' framework seems rather artificial, like the quasi-topographical basis of *Humphry Clinker*, or the alleged 'letters' into which Defoe's *Tour through Great Britain* is divided. It appears that Johnson did not read the book thus. This is even more surprising, given that Burney was persuaded by his friends to cut down the non-musical matter in favour of strictly technical content. The committee of taste involved included Garrick, William Mason, the well-known amateur Lord Holderness,

---

[13] Another significant book of this period was the translation by John Reinhold Forster (1772) of Bougainville's *Voyage autour de monde*, best known today as provoking Diderot's *Supplément* (see below, p. 216).

[14] *Memoirs of Doctor Burney*, ii. 78.

and none other than Dr Hawkesworth. Their activities have been described by Roger Lonsdale:

These friends were unanimous in assuring Burney that 'France and Italy had been so often described, that there was nothing new to tell,' with the possible exception of the musical life of these nations, to which previous travellers had paid little attention. This advice was by no means unreasonable, for travel books at this period were pouring from the press and the reviewers were already showing signs of impatience ... In 1778 Samuel Johnson told Boswell, who was thinking of publishing an account of his travels in Europe: 'I give you my opinion, that you would lessen yourself by it. What can you tell of countries so well as those upon the continent of Europe, which you have visited? ... The world is now not contented to be merrily entertained by a traveller's narrative; they want to learn something.' [*LSJ* iii. 300][15]

Evidently, the informational value of Burney's work overcame Johnson's well-documented indifference towards music ('All animated nature loves music—except myself!', Fanny Burney has him crying[16]).

It is unclear when Johnson read the two volumes of musical travels. In February 1773, a few months before setting off for the north, he had asked Mrs Thrale for the loan of the first part, dealing with France and Italy—but this was on behalf of his awkward lodger, Anna Williams (*L* i. 301). A couple of years earlier Johnson had seemingly tried and failed: at all events, Boswell noted in his journal: 'He said Dr Burney was a very pretty kind of man: but he could not read through his book. I asked him why. He said, "Because I could not read about fiddles and fiddlestrings." '[17] Was this the real truth of the matter, even in later years? Perhaps not, because in May 1773 Fanny Burney was able to make this flattering entry in her diary: 'Mr Baretti called here last Sunday. He told my father that Dr Johnson will be very glad to see him; that he has read both his Tours with great pleasure, and has pronounced him to be *one of the first writers of the age for travels!*'[18] The crucial difference, Lonsdale has observed, must be that in the second volume Burney had included more 'miscellaneous'

[15] Roger Lonsdale, *Dr Charles Burney: A Literary Biography* (Oxford: Clarendon Press, 1965), 98–9.   [16] *Memoirs of Doctor Burney*, ii. 78.
[17] *Boswell for the Defence*, 51.
[18] *Early Diary of Frances Burney*, i. 221–2; *Memoirs of Doctor Burney*, i. 255.

remarks on subjects other than music, and had provided more of a narrative linkage.[19] Possibly, Johnson was sufficiently impressed to go back to the French and Italian tour and reassess its qualities.

Despite all this, it is still puzzling that Johnson should have gone so far as to tell William Seward that he had kept Burney's 'elegant and entertaining' travels 'in his eye' when writing the *Journey (LSJ* v. 186). One could point to a few external matters of presentation: most obviously, the organization of the narrative into subheadings, often (in Burney) and always (in Johnson) relating to a named location. Thus, Burney in his German tour has entries for Koblenz, Frankfurt am Main, Darmstadt, and so on; whereas Johnson has Ullinish, Talisker in Skye, and so on. But Burney's sections are generally shorter, and in any case he did not invent this method: one variant appears in a recent work that Johnson assuredly did not seek to emulate, that is Sterne's *Sentimental Journey* (1768). In very broad terms, one could discern a similarity in the reactions of two well-prepared visitors seeking enlightenment in countries which they had long encountered through the medium of books. Each is testing the value of certain preconceptions and stock assumptions; for instance, when Johnson comments: 'The general conversation of the Islanders has nothing particular. I did not meet with the Inquisitiveness of which I have read, and suspect the judgment to have been rashly made' *(JWI* 103). And when Burney exclaims: 'In travelling on the banks of the Rhine, from Cologn to Coblentz, I must own, that I was astonished and disappointed at finding no proofs of that passion for music, which the Germans are said to possess, particularly along the Rhine': but this, too, was something of a cliché in travel writing.[20] There are inevitably a few points of contact: both writers were men of mature years (though Burney, in his mid-forties, was distinctly the younger). Both were products of the west Midlands who had experienced a somewhat troubling family life, had started of with few advantages, and had finally achieved eminence in London. But if one seeks to move beyond the casual parallels which are bound to occur in these circumstances, and to find concrete signs of a close indebtedness, then one encounters more difficulty.

It is otherwise with Giuseppe Baretti's *Journey from London to*

[19] Lonsdale, *Dr Charles Burney*, 129.
[20] *An Eighteenth-Century Musical Tour in Central Europe and the Netherlands*, ed. P. A. Scholes (New York: Oxford University Press, 1969), 26.

Genoa (1770). The title is misleading, for most of the book is devoted to the narrator's progress through Portugal, Spain, and (briefly, at the end) France. It is based on a journey which Baretti had made in 1760, and whilst this is without doubt lightly fictionalized, there is more of the clear narrative drive which Johnson commends than anything in Burney's loose-knit travels. In this case, we know that Johnson took an instrumental role before rather than after the event. On 10 June 1761 he had written to Baretti in Milan, and had commended the latter's standing and credentials as an observer of the English scene: 'I am glad to have other nations made acquainted with the character of the English, by a traveller who has so nicely inspected our manners, and so successfully studied our literature.' Later in the same letter Johnson 'turns [his] attention' to Baretti again:

I hope you take care to keep an exact journal, and to register all occurrences and observations; for your friends here expect such a book of travels as has not been often seen. You have given us good specimens in your letters from Lisbon. I wish you had staid longer in Spain, for no country is less known to the rest of Europe; but the quickness of your discernment must make amends for the celerity of your motions. He that knows which way to direct his view, sees much in a little time. (*L* i. 132, 135)

In fact, Baretti took something like eleven weeks on the overland portion of his journey, an almost identical span (and at the same season of the year) as the Hebridean jaunt. Johnson, too, knew which way to direct his view during a fairly short sojourn in the Highlands.

Here we have both a recipe for Baretti's planned narrations, strikingly close to what was eventually achieved in some particulars, and at the same time an indication of the sort of travel book which Johnson would have liked to write, even as early as this. For 1761 is the earliest document that we have looked at so far with any attention; and it is reasonable to see Johnson here not as reacting on the spur of the moment, or rationalizing his ideas in response to fresh events—but, rather, as thinking out his position, as we should say 'from the ground up'. Of course, he had contributed to travel literature himself from his earliest days as a professional author, and had taken up the topic in the *Rambler* and *Adventurer*.[21] But

[21] See Curley, *Johnson and Travel*, 47–78.

the letter to Baretti is closer to the actual business of how to go about composing a travel account of one's own.

When it appeared in 1770, Baretti's *Journey from London to Genoa* proved distinctly Johnsonian in certain respects, much more so than either of Burney's narratives in the next few years. For example, Baretti exhibits a pervasive interest in language (as marked by a section on the 'Biscayan' or Basque languages) which precisely matches Johnson's description of the Erse tongue. Baretti sets out to discover what he can of the local speech: 'The Biscayan language, or *Bascuenze*, as they call it according to the idea that I have been able to form of it, must be divided at least into three dialects.'[22] Johnson is briefer and less energetic, but he is prompted by similar motives; 'of the Earse language, as I understand nothing, I cannot say more than I have been told' (*JWI* 114). For that matter, Baretti admits that he has looked into a grammar of the Biscayan dialects 'oddly entitled *El impossible vendico*, "*The impossibility conquered*"*. In that grammar the *Bascuenze* is explained by the Castilian. I have that, which was printed at Salamanca, in 1729, and have repeatedly looked into it; but not yet to any purpose.'[23] This was a large admission for a man who had attained note in England as a compiler of Italian–English and Spanish–English dictionaries, who was to become the Thrales' Italian tutor, and who was initially of interest to Johnson specially because of his linguistic skills.

Baretti's views on many topics that arise on his journey are expressed with a Johnsonian confidence in generality. At times, the actual sentiments chime in with Johnson's even though the expression lacks his full authority and weight:

Such is the natural perverseness of human nature, that it will never be possible for human wisdom to strike out a set of laws, sufficient to contain both the great and the small within just limits, and keep government equidistant from the rocks of tyranny and the shallows of licentiousness. Trust the better sort with any portion of arbitrary power, and you render them haughty and oppressive: but on the other hand, what will be the consequence if you shorten the distance between the great and small by means of laws of a levelling tendency, and thus attempt to allay the natural

---

[22] Joseph Baretti, *A Journey from London to Genoa* (Fontwell, Sussex: Centaur Press, 1970), pt. 2, p. 219 (an account drawing on information from Baretti's second trip to Spain, labelled 'digression'). Henceforth cited as Baretti.

[23] Ibid. 222; see generally pp. 213–26.

bitterness of the life that the poor multitude must lead? That same poor multitude will soon turn daring in this case; will prove untoward and disrespectful; and will even be tyrannical on many and many occasions. Which of the two evils will you decide to be the lighter? The insolence of the great to the small, or that of the small to the great?[24]

There have been few more compelling evocations of the natural bitterness of the life that the poor must lead than Johnson's clear-sighted account of the social circumstances in the Highlands: 'In pastoral countries the condition of the lowest rank of the people is sufficiently wretched' (*JWI* 101). Baretti does not command the same capacity for understanding or avoidance of trite moralism, but—far more than Burney and the majority of travellers—he does move from anecdote and impression towards reflection or analysis. Some of Baretti's flights of imagination are a little bizarre: 'While I stood gazing at our mariner thus violently employed, it came into my head that the satisfaction of a felucca would be very great, could a felucca but think, and be susceptible of satisfaction.'[25] That surely is the very accent of Boswell's journals.

The general tone is sceptical, yet enquiring; there is curiosity, in the sense of desire for information, but always a disinclination to swallow any tale that may be recounted by the natives. Here is Baretti, for example, on a French beggar whom he had encountered:

I would give much for an exact journey of such a rambler, and am sure it would prove very entertaining, if it were done with any degree of skill. He travels on leisurely, begging his way, and relying entirely upon the chance of people's charity. But since alms is easily obtained in this country, I wonder that the number of pilgrims is not greater, this being the only one I have yet seen in Spain.[26]

Another characteristic passage occurs earlier in the book, whilst Baretti is still in Portugal. He observes:

The large library at *Mafra*, I had not time to examine. Yet I have seen enough of it to know that it is a very good one. Besides the best books in

---

[24] Ibid. 278.   [25] Ibid. 327.

[26] Baretti advises the pilgrim to keep an account of his rambles (ibid. 149–50); cf. Johnson's recommendation in the letter of 1761 ('I hope you take care to keep an exact journal'). Such advice was, of course, commonplace, but in this case it proceeded from a man celebrated under the cognomen of 'the Rambler', or, as Paoli termed him in his broken accents, 'the great Vagabond' (*Memoirs of Dr Burney*, ii. 258).

the learned languages I am told that it contains some valuable manuscripts, particularly in Hebrew and in Arabic; and as I have seen several of the friars studying there, it is most probable that some of them are learned. But a traveller, had need to stay a considerable time in such places, in order to come away with just ideas of the people, and this unluckily was not in my power at *Mafra*.[27]

We may briefly recall Johnson at St Andrews: 'The doctor, by whom it was shewn, hoped to irritate or subdue my English vanity by telling me, that we had no such repository of books in England' (*JWI* 7).

There are two points of significant covergence. Both occur in the latter half of Baretti's *Journey from London to Genoa*, and indeed are found within a few pages of each other. The first concerns an episode in the harsh countryside of Aragon, as the traveller makes his way over the mountains towards Zaragoza:

Continuing my progress upwards, and reaching the top of the hill, I advanced a little on a narrow flat that is there, looked round, plucked up the mentioned plant [thyme], and looked round again and again on every side. After having thus considered the awfulness of the solitary wilderness, I sat myself down on a stone, and said to myself: 'What a place for meditation is here, in the midst of this eternal abode of silence! here is no man, no beast, no bird, nothing to make the least noise. Let me sink into some reverie, and try how far my undisturbed thoughts will go.'[28]

Here we have not just the 'wide extent of hopeless sterility' which Johnson discovered in the Highlands, 'quickened only with one sullen power of useless vegetation' (like Baretti's thyme, the only plant to be seen in the 'expanded wilderness') and amounting finally to a mere 'uniformity of barrenness' (*JWI* 39–40).[29] But the strikingly similar gesture in Johnson's narrative is this:

I sat down on a bank, such as a writer of romance might have delighted to feign. I had indeed not trees to whisper over my head, but a clear rivulet streamed at my feet. The day was calm, the air soft, and all was rudeness, silence, and solitude. Before me, and on either side, were high hills, which by hindering the eye from ranging, forced the mind to find entertainment for itself. Whether I spend the hour well I know not; for here I first conceived the thought of this narration. (*JWI* 40)

It must immediately be confessed that whereas Johnson moves on to a resounding passage concerned with what might be called the

[27] Baretti, i. 169.   [28] Ibid. ii. 155–6.   [29] Ibid. ii. 154.

concept of wilderness (ending up: 'Yet what are these hillocks to the ridges of Taurus, or these spots of wildness to the deserts of America?': *JWI* 40–1), all that Baretti can manage is an obsessive recollection of black-eyed Paolita of Badajoz, whom he had seen much earlier on first entering Spain.[30] The old Adam and Laurence Sterne combine to distract him. But for a moment there is a remarkable identity of mood, even of phrasing, as the two men confront a great silence and solitude, and compose themselves to reflect on what they have witnessed.

The very next 'letter', dealing with the next day's journey, shows Baretti coming close to Johnson on two occasions. The first is a passage which may have been inspired by *Rasselas*, especially chapter 19:

Like all men that have read much poetry in the prime of age, I have once entertained very high notions of pastoral happiness; nor have I forgot the time when I was tempted to run away from home, and go turn shepherd in the Alps. Those notions, indeed, have not been long effaced; yet I think I could willingly take a trip to Andelusia with the shepherds of to-day, was it not for that ugly circumstance of lying in an open field at night, and seldom under shelter. A twelve month of such a life would otherwise prove pleasing enough in my opinion, and afford very entertaining subjects for many letters, as numberless curious observations might be the fruit of such a peregrination.[31]

Very shortly afterwards Baretti turns to the hopes that the 'new reign' (that of Carlos III, who had acceded in 1759) has kindled among the Spanish people. He continues:

But every new reign in every country commonly raises expectations much greater than the nature of men and things will admit. I am therefore afraid that those of the Spaniards are of this cast, especially as their country has been equally drained of men and money by their late war in Italy, and too large a treasure will be wanting in my opinion to carry such mighty schemes into execution.[32]

Prudent measures and strict economies are needed; 'but what is easy in speculation, may not prove so in practice, and changes are not to be quickly brought about' (Johnson could have dictated that sentence).

Great works and new enterprises require a strong spirit of perseverance, nor is it in the power of kings to inspire their ministers and agents with that

---

[30] Ibid. ii. 156.   [31] Ibid. ii. 162.   [32] Ibid. ii. 166.

virtue, let us suppose them ever so much possessed with it themselves. However, I am too ignorant of what is transacting in the councils at Madrid, to venture upon prognostics. I am pleased with the sanguine confidence of my new acquaintance the canon, and, were I a Spaniard, I would endeavour to adopt it, because the dreams of hope are the most pleasing of all dreams.[33]

We are very close here to the central concerns of Johnson's account, with its consideration of the new 'commercial' prospects for the Highlands, and its scrutiny of what he calls 'national manners' (*JWI* 57, 91–2). Beyond this, there is in the cadences of Baretti's passage a true Johnsonian ring: one might recall the penultimate paragraph of the *Journey*: 'It was pleasing to see one of the most desperate of human calamities capable of so much help: whatever enlarges hope, will exalt courage; after having seen the deaf taught arithmetick, who would be afraid to cultivate the Hebrides?' (*JWI* 164); or, Baretti might add, to carry out the new king's plans in Spain, building roads, resettling the population, supporting agriculture, and cultivating the sciences.[34]

III

It is not so very surprising, in the end, that the travellers returning to Edinburgh should have been greeted as though they had spent a season in Greenland. (We are told that even 'to the Southern inhabitants of Scotland, the state of the mountains and the islands is equally unknown with that of Borneo or Sumatra': *JWI* 88.)[35] An enterprise such as theirs, in the year 1773, could not but carry with it echoes of the explorations that everyone was talking about. And if we look at the text of the two accounts of the Hebridean trip, we shall find that such echoes turn up—unobtrusively sometimes, and

[33] Baretti, ii. 166–7.

[34] In general I do not seek to argue for direct dependence between the two texts: e.g. Johnson's statement, 'Thus in Biscay, the original Cantabrian . . . still subsists', does not refer back precisely to anything in Baretti (a note in the *Journey* (*JWI* 44) suggests that Johnson is remembering the theories of John Wallis). It is worth noting that Baretti's informant mentions 'the tongue (much more ancient than our monarchy) called *Bascuenze*' (Baretti, ii. 208).

[35] Cf. Johnson's own notion of sending Mrs Thrale's salutation from this verge of European life (*L* i. 348). Johnson presents himself at the outset as a 'southern stranger' (*JWI* 4).

intermittently rather than in every paragraph. None the less, an attentive reading will show that both men were aware of their journey not just as a sociological mission, or a moral quest (the side most emphasized today, especially in the case of Johnson), or even as a literary undertaking—they also saw their experiences as marked on 'the great map of mankind' (in Burke's expressive phrase), as charted by recent voyagers.[36]

It is worth reminding ourselves here that the title of each work does refer to an actual itinerary—*A Journey to*, not a survey of, *the Western Islands*; the *Journal of a Tour to*, not a sojourn in, *the Hebrides*. What this means in practice is that even the broader and more abstract questions of politics, society, and culture which arise in the two narratives need to be judged against the insights of the travellers opening up the contemporary picture of human achievement. There is a characteristic passage near the end of Boswell's account: 'Our satisfaction at finding ourselves again in a comfortable carriage was very great. We had a pleasing conviction of the commodiousness of civilization, and heartily laughed at the ravings of those absurd visionaries who have attempted to persuade us of the superior advantages of a *state of nature*' (*LSJ* v. 365). This comment might be glossed by reference to Locke's two *Treatises of Government*, to Rousseau's *Émile*, and dozens of other Enlightenment texts. But in the 1770s and 1780s it would take a strong colouring from recent firsthand descriptions of primitive peoples. When contemporaries heard of a noble savage, they would have thought first not of Oroonoko or Crusoe's Friday, but of a more recent and real figure such as the Tahitian Omai—whom Banks patronized, Reynolds painted, the Burneys entertained, and Johnson admired for his elegance (see Chapter 4, below). And in the *Life* it is regularly in the context of South Sea travel that the issue of an alleged state of nature is discussed; witness a conversation in April 1776:

A gentleman [Boswell himself] expressed a wish to go and live three years at Otaheité, or New-Zealand, in order to obtain a full acquaintance with people, so totally different from all that we have ever known, and be satisfied what pure nature can do for man. JOHNSON. 'What could you

---

[36] *The Correspondence of Edmund Burke*, ed. G. H. Guttridge, 10 vols. (Cambridge: Cambridge University Press, 1961), iii. 351. See the valuable study by P. J. Marshall and Glynder Williams, *The Great Map of Mankind: British Perceptions of the World in the Age of Enlightenment* (London: J. M. Dent, 1982).

learn, Sir? What can savages tell, but what they themselves have seen? Of the past, or the invisible, they can tell nothing. The inhabitants of Otaheité and New-Zealand are not in a state of pure nature; for it is plain they broke off from some other people.' (*LSJ* iii. 49)

And on a more famous occasion, in the last summer of Johnson's life, Boswell remarked that he did not think the people of Otaheité could be reckoned as savages, and received the stinging reply: 'Don't cant in defence of Savages' (*LSJ* iv. 308–9). It is little, if any, exaggeration to say that Johnson set out for Scotland in order to 'obtain a full acquaintance with people . . . totally different from all [he] had ever known'. His reservations concerning any Tahitian ability to convey worthwhile knowledge have very close affinities with what he says in the *Journey* on the subject of oral culture among the Gaelic-speaking population of the Highlands ('the bard was a barbarian among barbarians, who, knowing nothing himself, lived with others that knew no more': *JWI* 116).

Consequently, some of the more general observations in Johnson's narrative must be seen not just as the fruit of long study and early acquirements, but as contributions to an urgent and even topical debate.[37] When he remarks at Ullinish: 'Savages, in all countries, have patience proportionate to their unskilfulness, and are content to attain their end by very tedious methods' (*JWI* 72), he could easily have recalled that the narrator of Cook's voyages drew attention to the 'infinite labour and fatigue involved in humdrum tasks performed by people with only the most primitive tools at their disposal'.[38] Again, when Johnson reflects on the Norse invasions of Scotland, he thinks of the destruction of forest cover caused by any major influx of population: 'The first effect of plenitude of inhabitants is the destruction of wood. As the Europeans spread over America, the lands are gradually laid naked' (*JWI* 98–9). So the travellers had reported.

[37] There is, as we have seen in Ch. 1, a personal topicality in Johnson's observation that 'To be told that any man has attained a hundred years, gives hope and comfort to him who stands trembling on the brink of his own climacterick' (*JWI* 84). The grand climacteric was the age of 63; Johnson passed his sixty-fourth birthday on Skye: see pp. 19–20 above.

[38] *Voyages of Discovery*, 35. Elsewhere Johnson says that on Skye the people's agricultural methods are 'laborious, and perhaps rather feeble than unskillful' (*JWI* 79). Of the Scottish nation more generally he says: 'Till the Union made them acquainted with English manners, the culture of their lands was unskillful, and their domestick life unformed; their tables were as coarse as the feasts of Eskimeaux, and their homes filthy as the cottages of Hottentots' (*JWI* 28).

Certain references are more explicit; of stone arrowheads at Raasay, we are told: 'They nearly resemble those which Mr Banks has lately brought back from the savage countries in the Pacifick Ocean.' More fleeting is the reference to Staffa, 'so lately raised to renown by Mr Banks' (*JWI* 63, 141). This was, of course, the description of Fingal's Cave which Banks had provided for Pennant's second tour. Brief comparisons fix Highland ways with relation to 'the boor of Norway'; or suggest that 'if the world has agreed to praise the travels and manual labours of the Czar of Muscovy, let Col have his share of the like applause, in the proportion of his dominions to the empire of Russia' (*JWI* 76, 101). Johnson knows perfectly well that the island of Coll is not equivalent to the empire of Muscovy; but to convey his sense of the places and people that he encounters, he feels the need to impose a wider geographical context on the material. He understands the Highlands better for having imaginatively surveyed the continents from China to Peru.

In this respect, as in others, Boswell's account provides an array of facts and ideas more closely comparable to Johnson's than is generally recognized. One reason for that circumstance is the presence of Johnson's own opinions in the Boswellian text. Thus, when the travellers make the very short crossing from Skye to Raasay, the rough sea prompts Johnson to remark: 'This now is the Atlantick. If I should tell at a tea-table in London, that I have crossed the Atlantick in an open boat, how they'd shudder, and what a fool they'd think me to expose myself to such danger!' (*LSJ* v. 163). At first this reads simply as comic self-aggrandizement, but the reference to the tea table does remind us that there was something authentically heroic about Johnson's trip, in places at least. On another occasion, Johnson raises the topic of Phipps's voyage to the polar regions (*LSJ* v. 236). But often it is Boswell himself who brings to the surface the world of exploration that we have been considering. Thus, on 23 September Boswell resolves to find out whether, among his varied accomplishments, Johnson knows anything of the trade of a butcher: 'I enticed him into the subject, by connecting it with the various researches into the manners and customs of uncivilized nations, that have been made by our late navigators to the South Seas. . . . I began with observing, that Mr (now Sir Joseph) Banks tells us, that the art of slaughtering animals was not known in Otaheité' (*LSJ* v. 246).

Much later in the trip, Boswell mentioned 'that I had heard Dr Solander say he was a Swedish Laplander'. Johnson gives a reply that may not be well-founded but which indicates previous acquaintance with the topic: 'Sir, I don't believe he is a Laplander. The Laplanders are not much above four feet high. He is as tall as you; and he has not the copper colours of a Laplander' (*LSJ* v. 328). Boswell retires, unsatisfied and puzzled, perhaps musing on the possibility that Johnson was related to the giant Patagonians of popular legend (abetted, of course, by travel books). Only a page later Boswell slips in some information about inheritance customs in Otaheité, as he has 'been told' of them—conceivably by Cook himself (*LSJ* v. 330). It should be stressed that the Tahitian craze had not died out when Boswell's book appeared in 1785. Two years later Anna Seward reports a party at the home of Richard Payne Knight in Herefordshire; one of the 'nymphs' disporting herself in this romantic setting is a black-haired girl who seeks to make the scene 'more perfectly "Otaheitéan" ' (i.e. idyllic) by dancing and singing grotesquely. As Anna Seward states it: she 'became the very figure we had seen represented in Cook's *Voyages*. We . . . exclaimed to each other "what a complete little savage—we are certainly in Otaheité." '[39] Thus durable was the impact of the tales of exploration, and it is something which constantly hovers behind Boswell's text.

IV

On 19 October the travellers reached Iona, and Johnson gave utterance to one of his most resounding and memorable thoughts. It occurs in a passage which Boswell could not resist grafting into his own text, as 'conveying my own sensations much more forcibly than I am capable of doing' (*LSJ* v. 334). The key sentence is this:

---

[39] H. Pearson (ed.), *The Swan of Lichfield* (London: Hamish Hamilton, 1936), 103–4. It should be recalled that Anna Seward's elegy on Captain Cook was one of her best-known works; Johnson evidently paid it high compliments. Boswell's account (*LSJ* iv. 331), should be supplemented by Seward's own, in a letter to Mrs Piozzi (*The Swan of Lichfield*, 112). In view of Boswell's relations with Seward, it is not likely that he would exaggerate any commendation which Johnson bestowed on her. There is a story that on his tour Johnson actually performed an elaborate imitation of the newly encountered kangaroo: Brady, *Boswell: The Later Years*, 62 (see p. 94 below).

'Whatever withdraws us from the power of our senses; whatever makes the past, the distant, or the future predominate over the present, advances us in the dignity of thinking beings' (*JWI* 148). Such a progression might be said to be the leading motif of Johnson's own existential journey, and the fact that it became a motto of Boswell's tour as well points to a deep significance in the utterance. The Hebridean journey was an escape from temporal limitations, an education in historical understanding. But, in the manner of the age, both narratives achieve this imaginative leap by envisaging human knowledge as a tract of land to be crossed. Johnson's transit of the Caledonian hemisphere turns out to be similar to a South Sea voyage, in its anthropological, scientific, and cultural framework. To a lesser extent, it may be seen as a personal and impressionistic survey, in the style which Baretti especially had evolved from Sterne and others; and, more tangentially still, a Burneian 'survey' of a neighbouring country. In each of these ways, however, the journey belongs very specifically to its immediate historic context, in its motivation, structure, and manner of reporting. It was the epic, physical quests of travellers like Cook which made Johnson's intellectual exploration of Scotland, as it was to be valiantly performed and (twice) nobly narrated, into something fully conceivable.

In a footnote to his *Tour* Boswell cites a warm tribute to the eloquence of Johnson's reflections on Iona: 'Had our Tour produced nothing else but this sublime passage, the world must have acknowledged that it was not made in vain. The present respectable President of the Royal Society was so much struck on reading it, that he clasped his hands together, and remained for some time in an attitude of silent admiration' (*LSJ* v. 334). The significance of this interpolated tribute is that it derives from Sir Joseph Banks, a prime figure in the explorations of the age. To have endorsement for the tour from such a person is a ratification of the entire undertaking. Boswell valued this support because it made good a connection he had been striving for—Cook's voyages, Johnson's journey, Boswell's own travels into certain remote nations.[40]

Johnson has already been cited as dramatizing the short crossing

---

[40] Boswell also cited Banks's explorations in his narratives: see *LSJ* v. 246–7. For Johnson's citations, see p. 85 above.

from Skye to Raasay (no more than three miles) into an epic voyage: 'This now is the Atlantick' (see above, p. 85). The comic hyperbole expresses not the literal dimensions of the trip, but its implicit cultural and ideological scope. London tea tables had been hearing plenty about Tahitians, Indians, and Laplanders; Johnson and Boswell were not able to venture so far afield, but they undertook an arduous journey which could be narrated as a quest of similar proportions.

4

The Noblest Savage of them All: Johnson, Omai, and Other Primitives

On 9 September 1773 a young man from the Society Islands embarked on the *Adventure* and set out for England. This was the second vessel attached to James Cook's first voyage to the South Seas, under the command of Tobias Furneaux. The young man went by the name of Tetuby Homy or, as he became known when he reached England ten months later, Omai. On that same day Samuel Johnson and James Boswell were in the middle of their Hebridean jaunt. More exactly, they had reached the small island of Raasay, off Skye. The previous day Johnson had discussed Fingal, the great talking point of the moment, the embodiment of natural 'inspiration', disputing a local minister's comparison of Ossian with Homer. It had been raining heavily—this was, after all, Scotland in the autumn.[1]

Here is a collision that is worth exploring. It is a temporal convergence which, it might be thought, conceals a deeper divergence. On the one hand we have a youthful and ignorant primitive being dragged from a remote Polynesian island to London, which was arguably the capital of the civilized world (only Paris or, some would suggest, Edinburgh could put in a strong rival claim). Omai was taken across oceans, largely unaware of what he was involved in. On the other hand a learned, elderly man of the world was leaving his home in London for a trip, long planned and indeed meditated, to the most remote regions of Britain. It was a journey measured only in hundreds of miles. And the contrast could be extended: Omai never progressed beyond halting English, whereas Johnson was the codifier of the language in his great *Dictionary*, and a master of eloquent speech. He was bookish, sophisticated, and something of a polymath.

Yet the two journeys are, paradoxically, quite comparable from

[1] I should like to thank Barbara Looney for help in locating and transcribing material for this chapter.

some angles; they have the parallel quality of mirror images. In the discussion which follows, the aim will be to trace likenesses as well as unlikenesses, and to establish the sense in which the two undertakings may cast light upon one another. The sources are fairly obvious—certainly so in the case of the Hebridean venture, where the famous accounts of Johnson himself and of Boswell will be used. In the case of Omai, most of the evidence will be drawn from E. H. McCormick's fine biography (1977).[2] I have no compunction about employing Boswell's *Tour*, as it renders Johnson's presence with incomparable directness and force. This immediacy is crucial to the case which follows, for we shall be concerned with the phenomenology of Johnson—the moral and physical impact that he made on observers—as much as with any inner essence or 'objective' identity. Moreover, Boswell's own Scottish angle of vision is useful for this enquiry. It might be said that Boswell textualizes Johnson's otherness: the life and landscape of Scotland become a norm against which the existential differences of the visitor show up clearly. He emerges as a vector of social forces, the embodiment of his own civilization in a foreign clime. Put briefly, my case will be that Johnson, setting out to conduct a limited expedition along the lines of Sir Joseph Banks (Cook's companion on his first Pacific voyage, the main guardian of Omai in England, and a visitor to the Hebrides in 1772), ended up replicating the experiences of the Tahitian in Europe.[3] What we have seen earlier as an anti-grand tour proves to have been a displaced Pacific voyage—a conclusion which chimes in with the findings of Chapter 3.

I

The basic story of Omai is simple. He was picked up by Captain Furneaux in the *Adventure* and reached England on what was then the less momentous date of 14 July in 1774. His stay lasted until 14

---

[2] E. H. McCormick, *Omai: Pacific Envoy* (Auckland: Auckland University Press, 1977). This supplants earlier treatments. Valuable background is supplied by J. C. Beaglehole, *The Life of Captain James Cook* (Stanford, Calif.: Stanford University Press, 1974), esp. pp. 462–71.

[3] For Banks I rely chiefly on H. B. Carter, *Sir Joseph Banks, 1743–1820* (London: British Museum (Natural History), 1988), esp. ch. 5, pp. 104–44.

July 1776, when he sailed from Plymouth, laden with presents and clothing bestowed on him by Banks. Once back in Huahine, he fell into bitterness and morose complaint. Unable to settle back in his native environment, he lingered on miserably for a few short years. Captain William Bligh later recorded seeing the remains of his house. His decline mirrors the unhappy fate of his people: the fatal impact of European explorers on Polynesian life has been graphically described by Alan Moorehead among others.[4] Omai's name lived on, and he even figured in a Christmas pantomime by John O'Keeffe at Covent Garden in 1785. The London missionaries who formed the next wave of European incomers to Tahiti regretted the time and effort that had gone into his transplantation to London. Their leader wrote: 'The foolish Omai was an expense more than would have maintained a mission to the island.' The whole episode is an allegory of deracination, mistaken ideals, cultural misunderstandings.[5]

At the time, much of the blame was heaped on poor Omai himself; indeed, his was in some respects an inadequate personality, ill-suited to the role asked of him. He was said to have got ideas above his station, and to have invested himself with a social dignity which his fellow-countrymen were unwilling to concede to him. He was dissatisfied with the house built for him—King George, he claimed, had promised him a dwelling of two storeys, and this had only one—it was a place 'such as was used for housing pigs in England'.[6] Like Gulliver on his return from Brobdingnag, Omai found himself unable to adjust to the ordinary scale of living in his native land. He was also upset when he surveyed his remaining possessions: hatchets of poor quality and a few nails, glass beads that would not buy him a coconut in exchange. He wound up trading his kitchenware with crew members for iron tools.

We do not, of course, have Omai's side of the story. Ours is a Eurocentric view, established mainly during the period of social prominence which Omai enjoyed throughout during his stay in

---

[4] Alan Moorehead, *The Fatal Impact: An Account of the Invasion of the South Pacific, 1767–1840* (London: Hamish Hamilton, 1966).

[5] For the expectations which had grown up in the European mind concerning Polynesian life, see a fine study by Bernard Smith, *European Vision and the South Pacific* (New Haven, Conn.: Yale University Press, 1985). Chiefly relevant to this essay are the sections on the early reaction to Cook and other travellers in the 1770s, pp. 1–132. The quotation in the text occurs on p. 144.

[6] McCormick, *Omai*, 254–5.

England. Having been greeted by Banks, he was promptly taken to
Kew to be presented to the King and Queen on 17 July 1774. He
was fêted and lionized. In August he went with Banks to the seat of
Lord Sandwich, First Lord of the Admiralty, and the main
promoter of the Pacific expeditions. Soon afterwards he visited the
University of Cambridge to mingle with doctors and professors in
the Senate House. He sampled balls and masquerades, concerts and
race meetings, as well as grouse-shooting. The newspapers were full
of such contrived cultural shocks for the hapless Omai, who figured
in indecent poems besides earning immortality as the subject of a
famous romantic portrait by Joshua Reynolds. He also met Fanny
Burney, whose brother James took part in Cook's second and third
expeditions. The German savant Georg Christoph Lichtenberg
encountered him at the British Museum and, with well-meaning
importunity, asked him how he enjoyed the English winter: 'Cold,
cold,' replied Omai, shaking his head. Lichtenberg described him as
'large and well-proportioned', with a yellowish-brown skin; there
was in his bearing 'something very pleasant and unassuming which
becomes him well and which is beyond the range of expression of
any African countenance'. His English, unfortunately, was 'far
from intelligible'. Omai never fully overcame these difficulties of
communication. He learnt, bizarrely, to play chess well.[7]

Unquestionably, Banks saw him at first as a specimen to be
shown off, almost like the botanical specimens which he had
brought back from the Antipodes. Whilst on the *Endeavour*
voyage, Banks had decided to bring back another native of the
Society Islands named Tupaia, who unfortunately died off the coast
of Batavia on the way home. Banks had written in his journal: 'I do
not know why I may not keep him as a curiosity, as well as my
neighbours do lions and tygers at a larger expense than he would
probably ever put me to.'[8] Banks later began to have doubts about
the propriety of such acts of transplantation; but initially, like all
who had been impressed by the 'natural' innocence of the

[7] McCormick, *Omai*, 138. See also Carter, *Sir Joseph Banks*, 125–35, on
Omai and Banks.

[8] Sir John Cullum regretted that no steps had been taken towards giving Omai
'any useful Knowledge, Mr Banks seeming to keep him, as an Object of Curiosity, to
observe the Workings of an untutored, unenlightened Mind' (quoted in McCormick,
Omai 129). Others thought that he ought to have been taught a trade: see
Beaglehole, *Captain James Cook* 449.

Polynesian peoples, he viewed Omai in the light of a tamed noble savage who exemplified a state of primitive nature.[9]

In the summer of 1775 Omai embarked on a grand tour of England. By this time he was more poised in society, and even in September 1774 the Leicester correspondent for the *General Evening Post* had noted: 'Omai is remarked to have behaved with great politeness, allowing for his short acquaintance with European manners.' At church, we are told, he saw a gentleman he had met briefly in Buxton, 'and bowed to him with the address of a well bred European'.[10] The irony we read into this comment would not have been apparent for some years to come. On 2 June 1775 a small party embarked on the Admiralty yacht *Augusta* at the Thames quay near the Tower of London: at their head were the Earl of Sandwich and Joseph Banks, but Omai was also among them. Dr Charles Burney was their guest for the day, as they headed down the river to Greenwich. Thereafter the yacht made its way to Sheerness and Chatham, and then, during the next five weeks, to Portsmouth and Plymouth amongst other important dockyard towns. This was basically an official tour of inspection by the First Lord, though there was time for shooting-trips and botanical expeditions ashore. No one seems to have thought it odd that Omai should be allowed to go along with the party.

A week after the *Augusta* returned, Omai set off with Banks for the north of England. They spent some time at York, the social centre for a large tract of the country; visited Skelton, the home of Sterne's eccentric friend John Hall Stevenson; and tried the new sea bathing at Scarborough. Omai is also reported to have performed a Tahitian song with grimaces and gestures, a mode of body language which Samuel Johnson practised less deliberately. Fanny Burney, who thought that 'his song is the only thing that is savage belonging to him', remarked on his excellent table manners (not, again, a strong point of Johnson), and suggested that he seemed 'to shame Education'.[11] This provides the focus of an entire *Kulturkampf*, concerned with the alleged moral superiority of native peoples and the 'decadence' of the western nations. Fanny Burney was not

---

[9] Carter, *Sir Joseph Banks*, 135. Cf. Beaglehole, *Captain James Cook*, 449: 'Though a child of nature, he was not one of nature's wise children.'

[10] McCormick, *Omai*, 114.

[11] Ibid. 127, citing Fanny Burney's diary for 1 Dec. 1774.

strongly infected by the ideas of Rousseau and Diderot, yet she would have seen a contrast between the 'polite, attentive, and easy' manners of Omai and the awkward behaviour of Philip Stanhope, despite all the tutelage in the graces that he had received from the Earl of Chesterfield. It is a remarkable fact in passing that Stanhope was to call his eldest son 'Charles Rasselas'.

It is peculiarly apt that Omai should chiefly have been under the protection of Banks. Had Banks already been elected to the Club (that did not happen until December 1778), the Tahitian might possibly have been admitted to one of its gatherings. As it was, he did have contacts with the Royal Society through Banks, a future President and current member of the Council. In fact, Omai was the only outsider to be admitted to meetings in 1775 of a dining-club of Royal Society members which Banks had established.[12] There is something odd about this circumstance, for it is almost as though one of the prize trophies had been appointed to sit on the board of governors of a museum. Among the other exhibits of Banks's Antipodean journey were depictions of the newly discovered kangaroo, a breed almost as exotic to the western imagination as the Tahitian native himself.[13] As we now know, Johnson had been intrigued by the account Banks gave of the kangaroo, and during the early stages of his Scottish tour, at an inn in Inverness, he actually performed an impression of the animal. It is one of the few good stories Boswell seems to have missed:

The appearance, conformation, and habits of this quadruped were of the most singular kind: and in order to render his description more vivid and graphic, Johnson rose from his chair and volunteered an imitation of the animal. The company stared; and Mr Grant said nothing could be more ludicrous than the appearance of a tall, heavy, grave-looking man, like Dr. Johnson, standing up to mimic the shape and motions of a kangaroo. He stood erect, put out his hands like feelers, and, gathering up the tails of his huge brown coat so as to resemble the pouch of the animal, made two or three vigorous bounds across the room! (*LSJ* v. 511)

Most people of the time would have thought it beneath their dignity

---

[12] Carter, *Sir Joseph Banks*, 133; for Banks and the Club, see pp. 147–9.

[13] For the discovery (as far as Europeans were concerned) of the kangaroo, see ibid. 90–1, and Beaglehole, *Captain James Cook*, 240. For the kangaroo painted by George Stubbs for Banks (probably the earliest well known depiction), see Smith, *European Vision*, 14, and pl. 1.

to imitate a kangaroo; even Johnson, the least stuffy of men, might have thought it unseemly to imitate Omai.

It was at this juncture that the meeting of Johnson and Omai took place. Travel and exploration were major topics of the moment; the travellers' tales of Banks and others from Cook's party were on all lips; the Ethiopian explorer James Bruce vied with figures such as Constantine Phipps for public attention. As recently as 1772 a group of Eskimos from Labrador had come to London, where they had met the anatomist John Hunter, dined with the Royal Society, and visited Drury Lane.[14] This is the context both for Omai's sojourn in England and for Johnson's tour of the Scottish Highlands and Islands. As contemporaries debated the difference between the savage and the barbarian, as primitive ethnology theorized over the sons of Noah, as the cult of Ossian somehow ennobled all primitive cultures, as unexplored regions of the world came into a state of high cultural visibility, so Omai entered Johnson's world—and Johnson entered the 'primitive' world.[15]

There is a well-known passage in Hester Thrale's marginalia to Boswell's *Life*, in which she observes: 'When Omai played at Chess & at Backgammon with Baretti, everybody admired at the Savage's good Breeding and at the European's impatient Spirit.' There is another version: 'You would have thought Omai the Christian, and Baretti the Savage.' (*LSJ* iii. 469).[16] The presence of Omai had inspired a gentleman, who is readily identifiable as Boswell himself (see p. 83 above), to go and live in 'Otaheité' or New Zealand in order to obtain 'a full acquaintance with people, so different from all that we have ever known, and be satisfied what pure nature can do for man'. He received a dusty answer:

[14] McCormick, *Omai*, 76.

[15] See a helpful study by Margaret M. Rubel, *Savage and Barbarian* (Amsterdam: North Holland, 1978). See also Beaglehole, *Captain James Cook*, 448: 'The popular verse-satirists found [Omai] useful, unsophisticated nature in the midst of the sophistries of civilisation. He could himself annotate this theory on a social excursion . . . when, while Phipps dug up ancient barrows and Banks botanised, he prepared luncheon in a Polynesian *umu*, or earth-oven.'

[16] McCormick, *Omai*, 169; for Baretti's recollections of the chess game, see p. 333. Mrs Piozzi in old age retained a strong recollection of Omai; as late as 1819 she wrote: 'When Miss Burney asked Omiah, the savage, if he should like to go back to Otaheite, "Yes, Miss," said he, "no mutton there, no coach, no dish of tea, no pretty Miss Horneck; good air, good sea, and *very good dog*. I happy at Otaheite." My tastes and his are similar' (cited ibid. 333).

What could you learn, Sir? What can savages tell, but what they themselves have seen? Of the past, or the invisible, they can tell nothing. The inhabitants of Otaheité and New-Zealand are not in a state of pure nature; for it is plain they broke off from some other people. Had they grown out of the ground, you might have judged a state of pure nature. (*LSJ* iii, 49–50)

This exchange took place on 29 April 1776. The actual meeting of Johnson and Omai is recorded by Boswell in the *Life* under 3 April, where it is called up by a conversation which Boswell had just had with Captain Cook. The passage runs as follows:

He had been in company with Omai, a native of one of the South Sea Islands, after he had been some time in this country. He was struck with the elegance of his behaviour, and accounted for it thus: 'Sir, he had passed his time, while in England, only in the best company; so that all that he had acquired of our manners was genteel. As a proof of this, Sir, Lord Mulgrave and he dined one day at Streatham; they sat with their backs to the light fronting me, so that I could not see distinctly; and there was so little of the savage in Omai, that I was afraid to speak to either, lest I should mistake one for the other.' (*LSJ* iii. 8)

This indicates a degree of amused surprise at the rapid acculturation of Omai. It naturally does not involve any admission on Johnson's part of *innate* civility in the Tahitian islander. In this moment of commendation, Johnson seems to stand at his farthest from Omai; the very terms of his praise reflect a distance and a lack of real affinity. If this were all we had to go on, we should be ready to decide that Johnson's travels had not opened his mind very fully. But elsewhere we can see that Johnson had other concerns than simply the genteel.

II

To see the savage islander, Europeans had to take him out of his native context and project him into a Western setting. In order to see Samuel Johnson truly, we may need to remove him from his familiar stamping-ground (London especially) and plant him down in the foreign fields of remote north Britain.

The entire Scottish trip can be interpreted as a prolonged replay of Cook's first voyage to the South Pacific (see also Chapter 3, above).[17] What Barbara Maria Stafford has called 'the taste for discovery' had a complex set of underlying motives.[18] There were colonial and economic goals; there were strictly scientific ends; there were advances in the sphere of navigation and geography; there was the simple lure of adventure. But the most pervasive quality of curiosity nurturing the Pacific imperative was a kind of anthropological urge—a desire to test hypotheses about the nature of man. Johnson, with his abiding moral concerns, was incapable of ignoring these human implications. And he was brave enough to anticipate modern anthropology by making himself the object as well as the subject of his enquiry.

For much of the time in Scotland, we observe Johnson (in his own account and his letters to Mrs Thrale, but above all in Boswell's narrative) as a benighted innocent, as a sight to be shown off, as a mysterious prodigy, as the uncomprehending primitive among cunning and worldly denizens of the Highlands. It is clear that, from the start of the tour, Boswell planned to display his friend as an exotic. He takes Johnson round the Edinburgh literati on their arrival, and writes to James Beattie of the 'valuable acquisition' which the great man will be for the Scottish people (*LSJ* v. 15). In turn, Dr William Robertson had expressed the hope that Johnson would 'make the experiment', much like a curious botanist making a survey of the exiguous plant life of Spitzbergen (*LSJ* v. 15). Boswell was anxious to dispel what he regarded as a vein of provincialism in his revered friend: 'The truth is,' writes Boswell of *London* (1738), 'like the ancient Greeks and Romans he allowed

---

[17] As Smith remarks (*European Vision*, 1): 'In the year 1768 the Royal Academy was established and the Royal Society promoted Cook's first voyage to the South Seas. The two events fittingly represent two influential attitudes to nature current in eighteenth-century English thought . . . The opening of the Pacific provided a new world for the philosophers of nature.' Johnson was, of course, a close friend of Joshua Reynolds, the first President of the Academy, and had been active in earlier moves to form an English academy of art. He was given the honorary office of Professor of Ancient Literature on the prompting of Reynolds. He also knew Joseph Banks quite well, even before Banks was admitted to the Club.

[18] See Barbara Maria Stafford, *Voyage into Substance: Art, Science, Nature, and the Illustrated Travel Account, 1760–1840* (Cambridge, Mass.: MIT Press, 1984), 1–29. When Stafford writes of the capacity of the illustrated travel narrative 'for getting to the bottom of things', she primarily has in mind accurate scientific description, but the comment also applies to the kind of human enquiry which Johnson undertook.

himself to look upon all nations but his own as barbarians: not only Hibernia, and Scotland, but Spain, Italy, and France, are attacked in the same poem' (*LSJ* v. 20). It is strange that this poem, written thirty-five years earlier, should be invoked at the beginning of the *Tour* in 1773. The explanation is that Boswell was seeking to emphasize and even to exaggerate Johnson's status as an outsider visiting a land of 'barbarians'. The book was to show Johnson's partial conversion—this much is, more or less, Boswell's conscious intent. At a more submerged level, the book suggests that Johnson is the uncomprehending primitive who comes upon an ancient civilization operating by complex social rules which he cannot fathom.

At this same juncture, even before the Edinburgh visits have begun, Boswell gives his famous description of Johnson's appearance. This was the first detailed physical picture he had supplied of his subject; indeed, it was the first time in a prominent and serious work of biography that the characteristic Johnsonian image which we all carry with us had been set out with such particularity. Here, then, is the massive scale of the man: 'his person was large, robust, I may say approaching to the gigantick, and grown unwieldy from corpulency'. Instantly we are given suggestions of some immemorial quality in his features: 'his countenance was naturally of the craft of an ancient statue'. Boswell goes on to describe Johnson's convulsions and palsied jerking gestures. 'Upon this tour,' the narrator adds, 'when journeying, he wore boots, and a very wide brown cloth great coat, with pockets which might have almost held the two volumes of his folio dictionary; and he carried in his hand a large English oak stick.' Boswell pretends that he will be censured for such 'minute particulars', and defends himself by saying: 'When I mention the oak stick, it is but letting *Hercules* have his club' (*LSJ* v. 18–19).

This portrait serves more interesting rhetorical ends than its familiarity generally allows us to see. For example, the mention of the pockets which could hold the *Dictionary* is a remarkable touch: it reminds us of the man's intellectual history whilst drawing attention to the lumpish size of his physical appurtenances. (And, of course, there is nowhere an English dictionary would be less useful to carry around than in the Gaelic-speaking Highlands: what Johnson really needs is one of the non-existent Erse manuals.) Throughout the passage, Boswell is building up Johnson's moral stature whilst presenting him as a 'real sight' (as the old slang phrase had it)—someone imposing, yet undeniably comic under one aspect.

It is unfashionable to place too much emphasis on the personal oddities of Johnson, either in appearance or behaviour. But these were something that no contemporary could overlook—Garrick mimicked Johnson much as Johnson mimicked the kangaroo—and we have repeated testimonies to show that they influenced the first perceptions of those who met him. To take only the most striking and less familiar examples: Thomas Gainsborough said that he twitched and gesticulated for a month after meeting Johnson, and became 'as full of megrims as the old literary leviathan himself' (he thought he had been turned into a Chinese automaton).[19] Lady Knight fled from Johnson's lumbering bear-like presence when she first encountered it, adding that when he tried to adopt a more courteous address, 'He did it as awkwardly as a monkey nursing a child'.[20] Many observers thought that Johnson presented himself 'as if he had been nurtured at the cape of Good Hope'; a Scottish critic of the published *Journey* asserted: 'No man has ever yet seen Dr Johnson in the act of *feeding*, or beheld the inside of his *cell* in *Fleet-Street*, but would think the *feasts* of *Esquimeaux* or the *cottages* of *Hottentots* injured by a comparison.'[21] A slightly more complimentary style of comparison is illustrated by the art critic Fresnoy, in the *Middlesex Journal* in 1769, who sees him as 'Old Atlas'.[22] Mrs Montagu wrote, after she had quarrelled with Johnson: 'I wish his figure was put as a frontispiece to his works,

[19] See Jack Lindsay, *Gainsborough* (London: Granada, 1981), 135.
[20] Quoted by Barbara Luttrell, *The Prim Romantic* (London: Chatto and Windus, 1965), 26–7.
[21] Quoted from Sir John Hawkins's *Life of Johnson* (1787) by Frank Brady, 'Johnson as a Public Figure', in P. Korshin (ed.), *Johnson after Two Hundred Years* (Philadelphia: University of Pennsylvania Press, 1986), 51; see also Donald M'Nichol, *Remarks on Dr Samuel Johnson's Journey to the Hebrides* (1779), quoted by Robert F. Metzdorf, 'M'Nichol, Macpherson, and Johnson', in W. H. Bond (ed.), *Eighteenth-Century Studies in Honor of Donald F. Hyde* (New York: Grolier Club, 1970), 52.
[22] Quoted by W. T. Whitley, *Artists and their Friends in England*, 2 vols. (London: Medici Society, 1928), i. 252–3. John Gilbert Cooper called Johnson 'a literary Caliban': see Thomas Tyers's *Biographical Sketch of Johnson* (1785), repr. in *The Early Biographies of Samuel Johnson*, ed. O. M. Brack, jun., and R. E. Kelley (Iowa City, Ia.: University of Iowa Press, 1974), 69.

his squinting look and monstrous form would well explain his character.'[23]

We need to reclaim some of this material. Its interest lies not in vulgar 'eccentricity', but in the strong impression of a raw Johnsonian identity which his appearance and manners created. The apparent lack of polish in the man was something that critics of his *Journey* could seize on, to suggest that he was the real barbarian. Captain Edward Thompson, not by any means his most severe critic, reflects on the paradox: 'Behold this extraordinary man on his journey, in quest of barbarism.' Johnson 'met with some degree of civility in the most desert parts'; indeed, he found 'nothing more barbarous than himself'.[24] Boswell would have repudiated any direct statement to this effect, but the inner message of his *Tour* is not all that different. And though, naturally, Johnson himself does not carry with him quite the same sense of his exoticism, he was perfectly aware that there was a profound oddity attached to his being in the Highlands at all. He wrote to Mrs Thrale on 23 September 1773: 'You remember the Doge of Genoa who being asked what struck him most at the French Court, answered, "Myself." I cannot think many things here more likely to affect the fancy than to see Johnson ending his sixty fourth year in the wilderness of the Hebrides' (*L* i. 370). It is an oddity which we must continually bear in mind.

Early on in the *Tour* there is a significant moment when Boswell describes Johnson's encounter with Lord Monboddo (see below, pp. 226–31). It is well known that Johnson in his *Journey* passes over this episode with two brief sentences in the section headed 'Montrose' (*JWI* 12). It was in this very year of 1773 that Monboddo brought out the first volume of his most famous and scandalous work, *Of the Origin and Progress of Language*. His

---

[23] Letter of 3 Nov. 1781, quoted in Reginald Blunt, *Elizabeth Montagu, 'Queen of the Blues'*, 2 vols. (London: Constable, 1923), ii. 157. Johnson was termed both a 'savage' and a 'barbarian': for the first, see *St James' Chronicle*, 25 May 1786, cited by E. R. Page, *George Colman the Elder* (New York: Columbia University Press, 1935), 282; for the second, see Hugh Blair to David Hume, quoted in E. C. Mossner, *The Life of David Hume* (Oxford: Clarendon Press, 1980), 417. Anna Seward reports a description of the *Tour* as 'a most amusing history of a learned monster, written by his show-man': see Margaret Ashmun, *The Singing Swan* (New Haven, Conn.: Yale University Press, 1931), 140.

[24] Quoted by H. W. Thompson, *A Scottish Man of Feeling* (London: Oxford University Press, 1931), 142.

notoriously eccentric beliefs included the idea that original nature and original primitive society survived only in the South Seas, a version of primitivism in which the temporal nostalgia of the Golden Age was replaced by a geographical nostalgia for unspoilt and idyllic tropical retreats. Monboddo had talked to Banks since the latter's return from the Antipodes, although this had not diminished his conviction that men with tails probably did still exist somewhere in the remote corners of the world. Whilst his survey of voyages did not give prominence to the recent Pacific travellers, he had concluded that the peoples of New Zealand were not inhumane (i.e. barbarous) but brave and *savage*. Johnson met this potential adversary with some trepidation, in which respect mingled with a marked distrust of their anthropological theories. As John J. Burke Jr. has written, 'Boswell had a fondness for placing his friend in challenging situations to see how he would perform, and it is clear that he expected the sparks to fly . . . Johnson and Monboddo, however, both behaved creditably.'[25] It is worth stressing that the encounter took place when the prejudices of both men had been fed by the accounts of Cook's voyage and especially by the views of Banks.

It is unnecessary to transcribe every detail of this famous scene. We may recall that Boswell typically 'started the subject of emigration' (*LSJ* v. 78), thus giving Johnson the chance to expatiate on a matter of burning interest in Scotland—note that the travellers had not yet reached the districts from which emigration was taking place on a large scale. This indicates the element of preparation for the northern tour which Johnson had put in. The two venerable philosophers debate Homer, the state of learning, and other topics, with Boswell occasionally chipping in when the conversational flame threatens to sputter:

MONBODDO. 'The history of manners is the most valuable. I never set a high value on any other history.' JOHNSON. 'Nor I; and therefore I esteem biography, as giving us what comes closest to ourselves, what we can turn to use.' BOSWELL. 'But in the course of general history, we find manners. In wars, we see the dispositions of people, their degrees of humanity, and other particulars.' JOHNSON. 'Yes; but then you must take all the facts to

[25] John J. Burke, jun., 'The Documentary Value of Boswell's *Journal of a Tour to the Hebrides*', in Prem Nath (ed.), *Fresh Reflections on Samuel Johnson: Essays in Criticism* (Troy, NY: Whitston, 1987), 351.

get this; and it is but a little you get.' MONBODDO. 'And it is that little which makes history valuable.' Bravo! thought I; they agree like two brothers. (*LSJ* v. 79–80)

Actually, it is unclear whether Monboddo and Johnson are not at cross-purposes by the end of this exchange (the rustic sage appears to think he is agreeing with his visitor, but Johnson gives no direct assent). But note Boswell's description of the revelatory insights afforded by the treatment of war in historical works: 'the dispositions of the people, their degrees of humanity, and other particulars'. Along with 'manners', this is what the travellers had come to observe in the Highlands. The trip is a substitute for reading historical literature.

Among other issues relevant to the broad ideological aims of the tour is the dispute as to whether 'the Savage' or 'the London Shopkeeper' had the best existence; 'his lordship, as usual, preferring the Savage' (*LSJ* v. 81). Johnson later wrote to Mrs Thrale of this argument, without Boswell's knowledge; he asserted that he and Monboddo had disagreed only on this point: 'Monbodo declared boldly for the Savage, and I perhaps for that reason sided with the Citizen' (*L* i. 344–5; *LSJ* v. 83). For his part, Boswell was surprised to see how well these putative intellectual rivals took to one another. The discussion later turned to politeness, and, as usual, Johnson adopted what has seemed to some to be his paradoxical position, insisting that 'politeness was of great consequence in society' (*LSJ* v. 82). Boswell, ever eager to draw out features of a piquant and culturally salient nature, remarked that 'The circumstance of each of them having a black servant was another point of similarity between Johnson and Monboddo. I observed how curious it was to see an African in the north of Scotland with little or no difference in manners from those of the natives' (*LSJ* v. 82–3). He is referring to Monboddo's retainer Gory and to Johnson's servant in London, Frank Barber. But on this trip the travellers were attended by Boswell's man, 'Joseph Ritter, a Bohemian: a fine stately fellow above six feet high, who had been over a great part of Europe, and spoke many languages'. Johnson called Joseph 'a civil man' (*LSJ* v. 53). Here, at Monboddo's house, Johnson 'laughed to see Gory and Joseph riding together most cordially. "These two fellows," (said he), "one from Africa, one from Bohemia, seem quite at home" ' (*LSJ* v. 83). The joke is that Johnson himself was not at home; and in this welter of mixed races, he seems to be the person least adjusted to his surroundings.

There are two small after-shocks from this scene in the text of the *Tour*. Five days later, at Cullen, Johnson unleashes his famous dictum on Monboddo: 'Other people have strange notions; but they conceal them. If they have tails, they hide them; but Monboddo is as jealous of his tail as a squirrel' (*LSJ* v. 111). Much further on, under 23 September, Boswell records this among 'one of his [Johnson's] fits of railing at the Scots': "We have taught you," said he, "and we'll do the same in time to all barbarous nations,— to the Cherokees,—and at last to the Ouran-Outangs"; laughing with as much glee as if Monboddo had been present' (*LSJ* v. 248).[26] We are distracted by the jocular tone and by the targeting of Monboddo; what is essentially called into question is the status of Scotland as a 'barbarous' nation. Johnson does not have to be entirely serious (as he plainly is not) for the nature of the innuendo to emerge. Boswell was always on the look-out for material in this area, and rarely failed to bring up Monboddo's ideas when it served his purpose. For example, when Banks and Dr Solander returned to Edinburgh in November 1772 from their voyage to the Hebrides and Iceland, Boswell took care to arrange a dinner with them, and found that Monboddo had been disappointed to learn that they had discovered no men with tails on their South Sea adventure.[27] The more one looks at such evidence, the plainer it becomes that the Highland jaunt was not an innocent event born of mild curiosity and a desire for novelty. The entire trip was overladen with cultural baggage, and almost every step was dogged by some echo of the prevailing debates about the nature of civilization. The famous exchange between Johnson and Lady Macleod about the natural goodness of man (14 September 1773) is only one striking instance of this quality in the *Tour* (*LSJ* v. 211).[28]

---

[26] Topics which came up on the same day included the other great primitive sought in the Highlands, Macpherson's Ossian, and the absence of animal slaughter in Tahiti, where Boswell cites a conversation with Banks (*LSJ* v. 246–7).

[27] See Carter, *Sir Joseph Banks*, 114.

[28] There is a curious link between Johnson's views and those of Monboddo, who wrote that man 'has so much of the nature of the solitary wild beast, that he has no natural propensity to enter society, but was urged to it by motives to be afterwards explained' (quoted from *The Origin and Progress of Language* by Gladys Bryson in her *Man and Society: The Scottish Inquiry of the Eighteenth Century* (Princeton, NJ: Princeton University Press, 1945), 68–9). Monboddo, in his 'rustick

Johnson could not have failed to be aware that there was a good deal of curiosity among the people he visited regarding this strange incomer. On Skye the celebrated Flora Macdonald passed on one rumour: she had heard on the mainland that 'Mr Boswell was coming to Sky, and one Mr Johnson, a young English buck, with him; Johnson was "highly entertained with this fancy" ' (*LSJ* v. 184–5).[29] Shortly afterwards, on a wild moor, the elderly traveller was forced to dismount on a steep declivity: 'he tried to alight on the other side, as if he had been a "young buck" indeed, but in the attempt he fell at his length upon the ground' (*LSJ* v. 207). There are moments when Johnson tries to live up to the unreal image which had preceded him. Like Omai, he seems to be attempting gamely to meet the incomprehensible expectations of his hosts. Part of the charm of the Highland trip resides in the willingness of the venerable sage 'to do as the Romans do', at some cost to dignity and convenience.

One reason that Johnson is thus placed at this disadvantage lies in Boswell's unconcealed desire to thrust him into unfamiliar postures. The ambition is made explicit in the entry in the *Tour* for 30 August:

To see Dr Johnson in any new situation is always an interesting object to me; and, as I saw him now for the first time on horseback, jaunting about at his ease in quest of pleasure and novelty, the very different occupations of his former laborious life, his admirable productions, his *London*, his *Rambler*, &c. &c. immediately presented themselves to my mind, and the contrast made a strong impression on my imagination. (*LSJ* v. 132)

This again is a mirror image of Omai's situation in London, where the Tahitian is introduced to a world of leisure and sumptuous living quite at odds with anything he had experienced previously. At the same time, Boswell's proprietorial attitude towards Johnson allows him to forget who the 'real' Johnson is, beneath the disguise of a free-wheeling tourist:

The fellow cried, with a very Highland accent, 'See such pretty goats!' Then he whistled, *whu*! and made them jump.—Little did he conceive what Dr

---

suit' and styling himself '*Farmer Burnett*' (*LSJ* v. 77), is another variant of the savage—the pseudo-primitive.

[29] Johnson's response was to observe that in Anoch 'I, being a *buck*, had miss in to make tea'.

Johnson was. Here now was a common ignorant Highland clown imagining that he could divert, as one does a child,—*Dr Samuel Johnson!*—The ludicrousness, absurdity, and extraordinary contrast between what the fellow fancied, and the reality, was truly comick. (*LSJ* v. 144).

Ironically, the 'reality' is that Dr Samuel Johnson, italics and all, *is* forced to adopt the role of a child in many of his encounters with an unknown world.

Some of the best-known episodes in the narrative describe Johnson strutting and cavorting in improbable guises. In his letter to David Garrick of 29 August 1773 Boswell finds an evocative image to capture the effect this produces:

This day we visited the ruins of Macbeth's castle at Inverness. I have had great romantick satisfaction in seeing Johnson upon the classic scenes of Shakspeare in Scotland; which I really looked upon as almost as improbable as that 'Birnam wood should come to Dunsinane.' Indeed, as I have always been accustomed to view him as a permanent London object, it would not be much more wonderful to me to see St Paul's church moving along where we now are. (*LSJ* v. 347)

Earlier in the *Tour* Boswell had delighted to see Johnson declaiming lines from the play on 'the very heath where Macbeth met the witches, according to tradition' (*LSJ* v. 115).[30] Then there is the kangaroo performance, and much strutting about 'with a broad sword and target' to exemplify 'the spirit of a Highlander' (*LSJ* v. 324). We witness in such scenes a kind of radical openness, an undisguised childlike zest for novelty, an uninhibited indulgence of sensation. Johnson becomes more of a free agent, for he has cast off some of the trappings of civilized behaviour.

A visiting Italian, Prince Gonzaga de Castiglione, once inadvertently gave a toast to the author of the *Rambler* as 'the great vagabond'.[31] It is a suggestive phrase. There was a personal force in Johnson which proceeded in part from a defect in expected qualities: a lack of respectable inertia and a conventional insensitivity to the drama of the moment. This want of inhibition was thrown into dramatic prominence during the tour. He considered himself well-mannered, but the carapace was thin and always liable

---

[30] See also *LSJ* v. 76. Cf. Johnson's more subdued account (*JWI* 25).

[31] The story (from *c.*1777) is reported by Mrs Piozzi: see James L. Clifford, *Hester Lynch Piozzi (Mrs Thrale)* (Oxford: Clarendon Press, 1971), 370.

to crack. One of the more surprising of Boswell's remarks was to
the effect that, regrettably, 'Dr Johnson did not practice the art of
accommodating himself to different sorts of people' (*LSJ* v. 288).
The truth is that he was always himself, wherever he was set down,
but that his personality was complex enough to encompass a wide
range of behavioural styles and modes of self-presentation. A close
reading of either narrative of the Highland jaunt will show that
Johnson could act 'in character' whilst having to follow customs
and social protocols far removed from those to which he was
accustomed. Like a transplanted Tahitian, he attempts to conceal
his bemusement, but he knows that every gesture and every word
proclaim his inability to merge into the normal surroundings. Like
exiles and emigrés in all periods, he both conceals and vaunts his
difference. Once Boswell had got his man into the remote
Highlands, there could be no turning back; and the uprooted
metropolitan was at the mercy of his benign captors.[32]

III

If we review the evidence which has been assembled, the discrepancies between the two cases under consideration remain perfectly
obvious; but so do some surprising points of similarity. Both
Johnson and Omai define their own culture in the act not so much
of *seeing* another country, as of *being seen* in it. They resemble less
the fictional Chinese or Persian exploring the west than they do
Gulliver on his second voyage, displayed and bargained for in the
market-place. Travel was usually valued for the moral education
that it bestowed on the traveller; here we are asked to consider the
reaction of the *travelled* people. It is the effect on the imagination of
the host population which alone can make sense of the experiment.

A large paradox underlies Johnson's journey into the unknown.
The cosmopolitan goes to see a primitive society in action. He aims
to test the theories of Rousseau and others on natural man—but
finds he has *become* natural man. Even in the simple matter of
locomotion, he is forced to regress through the stages of civiliza-

[32] Extensive passages of the *Journey* reflect Johnson's inability to find what he is
looking for; to take a single example, his search for reliable information on second
sight: 'Thus hopeless are all attempts to find any traces of Highland learning' (*JWI*
112).

tion, travelling first by carriage, then on horseback, and then on foot. Unprotected from the elements, as rain lashes down on the bare moor, and then cast adrift in an open boat with the storm howling around him, he is cut adrift from all his familiar landmarks and the props of urban living—as distant, morally, from his customary cultivated habitat as Omai was from his ordinary background when he was removed to London. The anti-primitivist ('Don't cant in defence of Savages': *LSJ* iv. 308–9)[33] is obliged to replicate many of the conditions of primitive life.

Yet, where Omai was a hapless nobody, marked by destiny for his quarter of an hour of fame, a conspicuous coxcomb in a land far from his own, Samuel Johnson in some respects was never more himself than when thus uprooted from the externals of civilization. We feel as close to him as ever we do when he is living his normal London life. As he lumbers around the Highlands, he is often comic, but seldom absurd; he is often bemused, but never intellectually floored; often condemned to wretched fare, but never harsh or ungenerous. The Hebridean trip, mimicking in some details Omai's European adventure, gave us existentially, if not socially, a true picture of Samuel Johnson: more real, to many readers today, than that Johnson of the London fleshpots whom Boswell regarded as the true likeness of his mentor. Few great writers have had such a savage streak in them, and few have brought to everyday life a quality of such abiding nobility. 'Figure him there,' wrote Thomas Carlyle, 'with his scrofulous diseases, with his great greedy heart, and unspeakable chaos of thought; stalking mournful as a stranger in this Earth . . .'[34]

---

[33] For Johnson's rejection of the 'soft primitivism' to be found in accounts of Tahiti by Hawkesworth and Bougainville, see Smith, *European Vision*, 49.

[34] Thomas Carlyle, *On Heroes, Hero-Worship and the Heroic in History* (1841; New York; Chelsea House, 1983), 217.

5

Johnson's Letters to Hester Thrale and *A Journey to the Western Islands of Scotland*

In this chapter we move from large-scale to small-scale issues. Here we shall be looking at the process of composition, by setting Johnson's published *Journey to the Western Islands of Scotland* alongside the remarks he made, as it were, on the hoof. The aim will be to show how the final text of the book has been put together to create a particular view of Scotland and of Johnson's experiences on his trip.

I

It is well known that the materials which Johnson employed in the composition of his *Journey* (1775) included a series of letters which he had written to Hester Thrale while he was on tour with Boswell.[1] Indeed, of the recognized sources, the letters form the only surviving corpus of material to be utilized directly in the text of the *Journey*, so far as can be definitely established. It is therefore surprising that no full comparison has ever been made of the contents of the letters and of the relevant portions of the *Journey*. Major editions of Johnson's book have been prepared by R. W. Chapman, Mary Lascelles and J. D. Fleeman, but though they make reference in varying degrees to the series of letters, none of them has the space to record the variants, omissions, and additions.[2] It is the aim of this chapter to give a fuller account of the

---

[1] Since the letters are treated in order, and occupy little more than fifty pages in Chapman's edition (*L* i. 337–91), page references have not been supplied, though Chapman's running number for the letters is cited in each case.

[2] See, in addition to *JWI*, Johnson's *Journey to the Western Islands of Scotland*, ed. R. W. Chapman (London: Oxford University Press, 1970); and *A Journey to the Western Islands of Scotland*, ed. J. D. Fleeman (Oxford, Clarendon Press, 1985). Chapman's text of the *Journey* derives from his fuller edition (Oxford University Press, 1924).

relation between the two narratives of the tour, for those portions of the *Journey* where they correspond. This will enable us to identify the ways in which Johnson altered the focus of his private messages to Hester Thrale when he came to create his public version of Scotland.

The materials available to Johnson while he worked on his book in 1774 may be arranged as follows: (1) a lost 'book of remarks' which Johnson kept on his travels, as he reported to Mrs Thrale from Skye on 30 September 1773; (2) a series of fifteen newsletters to Hester Thrale, dated between 12 August and 18 November 1773 (the journey proper, as traced in the published narrative, is covered by letters 3–13 in this series, dated between 25 August and 3 November; in addition there were three short letters to Henry Thrale, written during the latter stages of the tour); (3) Boswell's manuscript journal of the trip, not quite complete, which he later revised and expanded to form the published *Journal of a Tour to the Hebrides* (1785) (the original manuscript has been edited by F. A. Pottle and C. H. Bennett (1936), and was revised in 1963[3]). To these authenticated items may be added a number of less well established materials: they include some books on Scotland which Johnson appears to have sought out to provide background information,[4] and a mysterious selection of 'various packets' which Boswell sent to Johnson in response to requests for information (the precise subject matter is not made clear.[5] Beyond this, we must recognize the fact that Johnson had his own unrecorded and unwritten memories of the tour to draw on. He may also have been goaded by conversation with Mrs Thrale to recall additional details.

Plainly, these circumstances do not allow us to reach absolutely firm conclusions regarding the source of every passage in the published *Journey*. None the less, it is perfectly possible to explore

---

[3] Occasional references are made to this, James Boswell, *Journal of a Tour to the Hebrides*, ed. F. A. Pottle and C. H. Bennett (London: Heinemann, 1963), cited as *Journal of Tour*, as well as to *LSJ*.

[4] See Johnson to George Steevens, 7 Feb. 1774, in *L* i. 396.

[5] See Boswell to Henry Thrale, 13 May 1774, cited by Mary Hyde, *The Impossible Friendship: Boswell and Mrs Thrale* (London: Chatto and Windus, 1973), 25. Johnson had written to Boswell on 29 Jan. 1774: 'You must make haste and gather me all you can, and do it quickly, or I will and shall do without it' (*L* i. 394). This almost certainly refers to information required for the composition of the *Journey*.

the relation between some of the materials listed above. Since we have item 3 in the fullest state of its existence during Johnson's lifetime, we ought to be able to identify anything which came specifically from this source. Very little falls with certainty to this category. Nor is the matter complicated by the 'remarks' which Boswell composed around the *Journey*, since he did not see Johnson's drafts for the volume before it was published, and so they are in every particular a *post facto* response to the printed *Journey*.[6] As for the imponderable items mentioned above, all that can be said here is that we need not invent memorial reconstructions where concrete parallels can be found in existing materials.

It is a great pity that Johnson's own book of remarks, item 1, should not have survived. We have no means of knowing how extensive this was.[7] It is only occasionally that Johnson mentions any note-taking during the trip. In his letter to Mrs Thrale of 15–21 September he describes the moment (now identified as occurring near Loch Cluanie) when he first conceived his plan of making a book from his travels. He writes: 'I sat down to take notes on a green bank, with a small stream running at my feet, in the midst of savage solitude' (*L* i. 355).[8] The reference to taking notes disappears in the passage devoted to this episode in the *Journey*. Obviously, the absence of any previous record of memoranda does not indicate that Johnson only began to write down his impressions at this point. Boswell makes no mention of a notebook along with the 'large English oak stick' and other travelling-appurtenances which Johnson took with him—but it would not have been a visible part of his dress.[9]

However, more attention than hitherto should perhaps be paid to a comment in a letter from Boswell to Henry Thrale on 22 November 1773. Boswell states that 'our much respected friend

---

[6] For these 'Remarks', see *Journey*, ed. Fleeman, pp. xxvi–xxvii.

[7] An easy, but not very secure, assumption would be that it resembled in its coverage the journal which Johnson kept of his tour of north Wales in 1775 (see *LSJ* v. 427–60). If that were the case, the entries would often have been thinner than those supplied in the journalized letters to Mrs Thrale; and the overall bulk of material would not have been very much greater than that found in the letters relating to the Hebridean tour. The north Wales diary covers 5 July–30 Sept. 1775, slightly less time than the full Scottish trip.

[8] For the precise identification of the location by Dr J. D. Fleeman, see *JWI* 40.

[9] Johnson's pockets were so capacious that they 'might have almost held the two volumes of his folio dictionary; and he carried in his hand a large English oak stick. Let me not be censured for mentioning such minute particulars' (*LSJ* v. 19).

and I have had a very long and curious tour of which his letters have I suppose given you and Mrs Thrale a pretty full account. The World however will have a still fuller account from him. I hope you and Mrs Thrale will not be wanting in keeping [him] in mind of the expectations which he has raised.'[10] These words were written just as the tour had come to an end, and when impressions were fresh. It is noteworthy that Boswell refers specifically to the letters Johnson had written to the Thrales, but at the same time says nothing of the 'book of remarks'. The two men had been brought together so intimately on their travels that Boswell could not possibly have been unaware of Johnson's habits in respect of 'journalizing', as Boswell called his own concomitant activity. It is reasonable to conclude that Boswell thought the newsletters to Southwark formed a major part of the record of the voyage, as Johnson had set this down along the way. In his own narrative of the tour, Boswell observed his friend at work in Banff: 'Dr Johnson wrote a long letter to Mrs Thrale. I wondered to see him write so much so easily' (*LSJ* v. 109–10).[11] At no point in the *Tour* is there any comparable allusion to lengthy composition in the 'book of record'.

All this suggests that the lost memoranda may not have been as extensive as one might suppose, although their shadowy presence can be detected in some passages of the *Journey* for which we cannot otherwise account. It is obviously impossible to determine how far the memoranda and the letters to Mrs Thrale overlapped. What we know of Johnson's working habits does not encourage the belief that he would willingly have written out the same information twice in a short space of time if this was unnecessary. The 'fatigues of travel' caused him to write only one letter in the first fourteen days of his trip (this is stated in the very letter from Banff which he was writing under Boswell's observation: *L* i. 342). We know, too, that Johnson wanted particular care to be taken of his missives from Scotland. He wrote to Henry Thrale on 15 October from Mull: 'I hope my mistress keeps all my very long letters, longer than I ever wrote before' (*L* i. 375).[12] Then, on arriving back

---

[10] Boswell to Henry Thrale, 22 Nov. 1773, MS in Hyde collection, quoted by Hyde, *Impossible Friendship*, 24.

[11] Cf. *Journal of Tour*, 79.

[12] In this letter Johnson tells Thrale that he may 'perhaps spin out one more' before returning to London. This could suggest that the accounts were extemporized rather than worked up from a full existing narrative.

in London, he was glad to find that Mrs Thrale had gone to the trouble of copying them out. This can be deduced from a passage in her *Anecdotes*: 'The letters written in his journey, I used to tell him, were better than the printed book; and he was not displeased at my having taken the pains to copy them all over' (*JM* i. 258). The same conclusion is prompted by the fact that these copies seem to have been the basis for the text in the volume of Johnson's correspondence which Mrs Piozzi (as she had now become) produced in 1788; there are even signs that Johnson may have 'made or approved' certain small changes in these texts (*L* i. 342 n.).

Previous commentators have made passing observations on the status of these newsletters *vis à vis* the *Journey*. R. W. Chapman stated that 'The numerous parallels between the *Journey* and the *Tour* are easily found', but he did not record these similarities in any systematic way, either in editing the *Journey* or in editing Johnson's letters. Mary Hyde has written that Boswell, 'as commanded' in Johnson's letter of 29 January 1774, 'sent some material which was useful, but Johnson depended in the main upon the long diary letters which he had written to the Thrales while on the trip' (*L* i. 342).[13] The last part of this statement is perhaps overconfident, unless or until we can recover the missing 'book of remarks', but I believe that it probably contains at least an element of truth.

The most serious attempt to formulate an accurate statement of the position is that of J. D. Fleeman, who has written:

The contents of Johnson's documentary letters to Mrs Thrale suggest that they were written up as records from notes, and the different order of many of the details and items mentioned in the letters from the order in the 'Journey' argues that the letters themselves were collateral descendants from the notebooks rather than intermediate sources for the eventual narrative manuscript of the 'Journey.' Nevertheless there is presumptive evidence that the letters were consulted when the manuscript of the 'Journey' was being written up: 'I hope my mistress keeps all my very long letters, longer than I ever wrote before' ('Letter 330'); but the error as to

---

[13] Hyde, *Impossible Friendship*, 25. Mary Lascelles (*JWI*, p. xiii) remarks that the originals of Johnson's letters 'survive almost intact, here and there relieving his retrospective account with the more vivid colours of immediate impression'. This is aptly said, but may fail to indicate the scale of adaptation, and may slightly understate the *conscious* desire to move the discourse away from 'immediate impression' towards retrospective judgement.

the magistrates of Aberdeen (10) set beside 'Letter 321' or the conflicting spelling of 'Glenmorrison' ('Letter 323') and 'Glenmollison' (27 n.) show that the consultation was uneven.

Johnson drew upon other sources, mainly printed but also from informants, and Boswell co-operated, although the amount of information was meagre and Johnson's inquiries may have been little more than a tactful way of making Boswell feel useful.

This may well be a correct interpretation of the facts before us. However, it is by no means self-evident that the letters were 'written up' from an independent set of notes (which perhaps did not exist in any sustained form for the entire journey). But even if that assumption were correct, it would not follow that the text of the printed volume was based on such notes, with only subsequent 'consultation' of the letters. The argument from the order of the topics is inconclusive: Johnson could just as easily have switched round material from the presumed notebook as from the letters. In discussing a small error that Johnson makes as early as the second page of his book, substituting 'Maria Reg.' for 'Maria Re.', Fleeman assumes that he made the mistake 'when he came to write up his notes'. But the letter to Mrs Thrale reads 'Maria Re.', and this could just as easily have been the misinterpreted source.[14]

In order to add to the present state of knowledge, we need to carry out a more thorough and detailed investigation of the surviving evidence. This means comparing the letters with the *Journey*, where they deal with the same subject-matter, and observing the changes, additions, and omissions with minute care. It is also necessary to keep in mind the possible influence of the manuscript of Boswell's *Tour*, which Johnson had been allowed to read, though in practice this does not seem to have affected any of the perceived disparities between the two Johnsonian accounts.

In the comparisons which follow, it should be borne in mind that the text of the lost 'book of remarks' might be closer to the *Journey* than anything which survives in the letters to Mrs Thrale. But this is of no great direct significance, because the focus of attention will be on the differences between a private and a public text. The interest of the comparison lies in the nature of the inclusions and exclusions, rather than in the precise archeological strata of text and *Urtext*. The inferences that I shall draw may or may not be

---

[14] See *Journey*, ed. Fleeman, pp. xxxviii–xxxix, 152.

valid, but in general their cogency ought not to depend on the nature or size of the lost memoranda.

II

Johnson left London on 6 August 1773. He first wrote to Mrs Thrale from Newcastle on 12 August, but 'forgot to send it', as a postscript from Edinburgh, dated 15 August, reveals (as a whole, this letter makes up Chapman's item no. 318 in the collected correspondence). No trace of the journey north survives in the printed account of the tour, but it is clear that Johnson had already begun to meditate on the larger themes of his book:

I have been taking a view of all that could be shown me, and find that all very near to nothing. You have often heard me complain of finding myself disappointed by books of travels, I am afraid travel itself will end likewise in disappointment. One town, one country is very like another. Civilized nations have the same customs, and barbarous nations have the same nature. There are indeed minute discriminations both of places and of manners, which perhaps are not unworthy of curiosity, but which a traveller seldom stays long enough to investigate and compare. The dull utterly neglect them, the acute see a little, and supply the rest by fancy and conjecture.

A second preliminary letter was sent from Edinburgh on 17 August, the day before the travellers set out on their expedition (this forms Chapman no. 320). In it Johnson gives some account of the Edinburgh illuminati whom he has met: William Robertson, Thomas Blacklock, 'The Lord Chief Baron [Ord], Sir Adolphus Oughton, and many more'; he also notes the places he has visited, including St· Giles Cathedral, the Parliament House, and the College. None of this appears in the *Journey*, where Johnson disposes of Edinburgh in a single phrase, 'a city too well known to admit description' (*JWI* 3). Naturally, Boswell made good the omission in his own *Tour*, devoting something like twenty pages, or a twelfth of his book, to the round of social calls and tourist sites (*LSJ* v. 21–53).[15] As remarked above (p. 5), it was one aim of the *Tour* to reinstate aspects of Scotland which the *Journey* had

---

[15] This section was written up later from scattered notes, as Boswell also had not begun a regular journal at this stage (*Journal of Tour*, p. xii).

slighted: but note that the letters to Mrs Thrale do contain mention of the leaders of the Edinburgh Enlightenment.

The third letter (Chapman no. 321) is the one from Banff on 25 August, which has already been mentioned. It incorporates journalized entries dated 18 August (Inchkeith, modulating into an undated entry for St Andrews, actually covering 19 August); 20 August (Aberbrothick to Montrose); and 21 August (Aberdeen, a stay actually extending to 24 August, and covered further in the next letter). One faintly odd feature at the outset is that Johnson does not tell Mrs Thrale that the travellers were accompanied as far as St Andrews by the lawyer William Nairne, though he does mention the presence of 'another gentleman' in the *Journey* (*JWI* 3). It is Boswell who identifies Nairne. All that would give a clue to Mrs Thrale is a reference to 'my companions' on the island of Inchkeith. This is not the only place where the letters are more reticent than the public document, although the reason here is perhaps no more than haste. After describing to Mrs. Thrale the visit to Inchkeith, Johnson adds: 'Look on your Maps'—an adjuration which could usefully be added to the printed book at times, if literary decorum did not preclude such directness. A more predictable piece of censorship occurs when the party reaches the burghs of Fife. The printed text has: 'We ... passed through Kinghorn, Kirkaldy [*sic*], and Cowpar [Cupar], places not unlike the small or straggling market-towns in those parts of England where commerce or manufactures have not yet produced opulence' (*JWI* 4). This is a masterly softening of the harsh reality reported in more brutal terms to Mrs Thrale: 'We ... landed at Kinghorn, a mean town, and travelling through Kirkaldie, a very long town meanly built, and Cowpar, which I could not see because it was night . . .' In view of the offence that some of Johnson's published comments were to cause in Scotland, it is as well that his less guarded observations did not appear until four years after his death.

The entry for St Andrews is considerably expanded in the *Journey*, and may depend on the printed sources that Johnson consulted as well as the lost memoranda.[16] One small disparity lies in the fact that the printed text informs us that 'A student of the

---

[16] In addition, it was now that Boswell could claim: 'My Journal, from this day inclusive, was read by Dr Johnson' (*LSJ* v. 58).

highest class may keep his annual session ... for about fifteen pounds, and one of lower rank for less than ten' (*JWI* 8), whereas the letter states that 'the students of the highest rank and greatest expence may pass here for twenty pounds'. It would not be worth noting such minor discrepancies were it not for two considerations: first, there are several such cases, and second, they are unlikely all to have arisen from mere inattention, in view of Johnson's known respect for arithmetic. It seems more probable that deliberate revision is indicated, after further checking or research. A more significant change is the omission of a sentence at the end of the story about an old woman who lived in the disused cathedral vaults (*JWI* 8–9). The printed text has nothing corresponding to this: 'Boswel asked her if she never heard any noises, but she could tell him of nothing supernatural, though she sometimes wandered in the night among graves and ruins, only she had some notice by dreams of the death of her relations.' It can be shown that one of Boswell's major acts of revision when he turned his manuscript diary into the published *Tour* was the suppression of many references to the supernatural.[17] Johnson obviously had some preliminary curiosity regarding the 'second sight' which he investigated in the Highlands (*JWI* 107–110), but he did not want to make too much of his companion's obsession with the macabre.

   Little of importance emerges from the Aberdeen section of this letter. There are minor disparities concerning the magistracy of Aberdeen and the length of terms at Scottish universities; more notable is the omission of a description sent to Mrs Thrale of children 'not dressed in rags' who yet go barefoot, as 'shoes are indeed not yet in universal use', followed by a joke about Cromwell and cabbages which Johnson wisely chose to exclude from the *Journey*. Comedy, as we shall see, is one of the regular casualties of revision. None of this, however, is as significant as the omission of an entire paragraph about the visit to Lord Monboddo on the way to Aberdeen. There is only a bland paragraph in the printed version (*JWI* 12). Nevertheless, it would have been no great revelation when Mrs Thrale printed the contents of the letter in 1788, since Boswell had already given a full description in his *Tour* of the lively debate between Johnson and the eccentric social

---

[17] I owe this point to Barbara Looney, whose unpublished Ph.D. dissertation for the University of South Florida (1992) documents the statement.

theorist concerning the savage and the polite (*LSJ* v. 74–83).[18] This would actually have made an excellent scene in the *Journey*, since it relates so closely to the overriding themes of the Highland quest (see above, pp. 100–3, and below pp. 226–31); but Johnson would have infringed the rules of good taste in a positively Boswellian way if he had given details of this private conversation.

The fourth letter (Chapman no. 322) was dated from Inverness on 28 August. It covers the end of the stay in Aberdeen, together with the visit to Slaines Castle and the Buller of Buchan: as usual, the principal heads of the letter are preserved in the sectional subheadings of the *Journey*. It is a much shorter letter, and the journal form has been dropped in favour of ordinary narrative. The differences are mostly trivial: at his installation as a freeman of Aberdeen, for example, Johnson found 'no petty officer bowing for a fee' (*JWI* 18); this figure was 'gaping for a fee' in the letter to Mrs Thrale. One revision may be stylistic: the printed text states that the coot 'lays eggs as large as those of a goose' (*JWI* 19), whereas the letter says that it 'lays a bigger egg than a goose', an alteration which is probably connected with linguistic propriety (*L* i. 347 n.). The last sentence of Johnson's letter is elegantly transposed in the published text. To Mrs Thrale, Johnson wrote: 'On each side was a cave of which the fishermen knew not the extent, in which smugglers hide their goods, and sometimes parties of a pleasure take a dinner.' The point is amplified in the *Journey*:

We were soon at leisure to examine the place with minute inspection, and found many cavities which, as the watermen told us, went backward to a depth which they had never explored. Their extent we had not time to try; they are said to serve different purposes. Ladies come hither sometimes in the summer with collations, and smugglers make them storehouses for clandestine merchandise. It is hardly to be doubted but the pirates of ancient times often used them as magazines of arms, or repositories of plunder. (*JWI* 20–1)

The expansion in general, and the concluding reflection in particular, are characteristic of Johnson's procedures throughout. We might also note the diplomatic attempt at the end to shift the nefarious activities of hiding plunder safely back into 'ancient times'.

The story is continued in the fifth letter (Chapman no. 323),

[18] Cf. *Journal of Tour*, 51–8.

which was written from Armadale on 6 September, just after the travellers had landed on Skye. Johnson now reports, as he tells Mrs Thrale, from the 'verge of European Life'. He returns to the events of 25 August, where the fourth letter had left off. His first comments relate to the countryside as 'not uncultivated but so denuded of its Woods, that in all this journey I had not travelled a hundred yards between hedges or seen five trees fit for the Carpenter. A few small plantations may be found but I believe scarcely any thirty years old, at least, as I do not forget to tell they are posterior to the Union.' This politically loaded joke is discreetly turned into a wry allusion to Johnson's own advancing years: 'I had now travelled two hundred miles in Scotland and seen only one tree not younger than myself' (*JWI* 21). Possibly Johnson had not wanted to remind Mrs Thrale of his age, a subject on which, as we have seen, he was always sensitive.

Soon afterwards, Johnson describes to Mrs Thrale the passage of the travellers across some hallowed Shakespearian ground: 'We went on to Foris over the heath where Macbeth met the witches, but had no adventure.' There is a more explicit touch in the printed text, where Johnson writes: 'we . . . next morning entered upon the road, in which Macbeth heard the fatal prediction; but we travelled on not interrupted by promises of kingdoms, and came to Nairn, a royal burgh, which, if it once flourished, is now in a state of miserable decay; but I know not whether its chief annual magistrate has still not the title of Lord Provost' (*JWI* 25). On Nairn itself, the letter had been more brutally abrupt: 'Next day we came to Nairn, a miserable town, but a royal burgh, of which the chief annual Magistrate is stiled Lord Provost.' There follows a visit to Fort George; the paragraph on this in the correspondence is closely paraphrased by that in the *Journey*, except that Johnson, naturally, omits a final compliment to Mrs Thrale: 'But nothing puts my honoured Mistress out of my mind.' At this stage the letters are growing more exiguous in detail, and the text of the published book incorporates many wider reflections on the state of Scotland.

From Inverness the travellers continued on horseback rather than by carriage. Johnson makes little of this in the letter, but he develops the point in the *Journey*, where he lays more emphasis on the difficulties along their way ('climbing crags, and treading bogs, and winding through narrow and obstructed passages': *JWI* 29). He tells Mrs Thrale that 'There is in these ways much labour but little danger,' and seems to have wished to allay any sense of alarm that she may have felt. As the party travelled along Lough (Loch) Ness, the road at one point was 'bordered with low trees' (*JWI* 31) which reminded Johnson of an English lane, though it was less muddy; he suppresses the thought, recorded in the letter, that 'Such a length of Shade perhaps Scotland cannot show in any other place.' This letter ends at Anoch, with the presentation of a book to the landlord's daughter. In the *Journey* the precise book is not specified, but Boswell wrote a long footnote to satisfy curiosity on this point, fixing it as a copy of Cocker's *Arithmetic* which Johnson had bought in Inverness (*LSJ* v. 138). When writing to Mrs Thrale, Johnson had mentioned the title, but obviously this was a matter below the dignity of printed history. The overall tendency is for the published version to remove detail and to pass over what would have been seen as accidentals—streaks of the tulip which need not be numbered.

The next letter, the sixth (Chapman no. 324), is the shortest so far. It was written on 14 September while Johnson was stranded at Dunvegan, and begins with an apology: 'The Post, which comes but once a week into these parts, is so soon to go that I have not time to go on where I left off in my last Letter.' He simply uses the opportunity to describe his present situation on Skye, and to give a brief account of his visit to Raasay. This stage of the journey is described more fully in the course of the next letter but one, a much longer dispatch which brought Mrs Thrale more or less up to date on the progress of the tour.

It was on the next day that Johnson began the seventh letter (Chapman no. 326), though it was not completed until 21 September. It may be added that on 14 September, along with the sixth letter, Johnson had written one of the few surviving letters to be sent from Scotland which was not addressed to the Thrales: it was a reply to Lord Elibank, and contains no details of the tour.[19] In the seventh letter Johnson carries the story from Anoch, which

---

[19] Other letters in this category are those to Macleod of Macleod on 28 Sept., a thank-you note; to Robert Chambers on 30 Sept.; to Chambers again on 15 Oct.; and to the Duke of Argyll on 27 Oct., another complimentary affair. Very little of relevance to this enquiry emerges from any of them. We cannot know if any of the lost letters were more informative, but the most defensible conclusion seems to be that Johnson confined any serious description of the trip to the Thrales, since it was these letters which were to be of use in compiling the planned narrative.

the travellers had reached on 31 August, as far as their arrival in Raasay on 8 September. This relatively short section contained some crucial episodes in the journey. It included Johnson's conception of the narrative on 1 September, with a reference in the letter to his note-taking, as we have already seen (p. 110); the quarrel with Boswell on the same day; and the unhappy stay at Armadale on 2–6 September. The disagreement with Boswell flared up suddenly on the last stage of the road to the Isles; it is totally ignored in both sources deriving from Johnson, and we only know of this brief antagonism from Boswell's journal and the *Tour* (*LSJ* v. 144–5).[20] The references to Boswell in the seventh letter, including those applying to this particular day, are quite kind; either Johnson wished to conceal the matter from Mrs Thrale, possibly feeling that he had acted hastily, or else he had forgotten about it two weeks later, when he came to write up his account. The latter explanation may seem the less plausible, but it should be remembered that a great deal had been happening in the intervening period.

As for the sojourn at Armadale, Johnson does not wholly conceal from Mrs Thrale his dislike of Sir Alexander Macdonald, whereas he maintained discretion in the printed text. However, it is again thanks to Boswell that we have become aware of the distaste that both men came to feel for Macdonald, as a cruel rack-renting landlord and a would-be genteel Anglified chieftain. Boswell himself was forced to suppress some of the abrasive exchanges as they appeared in his journal; even so, Macdonald was not pleased with the softened version which appeared in the *Journal of a Tour*, and complained to Boswell.[21]

The night before the travellers had passed over to Skye, they had stayed at Glenelg. What happened there forms the basis of a celebrated comic set piece in the *Journey*:

We were now to examine our lodging. Out of one of the beds, on which we were to repose, started up, at our entrance, a man as black as a Cyclops from the forge. Other circumstances of no elegant recital concurred to disgust us. We had been frightened by a lady at Edinburgh, with discouraging representations of Highland lodgings. Sleep, however, was necessary. Our Highlanders had at last found some hay, with which the inn could not supply them. I directed them to bring a bundle into the room,

---

[20] Cf. *Journal of Tour*, 110–11.   [21] See ibid. 114–15.

and slept upon it in my riding coat. Mr Boswell being more delicate, laid himself sheets with hay over and under him, and lay in linen like a gentleman. (*JWI* 48–9)

The story as relayed originally to Mrs Thrale contained a few circumstances which had to be omitted from the elegant recital of the *Journey*, but it also reveals that Johnson declined sheets not through superior hardiness, but through lack of any confidence in their protective power:

When the repast was ended, we began to deliberate upon bed. Mrs Boswell had warned us that we should 'catch something,' and had given us Sheets for our security; for Sir Alexander and Lady Macdonald, she said, came back from Skie, so scratching themselves—. I thought sheets a slender defence, against the confederacy with which we were threatened, and by this time our highlanders had found a place where they could get some hay; I ordered hay to be laid thick upon the bed, and slept upon it in my great coat. Boswell laid sheets upon his hay, and reposed in Linen like a Gentleman. The horses were turned out to grass, with a man to watch them.

This paragraph in the letter concludes: 'The hill Ratiken, and the inn at Glenelg, are the only things of which we or travellers yet more delicate, could find any pretensions to complain.' In general, Johnson permits himself few complaints in the printed text, and whilst in his private correspondence he refrains from exaggerating any difficulties, he naturally takes fewer pains to avoid offending Scottish sensibilities.

At this point in the printed narrative Johnson inserts his first separate section of general reflections, under the heading of 'The Highlands'. Naturally, there is no equivalent in the journalized information sent back to Mrs Thrale, although there is a notably reflective passage, partly playful and partly serious, on his present situation, in which he imagines that Mrs Thrale will be envisaging him 'withdrawn from the gay and the busy world into regions of peace and pastoral felicity'. It is clear that the enforced inactivity on Skye in mid-September gave Johnson the leisure both to speculate on what he had seen up to that point and to resume a more detailed narrative for Mrs Thrale.

This seventh letter ends with the trip across southern Skye and the voyage to Raasay. In the section for Corrichatachin Johnson fills out the published narrative with further reflections on Skye, seemingly based both on his impressions on the day in question and on things that he had noted since that time. The generalizing tendency is apparent in the means by which a visit to MacKinnon of Corrichatachin modulates into a survey of reading-habits on the islands; in the letter Johnson confines himself to mentioning the 'books, both English and Latin,' which were in the house. Similarly, the more concrete epistolary detail includes reference to 'a Minister's sister in very fine Brocade', who 'sung Earse songs'. The more impersonal equivalent in the *Journey* reads: 'we were treated with very liberal hospitality, among a more numerous and elegant company than it could have been supposed easy to collect' (*JWI* 53). This is a localized example of a difference that is apparent throughout. It has always been noticed that Johnson's book gives a much less specific treatment of people and events than Boswell's does. Such a contrast would still carry some truth, but a good deal less, if we compared the *Tour* not with the published version, but with the letters to Mrs Thrale. Of all forms of censorship which Johnson employed in creating the *Journey*, the most pervasive is simply the avoidance of excessive local and particularized fact. This is a procedure entirely in accordance with Johnson's known attitudes, but its workings here have not been drawn to our attention by any previous commentator.

Before moving on from this letter, we should pay brief attention to an interlude in which Johnson refers to his birthday. We have looked at this passage in another context (see p. 20 above): here it is relevant for another reason. This is by no means the only occasion on which the story of the Highland tour has to give way in the correspondence to other concerns; many other letters contain enquiries as to the health of the Thrale family, and other non-Scottish topics. This is, however, the clearest case of a direct incursion into the journal, signalled by Johnson at the start and the end: 'I cannot forbear to interrupt my Narrative. Boswel, with some of his troublesome kindness, has informed this family [the Macleods of Dunvegan], and reminded me that the eighteenth of September is my birthday . . . I will now complain no more, but tell my Mistress of my travels.' The interest of this break in the text, for our present purposes, lies in the evidence it provides that Johnson was conscious of transmitting a regular journal. In other words, the normal digressive habits of the epistolary style have been suspended; an apology is called for because the rhetorical form, a sustained travel narrative, requires some explanation for the sudden shift ten days forward from the present moment.

III

The transition from the seventh to the eighth letter (Chapman no. 327) is the smoothest of any in the series. A postscript to the former reads: 'We are this morning trying to get out of Skie;' the opening of the latter reads: 'I am still in Skie.' The new message is dated three days later, on 24 September, and comes from Talisker. After a brief updating exercise on the travellers' present location, the material relates entirely to the spell on Raasay; little by way of significant difference is apparent. Johnson expands his account of the pleasant welcome he and Boswell received ('We found nothing but civility, elegance and plenty': *JWI* 59), but he drops the hyperbole he used to Mrs Thrale ('politeness, which not the court of Versailles could have thought defective'). Naturally, a personal touch disappears: 'We went up into a dining room about as large as your blue room.'

There then ensues one of the best-known scenes in the entire journey, when an impromptu musical evening takes place before dinner. (In the published version Johnson has thirty-six sitting down to dinner, whereas the letter has only thirty-two. It is impossible to know whether such minor discrepancies arise from carelessness or from subsequent better information.) A young lady then sang some Erse songs; Johnson is quite brief about this in the printed text, and omits his comment to Mrs Thrale that he had consistently been unable to 'procure the translation of a line of Earse'. The *Journey* does, however, add the significant fact that one of the songs was about emigration to America, a theme which recurs in the book. Since there is no sign of this in the letter, we may reasonably suppose that this is one of the places where the lost notebook came to Johnson's aid when he wrote up his narrative. There are surprisingly few such moments.

The published account now moves on to an extensive survey of Raasay, which incorporates references to Martin's works and seems to have been assembled, in part at least, from external sources (*JWI* 64).[22] Some of the information concerning the island's

---

[22] See *JWI* 62 n.

laird was given at the end of the previous letter, though nowhere in the *Journey* does Johnson repeat the statement that 'The money which he raises by rent from all his dominions which contain at least fifty thousand acres, is not believed to exceed two hundred and fifty pounds.' In general, like most men and women of the eighteenth century, Johnson is not squeamish about money, but there is more reticence on this sort of thing in the printed text than in the private messages to Mrs Thrale. Although Johnson writes at the end of his published account: 'Raasay has little that can detain a traveller' (*JWI* 66), the island has actually detained his narrative for several pages. The material required may have come from various places, including his own independent observations, but little of it could have been found in the surviving letters to Mrs Thrale. Certainly, there is nothing corresponding to the comment in his report back to Southwark: 'You may guess at the opinions that prevail in this country, they are however content with fighting for their king, they do not drink for him; we had no foolish healths' (see further Chapter 6, below).

The ninth letter is the longest of all. It occupies ten pages in the standard edition (Chapman no. 329), and for the first time brings Mrs Thrale up to the present moment with its continuous journalized entries. It is dated from Ostaig on 30 September, but in fact the last portion of the letter contains a journal entry for 3 October. Johnson opens his letter with the words: 'I am still confined in Skie,' and then takes the story back to the time spent on Raasay. Again there are minor discrepancies in arithmetic. The letter surmised that the island 'maintains as near as I could collect about seven hundred inhabitants, perhaps ten to a square mile'. A different manner of calculation in the *Journey* yields a different result: 'The number of this little community has never been counted by its ruler, nor have I obtained any positive account, consistent with result of political computation. Not many years ago [in 1745], the late laird led out one hundred men upon a military expedition. The sixth part of a people is supposed capable of bearing arms, Raasay had therefore six hundred inhabitants' (*JWI* 63–4). The phrase 'nor have I obtained' may point to Johnson's additional researches when he returned to London; naturally, he was more anxious about precision in such matters when compiling the published work than in his relatively informal messages to Southwark. In the remaining sections on Raasay in the ninth letter, there is again much more specific and concrete detail. Johnson mentions a trip that Boswell made across the island to a ruined castle, an event suppressed in the *Journey*, and Johnson's own visit to a dilapidated Roman Catholic chapel is generalized away from the particular occasion towards a wider reflection on the 'malignant influence of Calvinism [which] has blasted ceremony and decency together' (*JWI* 65).

Eventually the travellers leave Raasay: there is a valedictory gesture in each account, but it is significantly different in the two cases. 'Thus we left Raarsa, the seat of plenty, civility, and cheerfulness,' reads the letter to Mrs Thrale. The farewell in the *Journey* is both more literary and more mixed in its judgement: 'Without is the rough ocean and the rocky land, the beating billows and the howling storm: within is plenty and elegance, beauty and gaiety, the song and the dance. In Raasay, if I could have found an Ulysses, I had fancied a Phaeacia' (*JWI* 66). The difference lies mainly in the enhanced elevation of the published form, and its greater readiness to move from the local and the actual. Johnson had no hesitation at other times in citing classical sources to Mrs Thrale (she was fond of doing as much herself), but here it is the demands of public as against private rhetoric, rather than the personality of the correspondents, which explain the asymmetry.

The travellers then returned to the mainland of Skye, landing at Portree. In his published version Johnson identifies the Scottish king commemorated in this place-name as James V, whereas the letter had merely stated 'one of the Scottish Kings'. A more significant addendum is the brief allusion to a ship lying in port 'waiting to dispeople Sky, by carrying the natives away to America' (*JWI* 67). There is no trace of this in the letter; since there would be little reason to conceal such matters from Mrs Thrale, the most likely explanation is that Johnson had chosen to concentrate on the theme of emigration in his *Journey*, introducing every instance, however tiny, which confirmed the importance of this phenomenon. When he originally wrote back to Mrs Thrale, he does not appear to have isolated this theme for attention. On the other hand he is much less detailed in his account of Flora Macdonald in the *Journey*, and one of several items of information to disappear is, oddly, the fact that 'She and her husband are poor, and are going to try their fortune in America.' The desire to reinforce the theme apparently clashed with the requirements of private decorum. What has happened in this section is that the direct rendering of an encounter and a conversation has been replaced in the printed book by a tactful overall summary, delivered almost in terms of a newspaper obituary.

The stay at Dunvegan yields some description of the locality, in which traces of the letter (if they are not also those of equivalent passages in the lost journal) can be seen sporadically. Again, as with Raasay, one of the most significant alterations occurs at the moment of departure. In the correspondence there is no more than a brief reference to the hospitality of this 'remote region' as 'like that of the golden age'. This is developed in the published *Journey* into a famous little flourish of rhetoric: 'At Dunvegan I had tasted lotus, and was in danger of forgetting that I was ever to depart, till Mr Boswell sagely reproached me with my sluggishness and softness' (*JWI* 71). One would scarcely have guessed that this remarkable flight of poetic invention has behind it the relatively banal words with which the golden age was summoned up to Mrs Thrale.

The following section of the printed book is devoted to Ullinish, and here the closest correspondence with the material sent back to Southwark occurs in the visit to a cave on the sea-shore, famous for its echo. In the event the travellers heard no echo, but Johnson at least saw mussels and whelks for the first time, as recorded in both accounts. Again a simple piece of narrative is polished in the *Journey* to produce a more resonant effect. What Mrs Thrale read was this: 'The Boatmen said, as I heard afterwards, that they perceived the cry of an English Ghost, this, Boswell says disturbed him.' The superstitious fears of his travelling companion are, as usual, deleted by Johnson when composing the published version— if anything, the faint joke is against Johnson himself: 'They expected no good omen of the voyage; for one of them declared that he heard the cry of an English ghost. This omen I was not told till after our return, and therefore cannot claim the dignity of despising it' (*JWI* 74). The following section is devoted to the stay at Talisker, and in both accounts the major event is the meeting with the young laird of Coll, who was to accompany the travellers on the next stages of their trip. Once more there is a loss of localized detail: the printed *Journey* states that the village is 'situated . . . upon a coast where no vessel lands but when it is driven by a tempest on the rocks' (*JWI* 75); the letter had also conveyed this information, but in the same breath had added the fact that three ships had almost been driven on to the rocks just two days prior to Johnson's arrival. The story ends: 'The crews crept to Talisker almost lifeless with wet, cold, fatigue, and terrour, but the Lady took care of them.' Boswell, surprisingly, also misses out this graphic episode. Perhaps Johnson was told of what had happened while Boswell was absent. It is a warning that Johnson's prevailing habit of generalizing the narrative may conceal other significant episodes which, for one reason or another, failed to reach Boswell's notice.

The next portion of the book concerns the journey southwards to Ostaig, not far from the earlier stopping-place at Armadale. At this point the printed narrative launches into the major consideration of all matters relating to Skye—and, indeed, the fullest analysis of Hebridean life—to be found anywhere in the book. At an equivalent point in the ninth letter there is a broadly parallel passage setting out Johnson's impressions of the island, and the information about its mores which he had gleaned. This is introduced with the formula: 'Mr Thrale, probably, wonders how I live all this time without sending to him for money.' Clearly, by this stage of the tour, during prolonged inactivity as the travellers waited for the weather to break and so allow them to continue their journey, Johnson felt the impulse to sum up his overall sense of the island community. The published analysis draws on relatively few details in the letter,[23] and the two surveys appear to have been composed independently. Certainly Johnson had access to facts for his *Journey* which were not reported in the letter; for example, the after-effects of the 'Black Spring' in 1771, down to the information that 'Many of the roebucks perished' (*JWI* 78). Johnson ends his letter with news of his own indifferent health, reflecting that 'This Climate perhaps is not within my degrees of healthy Latitude.'

This ninth letter ends with a résumé and a promise of things to come: 'Thus have I given my most honoured Mistress the story of me and my little ramble. We are now going to some other Isle, to what we know not, the Wind will tell us.' This note of uncertainty is smoothed over in the published account. In the event, the promise could not be kept immediately. The tenth letter (Chapman no. 330)

---

[23] Cf. e.g. the remarks on the size of cattle in *L* i. 373 and *JWI* 81; but even the same facts are stated in quite different ways: cf. *L* i. 373, on small gooseberries, with *JWI* 78.

was the first addressed to Henry Thrale; it was dated from Mull on
15 October. The short message contains little more than a
paraphrase of the travellers' present situation: 'Since I had the
honour of writing to my mistress, we have been hindered from
returning, by a tempest almost continual. We tried eight days ago to
come hither, but were driven by the wind into the isle of *Col*, in
which we were confined eight days.' There is no further mention of
their eventful passage, and no reference to the visit to Iona. This
letter would have been of scant help to Johnson in compiling his
fuller description for the *Journey*. After this the letter turns to other
matters.

However, Johnson also wrote to Mrs Thrale under the same
cover, and resumed his journalized narrative from the time that the
travellers left Skye on 3 October. He starts with an apologetic
formula: his correspondent 'I suppose expects the usual tribute of
intelligence, a tribute which I am not now very able to pay.' It is
true that the period of inactivity had dampened Johnson's
enthusiasm for exploring minutiae; by this time he was beginning
to grow weary and was looking forward to his return (as the letter
to Henry Thrale reveals). None the less, he was able to put together
a certain amount of material on the time spent on Coll. One
characteristic alteration in this letter (Chapman no. 331) occurs in
the description of the storm which blew them towards Coll; the
letter refers to 'a violent gust which Bos: had a great mind to call a
tempest', a touch which, in the corresponding passage in the
Journey, is turned into an impersonal form: 'the wind, which blew
against us, in a short time, with such violence, that we, being no
seasoned sailors, were willing to call a tempest' (*JWI* 119–20). In
his later 'Remarks' on the *Journey* Boswell wrote: 'You treat the
storm too lightly.'[24] As his own *Tour* discloses, he was certainly the
more anxious of the two men during the storm, and Johnson's
decision to edit out the reference to his companion may be seen not
so much as decorum as concern for Boswell's feelings.

Otherwise the reasonably full treatment of Coll in the published
book owes little to the private letter. Johnson told Mrs Thrale;
'*Coll* is but a barren place, description has few opportunities here of
spreading her colours.' However, description is allowed greater

---

[24] For Boswell's more anxious account, see *LSJ* v. 282–3, deriving from *Journal
of Tour*, 250–2.

liberty in the *Journey*, and this could well be another place where the lost notebook supplied details over and above those recorded in the letter. Occasional snatches are present in both extant sources; as for instance, the comment that Coll 'seems to be little more than one continued rock, covered from space to space with a thin layer of rock', is restated with more dignity in the printed account: 'Col is not properly rocky; it is rather one continued rock, of a surface much diversified with protuberances, and covered with a thin layer of earth, which is often broken, and discovers the stone' (*JWI* 124). For the most part, however, this represents one stage of the *Journey* where the information sent back to Southwark would have been inadequate for Johnson's later needs.

The twelfth letter was written from Inveraray on 23 October (Chapman no. 332). Johnson resumes his journal on 16 October and relates to Mrs Thrale the events of his stay in Mull, including his visit to Iona at the end. Frustratingly, he concluded with the sentence: 'The Description I hope to give you another time.' Chapman glosses the remark as follows:

Unless, which is unlikely, a letter is lost, we must suppose that the 'description' was never written in that form, and that J's published account of his visit to Iona depended on his 'book of remarks' or wholly on memory. He no doubt made notes of the architecture as well as his 'rude measures inaccurately taken, and obscurely noted' [see *JWI* 149].

This seems to me to be soundly reasoned: the absence of a letter containing the promised description is by no means suspicious, as there would have been few good opportunities before the travellers reached Glasgow for Johnson to prepare a full-dress description. (He did write briefly to Henry Thrale, along with a thank-you note to the Duke of Argyll.) It seems most congruent with the facts to suppose that the measurements 'inaccurately taken, and obscurely noted' represent the state of many entries in the lost notebook, at any rate by this stage of the tour. Chapman's suggestion that Johnson had need of his excellent memory when he came to the section on Iona strikes me as solidly anchored in the facts as we can reconstruct them.

The most notable alteration in this section follows a familiar pattern. It occurs during the visit to Inch Kenneth, when the travellers explored a ruined chapel. The letter to Mrs Thrale takes this form:

The altar is not yet quite demolished, beside it on the right side is a Bas relief of the Virgin with her Child, and an Angel hovering over her, on the other side still stands a hand bell, which though it has no clapper neither presbyterian bigotry, nor barbarian wantonness has yet taken away. The Chappel is about thirty eight feet long, and eighteen broad. Boswel, who is very pious, went into it at night to perform his devotions, but came back in haste for fear of Spectres.

Apart from one of the regular adjustments in dimensions, and the avoidance of harsh expressions against 'presbyterian bigotry' and 'barbarian wantonness', the most striking difference in the *Journey* is the total omission of Boswell's superstitions: 'It is about sixty feet in length, and thirty in breadth. On one side of the altar is a bas relief of the blessed Virgin, and by it lies a little bell; which, though cracked, and without a clapper, has remained there for ages, guarded only by the venerableness of the place' (*JWI* 144).[25] During the passage to Iona, two days later, a possibly hurtful reference to Boswell is again deleted. The *Journey* has: 'The day soon failed us, and the moon presented a very solemn and pleasing scene. The sky was clear, so that the eye commanded a wide circle: the sea was neither still nor turbulent: the wind neither silent nor loud' (*JWI* 147–8). In the original letter this pleasant night–piece contains an added touch: 'We then entered the boat again, the night came upon us, the wind rose, the sea swelled, and Boswel desired to be set on dry ground. We however persued our navigation, and passed by several little Islands in the silent solemnity of faint moonshine, seeing little, and hearing only the wind and the water.' Whether or not the aside to Mrs Thrale was actuated by malice, it is a pity that literary decorum insisted on its removal. Comedy, however, was not a quality for which Johnson strove in his published work: the incidental fun which creeps into the epistolary journal is almost always suppressed.

Under the same cover, Johnson enclosed a letter to Henry Thrale of the same date (Chapman no. 333). Like the other missives to the male partner, this is short, but it does advance the narrative a little. Johnson begins by proclaiming that 'We have gotten at last out of the Hebrides,' adding: 'some account of our travels I have sent to my Mistress.' After setting out the planned itinerary for the

[25] Chapman (*L* i. 379) does note this difference, and refers to Boswell's more open account in the manuscript diary (*Journal of Tour*, 317). In the *Tour* this visit to the chapel is wholly suppressed (*LSJ* v. 327).

remainder of the journey, he continues the story of the sojourn on Mull from where he had left off in his letter to Mrs Thrale:

About ten miles of this days journey were uncommonly amusing. We travelled with very little light, in a storm of wind and rain, we passed about fifty five streams that crossed our way, and fell into a river that for a very great part of our road, foamed and roared beside us, all the rougher powers of Nature, except thunder were in motion, but there was no danger. I should have been sorry to have missed any of the inconveniences, to have had more light, or less rain, for their cooperation crowded the scene, and filled the mind.

This is an abbreviated and slightly more personal version of the description which was to appear in the *Journey*:

The night came on while we had yet a great part of the way to go, though not so dark, but that we could discern the cataracts which poured down the hills, on one side, and fell into one general channel that ran with great violence on the other. The wind was loud, the rain was heavy, and the whistling of the blast, the fall of the shower, the rush of the cataracts, and the roar of the torrent, made a nobler chorus of the rough musick of nature than it had ever been my chance to hear before. The streams, which ran cross the way from the hills to the main current, were so frequent, that after a while I began to count them; and, in ten miles, reckoned fifty-five, probably missing some, and having let some pass before they forced themselves upon my notice. (*JWI* 158)

Johnson's letters to Henry Thrale are less intimate in tone than those to Hester, as well as considerably briefer, and this is the only one which contains substantive narrative of the trip. Its successor was little more than a note, three days later, while the travellers were still at Inveraray (Chapman no. 334). It is really a business letter, and does not bear directly on the present enquiry.

IV

Now that the travellers had left the remote islands and were back in more accessible regions, their progress came to resemble a tour of country seats, most notably Inveraray and Auchinleck. Commensurately, there appears a sense of winding down, both in the letters to Southwark and in the published book. It is indicative that the last named section of the *Journey* is headed 'Inch Kenneth'.

Previous headings had represented, accurately enough, small stages in the journey. The final sections are in effect untitled, since the visit to Inch Kenneth was for only to two days (17–18 October), whereas the book covers events down to 22 November. It is safe to assume that, however diligently Johnson had filled his notebook earlier, there would not be a very full documentation of these later stages of the tour in the missing record.[26]

On 28 October Johnson directed quite a short letter to Mrs Thrale from Glasgow (Chapman no. 336). It is exclusively devoted to a journal of the three preceding days, covering the progress from Inveraray to Glasgow via Loch Lomond. The entry for 26 October contains this short section on an unnamed valley: 'We travelled along a deep valley between lofty Mountains covered only with brown heath; entertained with a succession of cataracts on the left hand, and roaring torrent on the other side. The Duke's horse went well, the road was good, and the journey pleasant except that we were incommoded by perpetual rain.' Johnson adds a detail concerning the weather which is not reproduced in the published book: 'In all September we had according to Boswel's register, only one day and a half of fair weather.' This is another indication that Johnson was highly aware of Boswell's meticulous record-keeping, which appears to have contrasted with his own lackadaisical methods. When he prepared the *Journey* for publication, he was able to give the valley a name, Glencroe, and proceeded as follows: 'In this rainy season the hills streamed with waterfalls, which, crossing the way, formed currents on the other side, that ran in contrary directions as they fell to the north or south of the summit. Being, by the favour of the Duke, well mounted, I went up and down the hill with great convenience' (*JWI* 159). Again there is a subtle shift of emphasis, with less sense of direct physical impact on the rain-battered travellers. In the *Journey* rain is a datum of climatology, a feature of interest to the observant natural historian; in the private letters it is an actual piece of phenomenology, cold and wet.

A boat trip on Loch Lomond was arranged on the following day, for which the printed account was able to summon up additional facts, including the presence of an osprey's nest on one of the

[26] The Welsh journal of 1775 grows rather more sporadic in the last two to three weeks: see *LSJ* v. 453–60.

islands. As in the previous entry, the letter is more blunt in stating that 'We then returned very wet', as against the less direct phrasing of the *Journey*: 'The heaviness of the rain shortened our voyage' (*JWI* 159). Shortly afterwards there comes a mention of an obelisk erected to the memory of Tobias Smollett by a relative; the letter reveals a fact that is concealed in the public version, namely that Johnson was asked to revise the inscription. Typically, Boswell's *Tour* was able to reproduce the new inscription: 'Dr Johnson sat down with an ardent and liberal earnestness to revise it, and greatly improved it by several additions and variations. I unfortunately did not take a copy of it, as it originally stood; but I have happily preserved every fragment of what Dr Johnson wrote' (*LSJ* v. 366–7). This is worth attention, because it shows Boswell apologizing for a tiny defect in his record, whereas there is no doubt that Johnson would have been completely unable to reproduce any material at all from the episode. It is also interesting that Johnson should be found making 'additions and variations', which exactly describes his task in producing the full-length *Journey*.

This letter concludes with a small anecdote concerning an attempt to tip a keeper on the island on Loch Lomond; it is one of many small stories which Johnson considered beneath the dignity of his published account. Even Boswell found no place for this particular recital. It is far from surprising to encounter such instances, but again no previous commentator on the *Journey* has drawn attention to several such anecdotes in the correspondence which Johnson chose to exclude from the printed text.

The sixteenth letter in the sequence (Chapman no. 337) was addressed to Mrs Thrale from Auchinleck on 3 November. It is longer than the previous three. In fact, its bulk is largely made up of a detailed response to six letters which Johnson had found awaiting him when he got to Glasgow, and which are now lost. Very little of the contents has immediate relevance to the Hebridean tour, and it need not concern us here. At one point Johnson writes: 'Of the various accidents of our voyage I have been careful to give you an account and hope you have received it.' Again the stress is laid on the journal transmitted to Mrs Thrale, and this confirms the impression that Johnson valued his postal narrative as a significant record of his trip—perhaps *the* most significant record, along with Boswell's more detailed diary of events. In response to one of Mrs Thrale's letters, Johnson pays Boswell some hearty compliments:

one phrase concerning his companion's 'goodhumour and perpetual cheerfulness' may be the basis of the tribute to Boswell in the opening paragraph of the *Journey*. Elsewhere in the correspondence Johnson has had some sly fun at the expense of Boswell, suppressed in the published work. When Johnson states here; 'It is very convenient to travel with him, for there is no house where he is not received with kindness and respect,' he sets the tone for the more favourable and, as it were, official attitudes expressed in the *Journey*.

Towards the end of this letter Johnson states: 'I will now continue my Narrative,' and resumes his journalized entries for the intervening days (29 October–2 November). This carries the story forward to the travellers' arrival at Auchinleck. A short entry for Glasgow is skilfully embroidered to form four paragraphs in the *Journey*. Three of these are devoted to the university; Johnson permits himself some criticism of the mode of education, and of the outcome as far as students were concerned; but obviously he is unable to repeat his sole comment to Mrs Thrale: 'I was not much pleased with any of the Professors.' The social round of visits *en route* to Auchinleck is also played down—again Boswell made good this omission in his *Tour* (*LSJ* v. 369–71).[27] The text of the *Journey* contains no reference whatsoever to the Countess of Eglinton, although Boswell informs us that Johnson enjoyed his time with her; indeed, he tells a story of the aged lady and the elderly visitor which had found room in Johnson's letter. Something Boswell does not report from this conversation, and probably did not know of in 1785, is the addendum: 'She called Boswel the boy, yes Madam, said I, we will send him to school. He is already, said she, in a good school, and expressed her hope of his improvement' (*L* i. 388–9; *LSJ* v. 373–5).[28] One can imagine the relish with which Mrs Thrale read these words and printed them in

[27] This helps to explain some of Johnson's reservations about the professors at Glasgow. For Boswell's desire to embellish the record in the university cities, see above, p. 5.

[28] It was at this point in his manuscript journal that Boswell deplored his own indolence in allowing himself to 'shrink from the labour of continuing my Journal with the same minuteness as before'. In fact, he had ceased to make regular daily entries some time earlier (*Journal of Tour*, 369). If Boswell flagged, it is not surprising that Johnson also was—as the signs suggest—far less careful about keeping a record by this stage in the trip.

1788. Of the visit to Auchinleck itself, there is only the most cursory record.[29]

Just two short letters remain. The first was written in Edinburgh on 12 November (Chapman no. 338). It is in effect 'a letter of consolation' regarding Mrs Thrale's disappointed hopes of a legacy. Johnson mentions briefly that the travellers had reached Edinburgh and had received an embarrassingly warm welcome, but otherwise the journey is not in question. Six days later, again whilst still in Edinburgh, Johnson announced to Mrs Thrale that this would be 'the last Letter that I shall write'. He states that he will be leaving on the London coach the following Monday. Like its predecessor, the eighteenth letter (Chapman no. 339) contains no information of Johnson's doings in the Scottish capital. It is well known that the *Journey* devotes little space to Edinburgh, at both the start and the end of the book, unlike Boswell's parallel account. One reason may simply be that Johnson took no notes here, certainly on the return leg.[30]

V

There is universal agreement that the letters to Mrs Thrale (and possibly one of the letters to her husband) formed a major recourse for Johnson in the composition of the *Journey*. However, the absence of any detailed investigation has meant that the amount of selection, editing, and rephrasing has gone unnoticed. The fact that there was once a notebook has caused commentators to ignore what has been before our eyes since 1788. There are two bodies of evidence, in practice: the passages in the correspondence which were used and, in one way or another, adapted for publication, but also the material in the correspondence which could have been used but was not.

In respect of the first category, we can point to many passages

[29] Johnson writes to Mrs Thrale: 'I shall find no kindness such as will suppress my desire of returning home' (*L* i. 389), which is probably to be regarded as a compliment to his friend rather than a barbed comment against Lord Auchinleck. The *Journey* (*JWI* 161–2) is predictably reticent, and it is only through Boswell's *Tour* (see *LSJ* v. 375–84) and, more fully, the manuscript (*Journal of Tour*, 369–76) that we know of the altercations which took place.

[30] It is actually the case that Boswell also failed to keep notes for 6–9 Nov. (*Journal of Tour*, 442).

where the journalized entries in the letters to Southwark are reproduced fairly closely in the *Journey*. Examples include the arrival on Raasay and the trip on Loch Lomond. In all these passages, however, some degree of editing took place before publication, details are altered, figures revised, and names supplied where these were not available to Johnson when he wrote to Mrs Thrale. More generally, the tone and manner become impersonal: as some of the earlier comparisons have shown, less use is made of the first person, and the immediate physical experience is rendered less directly. Detail is often suppressed, and narrative switches more readily into general reflection.

As regards the second category, we may begin with certain predictable kinds of omission. It is not surprising that the printed text avoids small intimate references to Mrs Thrale's blue room and so on. Offensive and potentially libellous observations are removed, as are comments on identifiable groups such as the Glasgow professoriate. Johnson exercised considerable caution with respect to Scottish sensibilities, and the relatively mild criticism which was to occasion such an adverse reaction in Scotland represents a softened version of the commentary to be gleaned from the letters. The more blunt remarks about some of the towns visited in the first part of the tour are regularly toned down. Another element which is to a great extent lost in the published *Journey* is comedy: some of this incidental fun (though by no means all) is directed at Boswell in a spirit of private complicity with Mrs Thrale, but a measure of wry self-dramatization also disappears from the *Journey*. These changes are consonant with the overall aim of dignifying the narrative, and amplifying its larger meanings whilst subordinating local and personal detail. To this end, Johnson deletes anecdotes, however amusing; conceals Boswell's superstitious fears, and renders unspecific what he had reported to Southwark with much more stress on the 'petty particular'.[31]

Finally, it can be claimed that one further conclusion emerges from this enquiry: most portions of the text can be accounted for without attributing excessive importance to the lost notebook. Much of the published work could have been compiled from the journalized entries (whether or not these reproduced what Johnson

---

[31] See Howard Erskine-Hill, 'Johnson and the Petty Particular', *Johnson Society Transactions* (1976), 40–6.

had already written in his notes), aided by Johnson's memory of what was still a recent experience. Only one clear-cut example has ever been identified where Johnson seems to rely on Boswell's manuscript journal, but it may well be that he drew on this source elsewhere.[32] This judgement is supported by a number of facts: the high praise which Johnson gave the journal when he saw portions of it at Dunvegan; the frequency with which he comments on Boswell's note-taking (compared with the paucity of references to his own memoranda); and the warmth with which he urged Mrs Thrale to read it in 1775, evidently in the full assurance that she would find no serious conflict with his own published account.[33]

None of this proves that the notebook was a mere thing of shreds and patches, uniformly a matter of jottings 'such as I cannot much trust myself, inaccurately taken, and obscurely noted' (*JWI* 149). But it may be stated with due temperance that only isolated passages of the *Journey* seem to require further personal memoranda to have been made on the spot by Johnson. It would still be a wonderful advance if we could, by some great good fortune, recover the lost 'book of remarks', for it would certainly illuminate the process of composing the *Journey*—just as, as this chapter aims to show, the letters to Mrs Thrale serve to illuminate the means by which Johnson generalized and deepened his view of Scotland.

This enquiry may also have strengthened our sense of the narrative of the *Journey* as a shaped process, whilst the work obviously relies on close firsthand observation. Johnson was aware, before he ever set out, that his views on Scotland were controversial; and as Chapter 8 seeks to show, he must also have known well in advance of the publication of the *Journey* that it was likely to stir up controversy. We can see from the comparisons set out in this chapter that his public report on the nation is often gentler than the private messages he sent to Hester Thrale. Where the two sources deal with identical material (as they do for large stretches of the

---

[32] Johnson appears to have been misled by Boswell's original entry concerning the rival claims of Raasay and the Laird of Macleod. His comments (*JWI* 59) irritated Raasay, and he wrote to apologize. Boswell himself excised the offending statement from the *Tour* (see *Journal of Tour* 135).

[33] For Johnson's comments on the Boswellian record (as, of course, reported by Boswell), see *Journal of Tour*, 188, 193, 226, 241–2, 245, 293–4. For the recommendations to Mrs Thrale, see *L* ii. 31–2, 43, 47, 58, 73. Collectively these stress the adequacy of Boswell's account: 'you are now sufficiently informed of the whole transaction.'

correspondence), the published account is more serious, more impersonal, less detailed, more ready to shift into a generalizing mode. There is, of course, nothing very surprising in that: but we have tended for too long to accept the *Journey* as an unmediated recital of events and impressions. In reality, Johnson's Scotland is a mental construct, and we can witness some part of the assemblage by considering the evidence of the letters to the author's most intimate friend, Hester Thrale.

6

The Rambler and the Wanderer:
Boswell's Road to the Isles

On Saturday last, being the 30th of January, I . . . had solemn
conversation with the Reverend Mr Falconer, a nonjuring
bishop, a very learned and worthy man. He gave two toasts,
which you will believe I drank with cordiality, Dr. Samuel
Johnson, and Flora Macdonald.

(*LSJ* ii. 282)

Nobody believes any longer that the missing dates in Johnson's
diary during 1745 and 1746 indicate that he was busy supporting
the Pretender in Scotland. John Buchan made a lively story out of
this supposition in his novel *Midwinter*, but that is as far as it goes.
Yet in Boswell's picturesque imagination the dream of the rising as
a noble and (albeit perversely) loyal enterprise refused to be
dispelled. There are many signs that at some level Boswell was
undertaking the journey as a fantasy recreation of Charles
Edward's experiences in the Highlands. In order to sustain this
fantasy, he made use of Johnson as a kind of fetishistic aid, by
which his friend stood in for the missing prince. In this chapter I
shall try to provide evidence for the statements just made.[1] The
focus will be first on the Prince and second on Johnson; but less on
their historic reality, than on their role in the *Tour* as Boswell's own
identity crisis required them to act this out.

[1] There is of course a vast literature on Jacobitism, some of it unduly favourable
to the cause and to the leading actors. The most scholarly and fullest biography is
Frank McLynn, *Charles Edward Stuart: A Tragedy in Many Acts* (Oxford: Oxford
University Press, 1991). A valuable survey of the movement more generally is Bruce
Lenman, *The Jacobite Risings in Britain, 1689–1746* (London: Eyre Methuen,
1980). For the detailed itinerary of the Prince's flight, as first established by W. B.
Blaikie and others, I have used Eric Linklater, *The Prince in the Heather* (New York:
Harcourt Brace, 1965). Other particularized sources are employed *in situ*.

I

Few readers give much attention to the block of about thirteen pages in the first edition of the *Tour* where Boswell relates the information he had gleaned concerning the Pretender's flight (*LSJ* v. 187–205). It is an added section with no basis in the private journal, and thus less interesting to most students today. We are not well disposed towards interpolated stories either, unless we can wrench them into some kind of organic unity with the main portion of a text. Finally, it is a flashback into an earlier stage of Scottish history, and one which had been overtaken by the events of the intervening twenty-seven years. For all these reasons, we tend to concentrate on Johnson, and on the 'present' of 1773. I wish to argue that Boswell had an important subsidiary motive for his trip to the Hebrides, and that this merged with his desire to expose Johnson to the sights of his native country. This motive was a desire to re-create as much as was possible of Prince Charles's flight after Culloden.

The title of this chapter draws attention to an odd congruence. Boswell regularly refers to Charles in his interpolated narrative as 'the Wanderer' (having confessed to embarrassment about nomenclature).[2] But he also alludes to Johnson as 'the Rambler', a curiously similar notion. As we have seen in Chapter 4, a visitor toasted Johnson as 'the great vagabond'. Boswell tells us that his periodical of that name was translated into Italian as *Il vagabondo* (*LSJ* i. 201), and that this was Paoli's name for him. A representative quotation from the *Tour* is this:

Not finding a letter here [Inverness] that I expected, I felt a momentary impatience to be at home. Transient clouds darkened my imagination, and in those clouds I saw events from which I shrunk; but a sentence or two of the *Rambler*'s conversation gave me firmness, and I considered that I was upon an expedition for which I had wished for years, and the recollection of which would be a treasure to me for life. (*LSJ* v. 128)

---

[2] Boswell writes in a footnote, 'I do not call him the *Prince of Wales*, or the *Prince*, because I am quite satisfied that the right which the *House of Stuart* had to the throne is extinguished. I do not call him *the Pretender*, because it appears to me as an insult to one who is still alive, and, I suppose, thinks very differently' (*LSJ* v. 185). He had waited until after Johnson's death to publish the *Tour*; he did not need to hold out until the Prince died, because the latter was politically dead.

Moreover, there was another term sometimes applied to the Prince—'the Adventurer'. Duncan Forbes of Culloden, Lord President of the Court of Session, referred to him thus, and Johnson, of course, had written a series for a periodical with this title. For Boswell's purposes, he could be 'the Adventurer' as well as 'the Rambler'.

It is widely agreed that Boswell's dependent, hero-worshipping nature craved for a strong father-figure to give him 'firmness'.[3] I suggest that, together with the presence of Johnson, the endurance of the absent Charles Edward helped to lend him this strength, and that the 'expedition' was in part a quest for self-identification with the Prince. It was a way of expiating Boswell's guilty awareness that he was regarded by his real father as a renegade Scot who attached himself to southern and cosmopolitan values. Many commentators have argued that Boswell's career can be interpreted as a reaction against paternal values and, more broadly, against the values of Edinburgh—Whiggish, Hanoverian, and Presbyterian—for which Lord Auchinleck stood. If that is so, then Charles Edward was useful to Boswell simply as an alternative, even without the particular attractions of Jacobitism. On the Hebridean tour, Boswell could luxuriate in a feeling of having cast off paternal values and having found (in the company of Johnson) a more lasting role than he had discovered in his adolescent gestures and in his Corsican adventure. To put it shortly, he was still in a stage of rebellion, and the Prince was plainly a rebel, whatever the merits of his cause.

It is surely more than coincidence that Boswell should have given an account of the Pretender's wanderings in the middle of a narrative of his own peregrination with Johnson. The episode is interpolated at a critical juncture—when the travellers have reached Skye, the heart of their undertaking, and specifically when they are lodging at Kingsburgh, the home of Flora Macdonald. A crucial paragraph points to a secret significance of the tour, almost the hidden agenda behind Boswell's story of the trip:

To see Dr Samuel Johnson, the great champion of the English Tories, salute Miss Flora Macdonald in the Isle of Skye, was a striking sight; for though

---

[3] The best treatment of this issue comes in a book by William C. Dowling, *The Boswellian Hero* (Athens, Ga.: University of Georgia Press, 1979).

somewhat congenial in their notions, it was very improbable they should meet here. . . .

The room where we lay was a celebrated one. Dr Johnson's bed was the very bed which the grandson of the unfortunate King James the Second lay, on one of the nights after the failure of his rash attempt in 1745–6, while he was eluding the pursuit of the emissaries of government, which had offered thirty thousand pounds as a reward for apprehending him. To see Dr Samuel Johnson lying in that bed, in the isle of Sky, in the house of Miss Flora Macdonald, struck me with such a group of ideas as it is not easy for words to describe, as they have passed through the mind. He smiled, and said, 'I have had no ambitious thoughts in it.' (*LSJ* v. 185–6)

Here the twin vehicles of Boswell's fantasy are united in a single location—the bed at Kingsburgh. Boswell has stage-managed events so that his objects of wish-fulfilment can occupy the same space— the deluded, tragic, and fated prince, the noble and venerable hero of the mind. One was vanquished, and that is his appeal; the other is victorious, and that is comforting. Both display their endurance and their idealism; each provides a tumultuous 'group of ideas'.[4]

In this sense, Kingsburgh is the axis of the Tour: Flora Macdonald, a relatively small character in the Johnson narrative, occupies a large position in the Charles Edward narrative. Again, it can be no accident that Boswell brought Johnson to Skye, the site of the most dramatic stage in the Prince's escape after Culloden. But he had already ensured that the travellers' route should cross the path of the fleeing Prince, well before they reached Skye, they had entered a region with strong associations with the events of 1746. Only on Skye, however, did the tour embrace extensive firsthand contacts with survivors of the episode, and so it is here that Boswell locates his rehearsal of the earlier happenings. At Kingsburgh, one might say, the Rambler catches up with the Wanderer.

Although more and more travellers were passing beyond the

---

[4] Boswell describes a conversation between Johnson and Flora Macdonald, ending with this passage: 'Perceiving Dr Johnson's curiosity, though he had delicacy enough not to question her, [she] very obligingly entertained him with a recital of the particulars which does so much honour to the humanity, fidelity, and generosity of the highlanders. Dr Johnson listened to her with placid attention, and said, "All this should be written down" ' (*LSJ* v. 187). Boswell promptly takes the opportunity to insert his own narrative. Thus the interpolated account is implicitly endorsed by Johnson—indeed, it constitutes a natural prolongation of the exchange between Johnson and Flora Macdonald. Again this technique of integration seems to have been missed by previous commentators.

Highland line, there was as yet no set tourist itinerary. However, most of the trail followed by Johnson and Boswell is an obvious one. Once they had decided (or Boswell had) that they should proceed up the east coast to Aberdeen, the next stages were more or less predetermined. Inverness was the only major town to the north of the Highlands, and then it was necessary to follow the angle of the Great Glen (represented here by Loch Ness). To reach the west between Fort George and Inverness, the pair must have passed very close on 28 August to the site of the battle of Culloden—within two or three miles—but neither narrative alludes to this circumstance. It should be stressed that the itinerary for the remainder of the tour had been drawn up just a day earlier, at Calder, with the aid of the Reverend Kenneth Macaulay and Boswell's own map. At this stage Boswell thought there was plenty of time in hand, anticipating 'interruptions by bad days' amounting to no more than ten days. In fact, the hold-up on Skye was longer. This necessitated the cancellation of a plan that Boswell had formed that 'we might perhaps go to Benbecula, and visit Clanranald' (*LSJ* v. 120–1).

Why should this loop be added? The most obvious reason is that the Prince had spent weeks on Benbecula and South Uist in May and June 1746. This was the heart of the Clanranald Macdonalds, who were among the Prince's most loyal supporters. It was here that Charles Edward had met up with Flora Macdonald, and from Benbecula that his famous boat trip across the Minch to Skye had taken place on 28–9 June. Boswell, too, wished to sail over the sea to Skye as part of his pilgrimage; but the weather precluded this.

If we now return to the journey from Inverness, we find that our travellers took a parallel course up Loch Ness—the Prince followed a more secluded route a couple of miles to the east (he naturally had to steer clear of the government garrison at Fort Augustus). But at this point Boswell struck westward into Glenmoriston. Peter Levi has wondered why he did not take the easier route southwards, curving round to the west into Morar and heading for the better port of Mallaig.[5] Boswell's route was more direct but more

---

[5] See Peter Levi's edition of the *Journey* and the *Tour* (Harmondsworth: Penguin, 1984), 23–4. It is true that if the travellers had gone round by Morar, they would have replicated more of the Prince's route, but chiefly on his return from Skye; and, secondly, Boswell did not have the same contacts with survivors of the rising as he did on Skye. The prearranged invitations came from Macdonald and Macleod, and he wanted to get to the island as promptly as possible, whatever the cost to comfort.

arduous. One explanation may be that the easier route would have involved passing through Glenfinnan, where the Prince had raised his standard at the start of the rising.[6] One who was moved to tears by a passing word from an innkeeper at Anoch might not have trusted himself to remain calm at such a historic site. Moreover, Boswell might have disclosed more to Johnson than he wished to. Significantly, he felt obliged to omit from the published text one revealing passage in the manuscript of his *Tour*: 'We were shown the land of Moidart where Prince Charles first landed. That stirred my mind.'

We need to understand that the detailed itinerary was altogether of Boswell's making. Johnson put himself utterly in his friend's hands. The Englishman must have realized, as the tour progressed, that the route constantly involved places with Jacobite associations, and that the travellers were coming into contact at every turn with men and women who had taken some part, direct or indirect, in the Pretender's escape. He seems to have acquiesced in this. Neither published account suggests that there was a deliberate programme along these lines; but then it is not to be expected that they would make such an acknowledgement. Johnson wished to visit the Western Islands, principally in order to see 'a different system of life'. Boswell wanted to go anywhere the Prince had been, but especially to Skye, the primary locus of his flight and the place where the most solid core of his active assistants could now be encountered.

It is noteworthy that Boswell paid far less attention to the supposed haunts of Ossian. The travellers bypass Staffa, with no great sign of regret. Johnson says: 'Macquarry is proprietor both of Ulva and some adjacent islands, among which is Staffa, so lately raised to renown by Mr Banks (*JWI* 141). He then alludes to 'the wonders of Staffa', that is the geological formations. Boswell has simply: 'We saw the island of Staffa, at no very great distance, but could not land upon it, the surge was so high on its rocky coast' (*LSJ* v. 332). A true devotee of the bards would have fixed Fingal's Cave, at this juncture above all others, as a prime object of the pilgrimage (see above, p. 70). When Banks had made his historic

---

[6] For this intensely symbolic moment, which for the Prince was 'the culmination of all his childhood dreams and adolescent aspirations', see McLynn, *Charles Edward Stuart*, 136. The event also concentrated some of Boswell's adolescent fantasies of Scottish history, feudal loyalty, monarchical power, and military glory.

visit to Staffa in 1772, he had solemnly read Ossian to put himself in the right mood.[7] Boswell did not care for Macpherson or for his supposed ancient epic. Instead of the misty legend of the dark ages, Boswell sought the roots of the most powerful modern myth of Scotland. His dream of a lapsed nationhood centred not on Fingal's Cave, but on Cluny's Cage, where the Prince had sheltered.

Putting these facts together, we can see that the route was planned to allow maximum interaction with the Prince's own path through the Highlands. It would have been quite impossible to follow every twist and turn of the earlier progress, which veered erratically backwards and forwards, as the Prince sought to elude his pursuers. The aged Johnson would never have been able to re-enact the zigzags of the youthful Charles Edward, which carried him across many of the most remote parts of the Western Highlands. None the less, it was Boswell's aim to replicate as much as he could of that journey, and to simulate some of its ardours. This in itself explains why the travellers did not take the easy road south from Fort Augustus, and struck across country into Glenmoriston. The Prince had spent several days at the beginning of August 1746 under the protection of the people of Glenmoriston, after he had been forced to abort his plan to head for a ship at Poolewe, at the head of Loch Ewe. The 'Seven Men of Glenmoriston', who succoured the Prince at this moment of disappointment, have become a key part of the legend. Around 13 August the Pretender lay near the braes of Glenmoriston, at the eastern end of Loch Cluanie.[8] Here his path intersected that of the later travellers, as they left Anoch and went along the old military road towards Glen Shiel. Their landlord at Anoch had been out in 1745 and 1746, and it was he who had provoked Boswell to tears with his recollections of the uprising.

There follows one of Boswell's most impassioned flights of rhetoric concerning the Jacobite cause. What the text does not reveal is that the opportunity for indulging such feelings had been contrived by his own decisions to intersect the Prince's route at this point.

M'Queen walked some miles to give us a convoy. He had, in 1745, joined the Highland army at Fort Augustus, and continued in it till after the battle

---

[7] See H. B. Carter, *Sir Joseph Banks, 1743–1820* (London: British Museum (Natural History), 1988), 106–7.

[8] See Linklater, *Prince in the Heather*, 128–36.

of Culloden. As he narrated the particulars of that ill-advised, but brave attempt, I could not refrain from tears. There is a certain association of ideas in my mind upon that subject, by which I am strongly affected. The very Highland names, or the sound of a bag-pipe, will stir my blood, and fill me with a mixture of melancholy and respect for courage; with pity for an unfortunate and superstitious regard for antiquity, and thoughtless inclination for war; in short, with a crowd of sensations with which sober rationality has nothing to do. (*LSJ* v. 140)

This is a nodal passage, accompanied by other sections in the *Tour* which stress the solidarity of the Glenmoriston people and their surviving feudal traditions. For example, McQueen, the landlord, tells Johnson that 'the Laird of Glenmorison's people would bleed for him, if they were well used but that seventy men had gone out of the Glen to America. That he himself intended to go next year . . . Dr Johnson said, he wished M'Queen laird of Glenmorison, and the laird to go to America' (*LSJ* v. 136–7). Here the prevailing theme of economic penury and consequent emigration is linked to the theme of the integrity of the clans. On the previous page Boswell had cited Johnson as remarking: 'I am quite feudal, sir,' and had added: 'Here I agree with him. I said, I regretted I was not the head of a clan; however, though not possessed of such a hereditary advantage, I would always endeavour to make my tenants follow me. I could not be a *patriarchal* chief, but I would be a *feudal* chief' (*LSJ* v. 136). This is faintly absurd, but it undoubtedly expresses a real desire on Boswell's part. The Lowland laird imagines himself a Highland chieftain. (In a suppressed passage of the manuscript of the *Tour* he wrote of an episode among the men of Skye who had been out in 1745: 'I exerted myself in an extraordinary degree tonight, drinking heartily at intervals, and thinking that I was fit to lead on Highlanders.') Actually, this is a confession masking a deeper repressed identification. The true object of Boswell's yearnings in Glenmoriston was the man who had passed that way twenty-seven years before.[9]

Only three days later Boswell is impelled to 'Scottify' Johnson and, more than that, to cast him as a clan chief: 'He was pleased

---

[9] It should be added that, as the travellers move through Glen Shiel, Boswell mentions in passing: 'We saw where the battle was fought in the year 1719' (*LSJ* v. 140). This is a reminder of an earlier phase of Jacobite activity, the abortive 1719 uprising. For this battle, see Bruce Lenman, *The Jacobite Clans of the Great Glen, 1650–1786* (London: Methuen, 1984), 4. For Glenmoriston, see ibid. 129–31.

when I told him he would make a good Chief' (*LSJ* v. 143). A few paragraphs earlier Boswell had returned to the 1745 rising, hearing of 'that ill-advised, but brave attempt' and being unable to 'refrain from tears' (*LSJ*, v. 140). In such sections Johnson's nobility is insensibly merged with that of the grand enterprise of the Jacobites; foolish, Boswell concedes, but all the more admirable and touching for that. Throughout the text the almost incessant reminders of the rising are used to evoke a sense of flawed heroism, whilst Johnson represents an equivalent magnanimity, shorn of the fatalism and quixotism attached to the Stuart cause. It is as though Boswell wishes to inhabit the youth, physical prowess, and romantic ardour of the Wanderer, as he travels these historic routes with the aged, lame, English Rambler.

II

The travellers in 1773 then took the most direct course for Skye. Their landfall on the island was at Armadale, seat of Sir Alexander Macdonald. The chief's father had been fighting on the Hanoverian side at Culloden, and was still on the mainland when the Prince made his furtive arrival on Skye. But his wife was herself a Jacobite, although unwilling to compromise her husband by open support of the Pretender. When his boat reached the Trotternish peninsula on 29 June, after his famous journey from Benbecula, Lady Macdonald was at the family estate of Monkstadt, a bare couple of miles from his landfall. She was the first person to be consulted by Flora Macdonald and, although she could not receive the Prince openly, she helped arrange the next stage of his escape. Boswell describes this episode briefly, at the start of his interpolated narrative: he does not allude to Lady Margaret Macdonald's convictions; he does not connect her to his host (her son) in the main narrative; and he lets out only in a footnote that he was in personal communication with this formidable survivor of the epic events of June and July 1746.[10] (Nor is it disclosed that she was a daughter of

---

[10] See *LSJ* v. 153, where Boswell prints two letters from Sir James Macdonald to his mother, 'which her ladyship has been pleased to communicate to me'. Boswell's anthem for doomed youth, in the person of Sir James, occupies a surprising amount of space: the lengthy inscription on his monument erected by 'his much afflicted mother, the LADY MARGARET MACDONALD, Daughter to the Earl of Eglintoune', is

Boswell's friend, the Countess of Eglinton, whom the travellers met later in the tour.) This was disingenuous because, if the truth be told, it was these events which held the strongest attraction for Boswell. He would not have gone near Skye if all it had to offer was the grandeur of the Cuillin Hills.[11]

After arriving on the island, the Prince, still in his disguise as an Irish maidservant, went on to Kingsburgh. The current master of this house was the father of the 'Kingsburgh' who appears in the main narrative of the *Tour*, and who had married Flora Macdonald. Again the text of the *Tour* is not very explicit about these matters. Boswell observes that 'We were resolved to pay a visit at Kingsburgh, and see the celebrated Miss Flora Macdonald, who is married to the present Mr Macdonald of Kingsburgh; so took that road though not so near' (*LSJ* v. 179). What he does not say is that this curve away from the direct route to Dunvegan was made in order to visit the scene of a celebrated episode in 1746, described only a few pages further on in the text of the *Tour*. At this point the travellers were reversing the course of the Prince's flight: he made his way from Kingsburgh to Portree and Raasay, as outlined in Boswell's own interpolated narrative of 1746; they went from Raasay to Portree and then to Kingsburgh, as the accompanying narrative for 12 September 1773 reveals. The side-slip here is minimal; but it seems to have gone almost completely unnoticed. Boswell has displaced his Jacobite pilgrimage from the interpolated story; we have to read this back into the main narrative to see what was fully at stake on the tour.

At Raasay a whole gallery of local worthies assembled to greet

---

set out in full (*LSJ* v. 115–3). The fact that Boswell gives the details of Sir James's death in Rome suggests that he was recalling, along with his friend, his own experiences in the city, and also freely associating the dead man with Charles Edward, the lost hope of the defeated court at Rome. The Old Pretender had died in the city in Jan. 1766, a few months after Boswell himself had been living there. When Macdonald died on 26 July 1766, the Young Pretender had taken up residence in Rome, hoping for papal recognition as King Charles III. One of his main advisers here was Andrew Lumisden, 'my very worthy and ingenious friend' as Boswell calls him (*LSJ* v. 194). Through Lumisden, Boswell kept in touch with what was happening at the Jacobite court. Again there seems to be some transference here, with Macdonald trapping some of the sense of blighted youth which secretly applies to the Prince.

[11]   Cf. Boswell on Johnson: 'I have a notion that he at no time has had much taste for rural beauties. I have myself very little' (*LSJ* v. 112).

the visitors. As Boswell explains: 'There were Rasay himself; his brother Dr Macleod; his nephew the Laird of M'Kinnon; the Laird of Macleod; Colonel Macleod of Talisker, an officer in the Dutch service . . . Mr Macleod of Muriavenside, best known by the name of Sandie Macleod, who was long in exile on account of the part which he took in 1745; and several other persons' (*LSJ* v. 165). Of these, the chief of the Macleods was a Hanoverian; but several of the others had been involved on the Jacobite side in the Rising. Raasay himself was the son of the laird who had borne the title in 1746, and he figures as 'young Rasay' in Boswell's interpolated story. Briefly, it was this man, his brother (Dr Macleod, who had been wounded at Culloden), and their cousin Malcolm Macleod who took charge of the Prince at this perilous juncture and conveyed him to the island of Raasay. In a direct replay of this episode, it is the same Malcolm Macleod who superintends the passage of Boswell and Johnson to Raasay: 'Along with him came, as our pilot, Mr Malcolm Macleod, one of the Rasay family, celebrated in the year 1745–6' (*LSJ* v. 161). Boswell gives a vivid description of this man, ending with the comment: 'I never saw a figure that gave a more perfect representation of a Highland gentleman' (*LSJ* v. 162). This individual was one of the persons excepted by name from the general pardon issued by the King in 1747. It should be added that the Laird of Mackinnon also had strong family connections with the rising (again the interpolated story dwells on this); and that another unnamed figure in the text is 'John M'Kenzie [who] was at Rasay's house, when we were there' (*LSJ* v. 193), one of the very few occasions when the tacit separation of the two narratives is broken momentarily.

The small island was not well known to most travellers, and never became a fixture on the essential list of places to visit in the Hebrides, even after tourism enveloped Skye. It was on Boswell's list for reasons that had nothing to do with tourist amenities. Raasay had been a stage on the Prince's flight across Skye, and the central actors in the episode were still alive to recall it. It may not be without significance that Boswell sneaked off on 10 September, while the travellers were on the island, and spent a whole day out of Johnson's company. When we read the excuse that his fellow-traveller was 'unable to take so hardy a walk', our suspicions are aroused; and then we learn that 'Old Mr Malcolm M'Leod, who had obligingly promised to accompany me, was at my bedside between five and six' (*LSJ* v. 168). Uncharacteristically, Boswell 'sprang up immediately'. It is difficult to believe that Boswell did not pump the old man for some of his memories, but this is a matter on which even the private journal is silent.

The Prince was forced to flee from pillar to post during his time on Skye, and finally he had to take a ship back to the mainland. He sailed from Elgol, on the south-west of the island, in Mackinnon country; Malcolm Macleod's sister was married to Mackinnon of Elgol. Boswell's interpolated narrative stops at this point, with the statement: 'These are the particulars which I have collected concerning the extraordinary concealments and escapes of Prince Charles, in the Hebrides. He was often in imminent danger. The troops traced him from the Long Island, across Sky, to Portree, but there lost him' (*LSJ* v. 199)—that is, the trail was lost when the Macleods of Raasay took over his protection. Boswell proceeds: 'Here I stop,—having received no further authentick information of his fatigues and perils before he escaped to France.' The tour of 1773 does not loop back on to the mainland, to dog the Prince's footsteps—that would have been too obvious to everyone. Instead, the travellers fretted on Skye, regarding themselves as 'prisoners',[12] until the weather seemed fair enough to allow them to get away. They set out for Mull, but a storm blew up which made them consider heading for Eigg, Cann, or Coll, the eventual destination. This time, then, they intersect the Prince's journey whilst at sea. Boswell describes Johnson as 'fearless and unconcerned' during the storm, and as 'lying in philosophick tranquillity', whereas Boswell himself was 'very ill, and very desirous to get to shore' (*LSJ* v. 283). Similarly, the Prince is described as behaving with great courage when a storm blew up in the Cuillin Sound—'Eigg, Rum and Canna on their port side, the fierce coast of Skye to the starboard'—as he made for Benbecula. He 'bore up most surprisingly and never wanted spirits'.[13] Boswell could not match his hero, but he transferred Charles's virtues under pressure to his revered friend Johnson.

There are numerous small similarities in the two journeys. We are told that the Prince 'had a hard head for drink, and there is a story of a great carousal when a party of lively Macdonalds came to Corradale and drank all night'. Boswell stayed up drinking till five

---

[12] See e.g. *LSJ* v. 262.
[13] Linklater, *Prince in the Heather*, 133.

in the morning at Corrichatachin (near Broadfoot) on 25 September 1773—the Prince had been within a couple of miles of this spot on his way to Elgol on 4 July 1746.[14] When he landed in Scotland in 1745 and took his first night's rest, Charles had 'looked narrowly at the sheets before deciding to sit up all night'; later he became hardier and slept in the most primitive conditions.[15] Boswell famously 'lay in linen like a gentleman' at Glenelg (*JWI* 49: see p. 121, above). His own account admits that he was 'uneasy, and almost fretful' at the bad accommodation; but 'Dr Johnson was calm' (*LSJ* v. 146), a true princely indifference to the squalor of his situation. Like Johnson and Boswell, the Pretender had begun his journey on horseback, but he had also been forced to proceed on foot, as they were, when the going in the Highlands got tougher.

Of course, the rigours which the later party endured were to some extent of their own choosing, whereas the Prince had been struggling for his own life as well as for the future of his cause. There is an element of make-believe in Boswell's efforts to replay the events of 1746. But then there was a good deal of play-acting about the entire tour. Johnson assumes the role of Macbeth meeting the witches (*LSJ* v. 76); he recites another speech from the same play at Forres (*LSJ* v. 115); he sees Boswell take over the role at Inverness (*LSJ* v. 129), this last matter requiring a detailed dramatic description for the benefit of David Garrick (*LSJ* v. 347–8); and, as we have already seen, Johnson impersonates an Australian marsupial (*LSJ* v. 511). Johnson is constantly imbued with 'the old Highland spirit' (*LSJ* v. 324). Boswell dresses his friend up, figuratively, in a variety of guises, from a chieftain to a walking St Paul's Cathedral (see p. 105). On one occasion Boswell kits Johnson out in full Highland dress, or at least as near as he can get to it:

One night, in Col, he strutted about the room with a broad-sword and target, and made a formidable appearance; and, another night, I took the liberty to put a large blue bonnet on his head. His age, his size, and his bushy grey wig, with this covering on it, presented the image of a venerable Senachi: and, however unfavorable to the Lowland Scots, he seemed much pleased to assume the appearance of an ancient Caledonian. (*LSJ* v. 324–5)

---

[14] Ibid. 50; *LSJ* v. 258.
[15] Linklater, *Prince in the Heather*, 51.

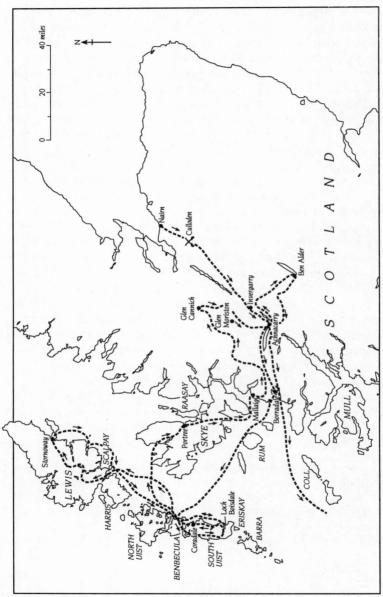

MAP 1. Route of Prince Charles Edward in 1746, from the Battle of Culloden to his departure for France.

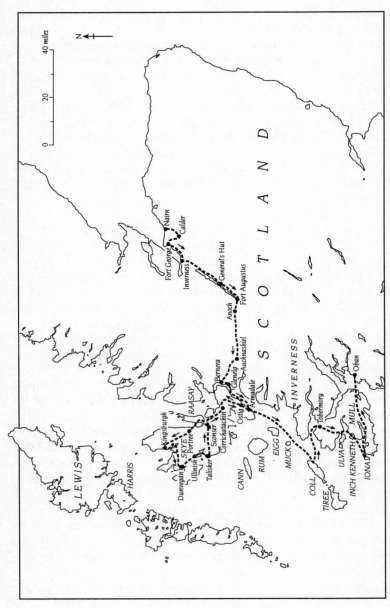

MAP 2. Route of Johnson and Boswell in 1773, from Nairn to Mull.

The 'liberty' that Boswell takes here, in putting his friend into Highland drag, is what he achieves rhetorically elsewhere, by stressing Johnson's openness to Highland culture. A few pages earlier he had described the daily playing of the bagpipe at Armadale, Dunvegan, and Coll: 'Dr Johnson appeared fond of it, and used often to stand for some time with his ear close to the great drone' (*LSJ* v. 315).

It is not far-fetched to extend this into a hidden analogy lurking beneath the surface of the text throughout, by which Boswell transfers his admiration for the Prince's heroic journey through the Highlands and Islands to Johnson—projects his admiration, that is, and indulges his emotional attachment to the doomed Jacobite cause without damaging his professed allegiance to the Hanoverian regime.

III

In using the words 'professed allegiance', I do not mean to suggest that Boswell harboured any serious commitment to a renewed Stuart bid for power. By 1773 the Prince had declined into a shadow of his old chivalric self and had become a drunken intriguer and womanizer whose self-destructive tendencies had already done most of their work. And, in effect, the dynasty lapsed with him. Boswell had enough of a realistic streak in him to forgo the adolescent dreams of a revived Stuart line which would prolong the greatness of the earlier centuries. It does not help much to call his hidden yearnings 'sentimental Jacobitism', since active Stuart sympathizers could nurture the same kind of fantasies—they simply tried to put their day-dreams into practice at a political and military level. Boswell was content to act out his imaginary identification with the wandering Prince by shepherding his intellectual hero across the same Scottish terrain that Charles Edward had traversed.

If Boswell had no strong attachment to Jacobitism as a live political option, why then should he associate himself with its living embodiment? Some further answers will be suggested later in this chapter, but one explanation must be considered immediately. This relates to the sheer sexual glamour of the Wanderer. That may seem a shallow enough consideration; but personal attractiveness is not a minor affair to most young men, and Boswell was still a young man at heart. 'All agreed that [Charles] was "a goodly person" ', writes A. J. Youngson. 'He was of well above average height, dark-eyed and sunburnt, his features regular, a graceful and masterly horseman, physically extremely fit. To some he looked like a man of fashion, and to others like a hero.'[16] To the short, undistinguished-looking Boswell, with his pudgy features and his indoor life as a lawyer, this combination was almost irresistible. If there was one thing he would have liked to be more than a hero, it was a man of fashion.

Having got the Prince to the mainland from Skye, as we have seen, Boswell announces that he will bring his narrative to a halt. In fact, there are still four pages to go before the story of the 1773 journey is resumed. First, Boswell quotes Voltaire's verdict on the house of Stuart, and then he briefly describes the subsequent fate of Malcolm Macleod and Flora Macdonald. After this he gives an elaborate show of loyalty to the existing regime.

Having related so many particulars concerning the grandson of the unfortunate King James the Second; having given due praise to fidelity and generous attachment, which however erroneous the judgement may be, are honourable for the heart; I must do the Highlanders the justice to attest, that I found every where amongst them a high opinion of the virtues of the King now upon the throne, and an honest disposition to be faithful subjects to his majesty, whose family has possessed the sovereignty of this country so long, that a change, even for the abdicated family, would now hurt the best feelings of all his subjects.

This modulates into a somewhat woolly and evasive appeal to pragmatic reasons as justification of the status quo:

The *abstract* point of *right* would involve us in a discussion of remote and perplexed questions; and after all, we should have no clear principle of decision. That establishment, which, from political necessity, took place in 1688, by a breach in the succession of our kings, and which whatever benefits may have accrued from it, certainly gave a shock to our monarchy,—the able and constitutional Blackstone wisely rest on the solid footing of authority.—'Our ancestors having most indisputably a competent jurisdiction to decide this great and important question, and having, in fact, decided it, it is now become our duty, at this distance of time, to acquiesce in their determination.' (*LSJ* v. 202)

---

[16] A. J. Youngson, *The Prince and the Pretender: A Study in the Writing of History* (London: Croom Helm, 1985), 19.

Archdeacon Paley is then cited to support the practical, if not the moral, claim to loyalty which the present regime could mount. Recognizing perhaps that this defence of Hanoverian legitimacy sounds an unconvincing note, Boswell attempts to introduce a more fervent air, and to attach his patriotic feelings to the present King. He makes the usual distinction between George III and his grandfather ('*born a Briton*'); he does not add that the current monarch had the further advantage of having no connection with Culloden and the suppression of the last rising.

However convinced I am of the justice of that principle, which holds allegiance and protection to be reciprocal, I do however acknowledge, that I am not satisfied with the cold sentiment which would confine the exertions of the subject within the strict line of duty. I would have every breast animated with the *fervour* of loyalty; with that generous attachment which delights in doing somewhat more than is required, and makes 'service perfect freedom.' And, therefore, as our most gracious Sovereign, on his accession to the throne, gloried in being *born a Briton*; so, in my more private sphere, *Ego me nunc denique natum, gratulor.* I am happy that a disputed succession no longer distracts our minds; and that a monarchy, established by law, is now so sanctioned by time, that we can fully indulge those feelings of loyalty which I am ambitious to excite. They are feelings which have ever actuated the inhabitants of the Highlands and the Hebrides. The plant of loyalty is there in full vigour, and the Brunswick graft now flourishes like a native root.

Having thus satisfactorily squared the circle, Boswell is finally able to bring his interpolated story to an end with a reference to the conversion of the former Jacobites. This he does in a curious way, by citing lines from a tragedy by John Home, which likens converts to 'birds new-caught' who at first 'struggle with captivity', but then 'smooth their plumes' and 'to new masters sing their former notes'. With evident self-satisfaction, Boswell applies his moral: 'Surely such notes are much better than the querulous growlings of suspicious Whigs and discontented Republicans' (*LSJ* v. 204–5). Few can seriously believe that such a wholesale conversion had taken place in the Highlands over a short period of time. Boswell seems to be writing about himself rather than the population of the Highlands.

It is fair to remark that these words were written in 1785. By that time Boswell had succeeded his father as Laird of Auchinleck; he had embarked upon his unwise English experiment, shifting his legal practice (in intention at least) to London; and he was pursuing his delusive hopes of a seat in Parliament, through the influence of a man who would repay his service with contempt, the Earl of Lonsdale. His father was dead; Johnson was dead; and many of his early heroes and surrogate parents (Rousseau, Voltaire, Kames, Hume) had quit the stage since 1773. In other words, Boswell was no longer young and he was more or less on his own. Even someone as quixotic as he was, and as reckless with regard to his own interests, could see that any overt disloyalty to the crown would have been imprudent. In any case, he had by this time convinced himself of his own orthodoxy. His breaches of decorum were now private lapses; he no longer dressed up as a Corsican chieftain, and he cultivated a pose of respectability as he followed his illusory quest for advancement at the bar and in politics.

It had been rather different in the 1770s. The evidence for this lies partly in Boswell's continuing efforts to placate the laird of Raasay, whose feelings had been hurt by a reference in Johnson's *Journey* which had suggested that Raasay had acknowledged Macleod of Dunvegan as his chief, unlike earlier members of his branch of the family. This had made him seem 'a much smaller man' in the community than he was generally reckoned to be. Boswell offered a conciliatory reply (which is very unlike his obstinacy with regard to Sir Alexander Macdonald's criticisms of his own book), and Johnson wrote a dignified letter of apology. All three letters—by Raasay, Boswell, and Johnson—were included in the text of the *Tour* in a brief coda (*LSJ* v. 409–13). Boswell says that the exchange 'shews Dr Johnson in a very amiable light', which is true. But the whole drift of the episode serves to indicate how anxious Boswell was to keep on good terms with the clan leaders he had met on Skye. The correspondence is printed at the end of a volume in which Raasay has figured as a selfless and resourceful supporter of the Prince when eluding goverment pursuers in June 1746. In his letter to Raasay Boswell recalls 'the happy hours' which he had spent on the small island, and he then adds a significant passage: 'You and Dr M'Leod were both so obliging as to promise me an account in writing, of all the particulars which each of you remember, concerning the transactions of 1745–6. Pray do not forget this, and be as minute and full as you can; put down every thing; I have a great curiosity to know as much as I can, authentically' (*LSJ* v. 411). We know from the earlier text that

Raasay did send 'a paper of information', which Boswell used to compile his interpolated narrative, censoring it a little. In addition, Boswell employed nuncupatory testimony that he had received from Flora Macdonald, Mrs Mackinnon of Corrichatachin, Malcolm Macleod, John Mackenzie, and possibly Dr Murdoch Macleod, Raasay's brother (*LSJ* v. 532–4).[17] There are very few slips in the account given by Boswell, and yet, as L. F. Powell remarks, it 'has been neglected by most historians'. This would have disappointed its author, who included it in the *Tour* ostensibly because it would 'not be uninteresting to [his] readers and, even, perhaps, be of some use to future historians' (*LSJ* v. 187).

Yet the 'authentic' quality of the story was only a part of the matter. Boswell's subjective needs called for an exciting and, indeed, romantic narrative. What is at stake is more than the literal recital of events. Consider the phrase that Boswell used in his letter to Raasay: 'put down every thing'. His urges as a writer made him strive to re-create the passion and the danger of those fraught hours in 1746. Again, it is not so much that Boswell is vindicating the Prince's conduct, from a political or military standpoint; rather, he is celebrating the enterprise, courage, and steadfastness of the Highlanders and the personal resolve of the Pretender. When we contemplate this section in the light of Boswell's life and character, it is easy to see the attraction which such an adventure would hold for him. The whole tour had been planned to allow such vicarious participation in the Prince's escape. Disregarding the university cities and such Lowland stops as Auchinleck, the visit to Skye was the only definite venue arranged in advance—invitations from Macleod and Macdonald are mentioned at the outset (*LSJ* v. 14).

This private identification with the fleeing Prince has its roots in Boswell's own history. Eric Linklater has quoted a description of the Pretender on the run, barefoot, with a dirty shirt on, 'a gun in his hand, a pistol and a dirk by his side'. Then Linklater adds: 'This is the picture of a man who, having been brought up in the tame luxury of an exiled court, had learnt how to live like an outlaw, a

---

[17] Boswell and his wife entertained Raasay's daughter Flora in Edinburgh, early in 1775 (*LSJ* v. 577). Boswell omits from the *Tour* a passage describing the burning of Raasay's house by the authorities as a reprisal against those who had given asylum to the Prince.

partisan, a folk-hero . . .'[18] Boswell spent most of his life trying to escape what seemed to him to represent a tame background. He had run away from home, briefly adopted Catholicism, used great efforts to get a commission in the army, and set himself up as rake in London—all repudiations of his decent Edinburgh home and respectable Lowland kinsfolk. As a correlative to Chapter 2, we may also note how he branched off from the usual idle and dissipated grand tour to take up the Corsican cause. Here he projected his dreams of heroism on to the redoubtable Pasquale Paoli. A vague youthful concept of liberty drew him to Corsica; but it was not just the liberty of the Corsican people, it was the independence and freedom of James Boswell which fed both his journey through Corsica and the book he made of it. Unquestionably, the Hebridean trip was meant to provide a renewal of these gratifications. There was no live hero on the spot, as with Paoli, so Boswell adapted Johnson for his purposes and resurrected the absent Prince.

The Corsican uprising was a real gift to Boswell, who always wished to be a vagabond with a cause. It enabled him to live quite dangerously, but to feel that he was doing his duty at the same time. At the start of his *Journal of a Tour to Corsica*, he states: 'I wished for something more than just the common course of what is called the tour of Europe,' and adds that he was drawn to the island as 'a place which nobody else had seen', where he would find 'a people actually fighting for liberty, and forming themselves from a poor inconsiderable oppressed nation, into a flourishing and independent state' (*JTC* 139–40). Despite the obvious differences, Scotland was able to present itself at times as 'a poor inconsiderable oppressed nation', reaching out for nationhood. There was a real sense in which the 1745–6 uprising could be interpreted as a fight for liberty, and Corsica's struggle against Genoa and France could be seen as an allegory of what had happened in Scotland. (In fact, Boswell seldom mentions the Genoese, just as he rarely alludes to the Hanoverian share in the events of 1745; the Duke of Cumberland is named only twice in the *Tour*, and these are passing references in

---

[18] Linklater, *Prince in the Heather*, 133. Boswell suppressed a sentimental story about Malcolm Macleod having kept a brandy bottle which the Prince had about him: *Journal of a Tour to the Hebrides*, ed. F. A. Pottle and C. H. Bennett (London: Heinemann, 1961), 129.

the interpolated narrative.) Up to this point, his sojourn on the Continent had conformed fairly closely to expected norms (see Chapter 2, above). It was only with the sudden excursion to Corsica that he transformed the nature of his initiation into manhood.

The tour was set up by a letter to Rousseau, the arch-primitivist, to whom Boswell had been recommended by the Earl Mareschal, a prominent Jacobite who had been under an attainder after his part in the rising of 1715. Boswell wrote to Rousseau from Rome, where he had encountered some of the Jacobite court. In his reply Rousseau observed that 'Mylord Mareschal est un des plus zelés partizans de la nation Corse' (*JTC* 142). The symbolic equivalence of Jacobites, Corsicans and 'partisans' is thus effected.

Boswell set out from Leghorn in June 1765, worried that he might be taken by the notorious Barbary pirates in his passage. In fact, it was an uneventful crossing, so that Boswell 'employed [himself] several hours in rowing' (*JTC* 147) as a means of boosting the quotient of adventure. The ship landed at Centuri, and Boswell began his journey to the interior. Characteristically, he managed to combine an element of roughing it with fairly comfortable stopovers in monasteries and private homes—there were scarcely any inns. He hired a man with an ass to take his baggage, but it proved to be such 'absolute scrambling along the face of a rock overhanging the sea' that he dispensed with the ass and got the man to carry the baggage on his own back (*JTC* 150). The rugged scenery is impressive, but it also reinforces the sense of an arduous enterprise—again Boswell seems to be dramatizing his journey to make it conform with the Prince's flight through the heather. Staying in convents 'appeared a little odd at first. But I soon learnt to repair to my dormitory as naturally as if I had been a friar for several years' (*JTC* 152). The traveller undergoes a change of religion in his fantasy, necessary for the suppressed day-dream to play itself out. As he moves into the interior of the island, he finds his progress through the mountains 'very entertaining', with 'immense ridges and vast woods'. He felt himself 'in great health and spirits, and fully able to enter into the ideas of the brave rude men whom I found in all quarters' (*JTC* 161). Such identification was part of the purpose of the tour, and it could be indulged more openly here than was the case with the Highlanders eight years later. Unable to restrain himself, Boswell 'harangued' the natives with a short essay on Enlightenment politics, commending the bravery of the Corsican people, but adjuring them to remember that 'they were much happier in their present state than in a state of refinement and vice, and that therefore they should beware of luxury' (*JTC* 162). If Johnson had been present, he would have urged his friend to clear his mind of primitivist cant. When the travellers made their way through the Highlands, Boswell held his tongue and forbore from lecturing the natives on the perils of luxury. He had grown up a little, and he had Johnson by his side.

Eventually Boswell reaches Paoli in his stronghold at Sollacarò. The two men have prolonged conversations, oddly reminiscent of Gulliver and the King of Brobdingnag. Boswell enjoys 'a sort of luxury of noble sentiment' when closeted with the chieftain (*JTC* 167). They run through both predictable and less predictable topics; it emerges that Paoli has even seen a copy of the *North Briton*. High-minded political reflections are swapped. Paoli praises the simple patriotism of the Corsicans, a thought which in 1765 perhaps made Boswell feel more of a displaced Scot than a progressive Briton. As we have seen with the Hebridean trip, the discourse is that of Enlightenment theorizing being put to the test of empirical experience.

The Corsicans briefly become idyllic Tahitians: 'The chief satisfaction of these islanders when not engaged in war or in hunting, seemed to be that of lying at their ease in the open air, recounting tales of the bravery of their countrymen, and singing songs in honour of the Corsicans, and against the Genoese' (*JTC* 185). It is Ossian in a warm climate. Boswell duly gets out his flute and joins in. 'I gave them one or two Italian airs, and then some of our beautiful old Scots tunes, Gilderoy, the Lass of Patie's mill, Corn riggs are Bonny. The pathetick simplicity and pastoral gaiety of the Scots musick, will always please those who have the genuine feelings of nature' (*JTC* 186). Boswell does not add that the traditional songs were now taking on further pathos, as remnants of an ancient culture in the course of destruction by the Hanoverian laws, the break-up of the clan system, the scourge of emigration, and the death-knell of the Jacobite cause.[19]

---

[19] An equivalent moment of pathos occurs in the *Tour* when Boswell joins the company in performing a dance which 'the emigration from Sky has occasioned. They call it *America*' (*LSJ* v. 277). As several commentators have observed, this is a moment fraught with cultural meanings; the couple whirl around in a circle to the

Subsequently, Boswell renews his conversations with Paoli. He finds out that the chieftain would like Boswell to persuade the English government to support his cause (something that Boswell duly attempted), and hopes that the ministry will listen: 'A man come from Corsica will be like a man come from the Antipodes' (*JTC* 188). This was a more natural figure of speech in 1773, when the voyages of Captain Cook, especially, had penetrated the European imagination (see Chapter 3). In 1765 Boswell takes it as a compliment to his own status as a cosmopolitan citizen and explorer of the remote parts of Europe. As 'a man of sensibility', he warms to the prospect of a union between Britain and Corsica 'both in commerce and war'.

From this point on, there is rather less in the *Journal of a Tour to Corsica* which directly illuminates Boswell's later quest. The most relevant sections concern Johnson. Boswell gives Paoli 'the character of my revered friend Mr Samuel Johnson', an advance version of the portrait that he was to attempt in the *Tour* and in the *Life*. He describes Johnson and Paoli as twin luminaries living (by exaggeration) at a distance of half the globe—they ought to be brought together. This was to happen, of course, but what is relevant here is Boswell's effort to make Johnson enter the space of Charles Edward. Then Boswell repeats several of Johnson's sayings, and cites two of them in the text—another foreshadowing of the method of the *Tour*. Paoli, delighted with these sayings, translates them 'with Italian energy to the Corsican heroes' (*JTC* 198–9). It should be added that later, in Corte, Boswell wrote to Johnson, directing his letter 'from the palace of Pascal Paoli, sacred to wisdom and liberty' (*JTC* 218). He did not keep a copy of the letter, but Johnson preserved it, and Boswell recalls it in the *Life* with affection, citing the expression, 'I dare to call this a spirited tour. I dare to challenge your approbation' (*LSJ* ii. 3). Johnson replied in January 1766, urging Boswell to come home (*L* i. 183–4). The most notable passage in the letter runs: 'Come home, and expect such a welcome as is due him, whom a wise and noble curiosity has led, where perhaps no native of this country ever was before.' It is possible that Boswell's 'spirited tour' had triggered old yearnings in

music of the bagpipes, re-enacting the dispersal of the community. This was the night when Johnson, made conscious of his years by the energetic dance, remarked: 'I cannot but laugh, to think of myself roving among the Hebrides at sixty. I wonder where I shall rove at fourscore!' (*LSJ* v. 278).

Johnson, and led him to reactivate his lifelong plan of a journey to the Hebrides; although, if that is the case, some years passed while the idea fermented in his mind (see Chapter 1).

The lasting effects of the Corsican adventure, as regards Boswell's life and literary career, are well known, and to reiterate them here would be to lose the thread of our present argument. After a time, everyone found Boswell's Anglo-Corsican attitudes tedious and affected, and Johnson had to rebuke him: 'I wish you would empty your head of Corsica' (*L* i. 208). What has not been fully understood is the importance of the expedition in confirming Boswell's vision of himself as a patriot chief, a partisan, a freedom-fighter, a beloved popular leader, a heroic adventurer, and much else—the same ingredients which were to go into his escapade in 1773, when he reran the Prince's flight across the Highlands and Islands.[20]

Boswell was intensely proud of what he had achieved in Corsica. In the preface to the third edition of the *Journal* (dated from Auchinleck on 29 August 1768) he wrote: 'Whatever clouds may overcast my days, I can now walk here among the rocks and woods of my ancestors, with an agreeable consciousness that I have done something worthy' (*JTC* 136). By 1773 the first clouds had indeed started to appear—what the Yale editors of his journals call 'the ominous years' (1774 to 1776) were almost upon him. He was beginning to feel that life had gone stale. It was a craving for something more than mere adventure which caused him to introduce Johnson into his day-dreams, as though he realized that the other man held the lease on his own immortality. It is striking that the words of the Corsican book are transferred to Johnson in the *Tour*, when Boswell smuggles into the text a letter he had written to Garrick from Inverness on 29 August, describing the visit to Macbeth's castle (see also p. 105). The passage now runs: 'Think what enthusiastick happiness I shall have to see Mr Samuel Johnson walking among the romantick rocks and woods of my ancestors at

---

[20] Another transference that we have already seen (see n. 10, above) occurs in a passage in which Boswell reflects on his own limited abilities: 'Ambitious to be the companion of Paoli, and to understand a country and a people which roused me so much, I wished to be a Sir James Macdonald' (*JTC* 210–11). Whenever Boswell felt small and defenceless, he imagined himself to be a brave chieftain. He had thought, incidentally, that if Macdonald had lived, he would have been able to prevail on his friend to visit Corsica.

Auchinleck!' (*LSJ* v. 348). The involved choreography of the tour became still more pointed when the travellers actually reached Auchinleck by way of the Countess of Eglinton's house near Troon—she was a fervent Jacobite, the mother of Lady Macdonald (see p. 147), and a living remnant of the old Scotland. Then the travellers arrive at Boswell's ancestral home, and again Boswell stresses the 'romantick scene', as well as dwelling on 'the antiquity and honourable alliances' of his family, with its relationship to James IV. He then brings up his distant kinship with Robert Bruce, and adds that he was sure Johnson 'would not think lightly of [his] relation to the Royal Personage, whose liberality, on his accession to the throne, had given him comfort and independence' (*LSJ* v. 379). The evasive syntax muffles these references to Bruce and to George III's award of a royal pension to Johnson. An elaborate rhetorical task is being covertly attempted: to link Johnson and himself with the Scottish royal family, though, as the editor of the *Tour* remarks, 'the relation . . . was remote even for Scotland'. Boswell had got himself into these contortions out of his suppressed desire to associate the 'romantick' aspect of his family history with Johnson, but also (safely removed) with the other royal personage who had wandered—unlike George III—among the rocks and woods of Scotland.

At Staffa, Banks had mused on how suitable it would be to read Ossian 'under the shade of those woods', which would amount to a 'Luxury above the reach of Kings'.[21] He had come, he felt, to 'the land of Heroes . . . the mother of the romantick Scenery of Ossian'. This prose, muddled by its very fervour, comes from a solid English scientist. A year later Boswell, a mercurial Scottish neurotic and would-be writer, tried to move these romantic vistas from the home of Ossian to the hills and glens which Charles Edward had crossed during his flight. In addition, the scene of historic romance was to be re-created at Boswell's own family home. A cluster of associations is gradually built up, wrapped around ideas of chivalry, history, monarchy, Scottish patriotism, and romantic scenery. Even if Boswell had cared for Ossian, that legend was a lost cause as far as engaging Johnson's vicarious participation in the fantasy was concerned. Instead Boswell was able to enlist an alternative myth to cement his dream—that is, Jacobitism.

[21] Quoted in Carter, *Banks*, pp. 106–7.

IV

I suggested earlier that Johnson acquiesced in Boswell's hidden programme for the tour. That may be understating the truth. Although the Pretender never appears by name in the *Journey*, Boswell as usual blows his friend's cover. He too was reticent about naming the Prince directly, and the one exception, outside the interpolated narrative, occurs in this passage:

When the punch went round, Dr Johnson kept a close whispering conference with Mrs M'Kinnon, which, however, was loud enough to let us hear that the subject of it was the particulars of Prince Charles's escape. The company were entertained and pleased to observe it. Upon that subject, there was something congenial between the soul of Dr Samuel Johnson, and that of an isle of Sky farmer's wife. It is curious to see how people, how far so ever removed from each other in the general system of their lives, come close together on a particular point which is common to each. We were merry with Corrichatachin, on Dr Johnson's whispering with his wife. (*LSJ* v. 264)

The by-play is hurriedly shifted into mock-amorous badinage. But what was 'congenial between the soul' of Johnson and that of a farmer's wife on Skye? It can only be an interest in the matter of their conversation. The dialogue is defined by Boswell as a 'whispering' which is audible enough to the assembled company for its gravamen to be clear. Either Boswell is falsely projecting his own concern with the Prince's flight on to Johnson (which, for various reasons, is implausible); or the Englishman was readily broaching the issue which underlay all of the tour—and which explained the route that his friend had chosen, the people to whom Johnson had been presented on Skye, and the kind of discourse such company prompted. What was faintly comic and embarrassing about the scene was not really the elderly sage's philandering with a woman in the presence of her husband; it was rather the fact that Johnson had shown such an avid (and imperfectly concealed) desire to learn the ways in which the Prince had been shielded from Hanoverian authorities.

It was no longer traitorous to permit such feelings to surface. The Pretender, though still alive, did not represent any real threat to the state. But to rejoice in his escape—as, we may surely deduce, Johnson did—was still a faintly indiscreet gesture. When Boswell presents him whispering with Mrs Mackinnon, there is an air of collusion: Johnson has become a secret sharer in the Jacobite family history. It was primarily Boswell who had put him in this position, but Johnson was perfectly capable of resisting the imputed role if he so desired. Apparently, he did not so desire.

Linda Colley has recently termed Johnson 'a Tory who sometimes leaned towards emotional Jacobitism'.[22] To be sure, 'emotional Jacobitism' is a somewhat nebulous concept, but the general sense of the phrase seems to be pointing in the right direction. Colley is certainly right to claim that Jacobitism was not just a matter of romantic ideologies, and that its success or failure related to hard issues of military power, economic opportunity, jobs, self-interest.[23] But this aspect of the overall situation is mostly effaced in the Hebridean venture. Johnson displays what might be called 'cultural' Jacobitism as the tour secularizes the hard issues I have mentioned. One of the recurrent topics in the *Journey* is the ravages left behind by the Reformation in Scotland; the author repeatedly draws attention to the effects caused by 'the tumult and violence of Knox's reformation' (*JWI* 5). In St Andrews 'we were reconciled to the sight of archiepiscopal ruins', owing to 'the distance of [this] calamity' in time (*JWI* 9). In Elgin 'The ruins of the cathedral ... afforded us another proof of the waste of reformation' (*JWI* 23)—here the pronoun 'us' seems to associate Boswell with the sentiment. On Skye 'the malignant influence of Calvinism has blasted ceremony and decency together; and if the remembrance of papal superstition is obliterated, the monuments of papal piety are likewise effaced' (*JWI* 65). Other examples could be given. Almost the only buildings which Johnson describes with approval in the entire *Journey* are the vestiges of the old religion and learning, destroyed by the progress of the Reformation. Of course, Calvinism did not represent the only form of Protestantism, even in Scotland, and Johnson's own Anglican loyalties were secure enough. But in his imaginative response to the Scottish landscape it was the remnants of 'papal piety' which triggered the strongest reaction.

All this comes to a head at the most eloquent moment of the book. As we have seen, Boswell signalled the description of Iona as

[22] Linda Colley, *Britons: Forging the Nation, 1707–1837* (New Haven, Conn.: Yale University Press, 1992), 76.   [23] Ibid. 72–85.

the key statement of the *Journey*, one that Joseph Banks read in silent wonder (see above, p. 87). The first and last sentences of the paragraph in question run as follows: 'We were now treading that illustrious island, which was once the luminary of the Caledonian regions, whence savage clans and roving barbarians derived the benefit of knowledge, and the blessings of religion. . . . That man is little to be envied, whose patriotism would not gain force upon the plain of Marathon, or whose piety would not grow warmer among the ruins of Iona.' (*JWI* 148). At this juncture, we are suddenly aware that Gibbon was to produce the first instalment of his masterpiece just one year after the *Journey* came out. Yet this 'timeless' reflection is prompted by the ruins of a fairly small religious settlement on a tiny island off the coast of Mull. Johnson's affection for the world-wide (or at least European) Catholic Church is evident from the warm accents of his prose. Whatever its other dimensions, Jacobitism could claim to have preserved a stronger sense of cultural community than the defensive nation-state of Hanoverian Britain.

As we have noted, the name of the Pretender may not crop up often in the two narratives of the tour, but there is a wider Stuart presence. Boswell soon provokes his friend into a sharp riposte:

I here began to indulge *old Scottish* sentiments, and to express a warm regret, that, by our Union with England, we were no more;—our independent kingdom was lost.—JOHNSON. 'Sir, never talk of your independency, who could let your Queen remain twenty years in captivity, and then let her be put to death, without even a pretence of justice, without your ever attempting to rescue her; and such a Queen too! as every man of any gallantry of spirit would have sacrificed his life for.' (*LSJ* v. 40)

I do not see how this can be explained away, unless one takes the extreme radical position that Boswell made it all up. Perhaps Queen Elizabeth had become too much of a Whig heroine; but, plainly, the 'gallantry of spirit' which should have come to the aid of Mary Queen of Scots was the very attribute which had sustained the Pretender's ill-fated attempt and, above all, his escape after Culloden. Only a couple of pages later Boswell conducts his friend to Holyrood, 'that beautiful piece of architecture, but, alas! that deserted mansion of royalty'. The visitors survey the staterooms, including that part 'in which our beautiful Queen Mary lived, and in which David Rizzio was murdered'. Here Boswell overhears

Johnson 'repeating, in a kind of muttering tone, a line of the old ballad, *Johnny Armstrong's Last Good-Night*: "And ran him through the fair body!" ' (*LSJ* v. 43). Who needs Ossian, or the Romantic revival, when a man of Johnson's age and background could be heard muttering border ballads on the scene of the stirring events of Stuart history? Walter Scott would scarcely have dared to put in as much. We might also note how the 'beautiful' but deserted palace and the 'beautiful' but doomed queen form a shadowy hieroglyph of the beautiful but exiled prince.

Let me reiterate that such passages are not cited in order to show that Johnson was a closet Jacobite, still anxious (if he ever had been) to restore the Stuarts. There is plenty of evidence, from the pages of Boswell's *Life* and elsewhere, to show that he accepted the *de facto* right of the Hanoverians, since by the 1770s there was no hope that 'he who has [the hereditary right] can be restored' (*LSJ* iii. 15–17).[24] Nevertheless, he understood Boswell's '*old Scottish enthusiasm*' (*LSJ* v. 374) well enough to be able to appreciate the motive that powered the journey, as his friend had constructed it. His own extensive knowledge of Scottish history, and his protective feelings towards the earlier Stuarts, equipped him for the role of a sympathetic visitor. What he actively disliked about Scotland was nearly all a product of the post-Reformation era, and to that extent he was able to enter into Boswell's nostalgia for a lost Scotland, however mythical a place that might have been.[25]

It may seem strained, if not perverse, to suggest that Boswell could have identified the elderly moralist with the young adventurer. To this objection there are two answers. The first is that Boswell had a remarkable capacity for picking up the likenesses between apparent dissimilarities. Consider his intuition regarding the links between Johnson and Monboddo (see also Appendix, pp. 226–31).

---

[24] See also a conversation as close in time to the tour as that of 15 Apr. 1773, in which Johnson admits that he was not sure that he could take the oath of loyalty to the crown, and reviews the issues with what Boswell calls 'conscientious' and 'delicate' appraisal of the subject (*LSJ* ii. 220).

[25] To mention just one of the further convolutions of the topic: Boswell regarded Lord Elibank as a key figure in the organization of the tour; letters passed to and from Skye between them, and we are told that Johnson 'had a very high opinion' of Elibank (*LSJ* v. 385). It was Alexander Murray of Elibank, the peer's brother, who proposed wild plots to kidnap or murder the Hanoverian family in 1751–2: see McLynn, *Charles Edward Stuart*, 403–14.

On the surface, these two men were chalk and cheese. But Boswell delves beneath the surface: 'There were several points of similarity between them; learning, clearness of head, precision of speech, and a love of research on many subjects which people in general do not investigate. Foote paid Lord Monboddo the compliment of saying, that he was "an Elzevir edition of Johnson".' A little later: 'The circumstance of each of them having a black servant was another point of similarity' (*LSJ* v. 74, 82). Hence Boswell was 'curious to see them together'. There are parallels with the encounter between Lord Auchinleck and Johnson. Boswell starts from the fact that 'My father was not quite a year and a half older than Dr Johnson' (*LSJ* v. 375), but then goes on to enumerate what look to be large disparities, political, religious, and human. However, it is obvious that the two men exercised a comparable influence on the life of Boswell, and by 1785 there was the additional factor that they had died within two years of each other. The reason that the intellectual gladiators were able to fight at equal weights lay in their shared pugnacity, vigour of mind, and professional standing.[26] Boswell cannot have supposed that the Prince and the sage were congenial figures overall; but his imagination seized on real affinities, and extrapolated from these to achieve a mythical consonance.

Second, as we have seen, Boswell was able to perceive qualities in his friend which were not always recognized by more conventional judges. He activated a primitive strain in Johnson's character which licensed the grave senior to unbend. One of the things that readers like Burke found reprehensible in the *Tour* was its protracted disclosure of the unofficial Johnson—a man who ate fish with his fingers, and relished informal contacts with people along the route. Perhaps Boswell even sensed that his friend shared in the imaginative pleasure afforded by the reconstruction of the great escape across the glens and moors in 1746.

---

[26] In fact, Lord Auchinleck did not always take a political stance which placed him in an adversarial position with Johnson. In 1759–60 he had been in touch with the Duke of Newcastle, and had joined with Elibank, Hailes, Monboddo, George Dempster, and Adam Ferguson (all moderates) in promoting the cause of the Scottish militia. The English Whig establishment rebuffed the proposal. Johnson himself had no love for Newcastle and his minions. See John Robertson, *The Scottish Enlightenment and the Militia Issue* (Edinburgh: John Donald, 1985), 108–13.

V

The Wanderer, then, represents Boswell in the guise of a physical adventurer, careless of bodily comfort; a freedom-fighter whose ultimate failure only added to his appeal; and as a sexually glamorous embodiment of historic Scottish values. The fact that Charles Edward had turned into a drunken reprobate would not have made it any harder to identify with him. However, if the Prince stood in for Boswell's id, Johnson was far from representing his super-ego, which is what one might expect. As we have seen repeatedly in this book, Johnson is seen as daring, tenacious, physically enduring, brave, and unconventional. He adopts a number of histrionic poses, and he defies his years with feats of spirited energy. He allows himself to be Scotticized, entering into the experiences of the Highlanders with extraordinary powers of sympathy—something of which most elderly English notabilities would have been totally incapable. Accordingly, Boswell bestows on him the honorific title of 'the Rambler'. This could suggest the intellectual or the severe moralist. In Boswell's text the word reclaims its original, non-literary associations. Johnson is a rambler as Charles Edward is a wanderer. Both have made an existential leap out of safety, habit, and comfort.[27] Each is required to fuel Boswell's dreams of a freer life, led in opposition to the prudential values which increasingly guided his normal behaviour. Astonishingly—whatever the historic truth—each lives up to the role they had been assigned in Boswell's imagination. By a great rhetorical coup in the *Tour*, the main action and the interpolated narrative merge into a single dramatization of their author's fantasy. The Wanderer and the Rambler join hands to preside over Boswell's mythical and actual journey through the Highlands to Skye. The *Tour* tells the story of their adventures, but the displaced hero is the unnamed traveller—James Boswell.

[27] 'If this be not *roving among the Hebrides*, nothing is,' exclaimed Johnson as his small boat sailed by moonlight 'in a sea somewhat rough, and often between black and gloomy rocks' (*LSJ* v. 333). 'Roving' was evidently more than a leisurely tour: it was, to take a cant phrase literally, no picnic.

7

Boswell and the Scotticism

About four years after undertaking his journey to the Hebrides, Johnson wrote a letter in which he renewed his acquaintance with the members of Boswell's family, whom he had met in Edinburgh in 1773. Almost at once he took up the issue of the accent which young Veronica Boswell was acquiring: 'As to Miss Veronica's Scotch, I think it cannot be helped. An English maid you might easily have; but she would still imitate the greater number, as they would be likewise those whom she must most respect. Her dialect will not be gross. Her Mamma has not much Scotch, and you have yourself very little' (*L* ii. 164). The passage serves to remind us of the concern which men and women felt at this time about audible or visible signs of 'Scottish' usages in the English language. Boswell's complicated feelings about his own national origin under-lie the enquiry which he had obviously made of Johnson. Words, syntax, pronunciation might all reveal an identifiably Scottish identity—something which could induce discomfort, puzzling to us, even among citizens of the Athens of the north during the heyday of the Enlightenment. In the case of Boswell himself, this common anxiety translated itself into a wider uncertainty than the merely linguistic. One of Boswell's motives for conducting Johnson around the Highlands and Islands may have been a desire to reassert his own Scottishness in a way which was impossible in the Lowlands, and especially in the quasi-metropolitan and sophisticated surroundings of the capital. To direct the travels of an elderly Englishman who had never been north of the Tweed before was one means of regaining an acceptable and, as it were, a 'willed' Scottish identity, instead of the imputed nationality assigned on the basis of language.

A well-known passage in *Humphry Clinker* (1771) serves to focus linguistic issues which bear on the Scottish Enlightenment, and which help to illuminate Boswell's attitudes in relation to the dominant intellectual movement of his time. At Durham Smollett's party of travellers have encountered the eccentric, indeed consciously Quixotic, figure of Lismahago. Soon afterwards, on 13 July, Jery

Melford writes to his friend Sir Watkin Phillips of the first major contretemps involving Lismahago, when the grizzled lieutenant sets out a paradoxical case:

He proceeded to set out his assertion that the English language was spoken with greater propriety at Edinburgh than in London.—He said, what we generally called the Scottish dialect was, in fact, true, genuine old English, with a mixture of some French terms and idioms, adopted in a long intercourse betwixt the French and Scots nations; that the modern English, from affection and false refinement, had weakened, and even corrupted their language, by throwing out the guttural sounds, altering the pronunciation and the quantity, and disusing many words and terms of great significance. In consequence of these innovations, the works of our best poets, such as Chaucer, Spenser, and even Shakespeare, were become, in many parts, unintelligible to the natives of South-Britain, whereas the Scots, who retain the ancient language, understand them without the help of a glossary.

Lismahago goes on to give a number of detailed instances in support of his claim, arguing that the 'energy' of southern English had been 'impaired' by the false refinements mentioned, and that an overall vowel-shift had made the language unlike any other European tongue, and thus difficult for foreigners to acquire.

Naturally, the belligerent Matthew Bramble is impelled to offer some corrective to this view, but Lismahago is undaunted, and the check serves 'only to agitate his humour for disputation':

He said, if every nation had is own recitative or music the Scots had theirs, and the Scotchman who had not yet acquired the cadence of the English, would naturally use his own in speaking their language; therefore, if he was better understood than the native, his recitative must be more intelligible than that of the English; of consequence, the dialect of the Scots had an advantage over their fellow subjects, and this was another strong presumption that the modern English had corrupted their language in the article of pronunciation.[1]

The argument dissolves into a wider set of paradoxical assertions, and then peters out. But there are several expressions here which point to a major debate of the time. The phrase 'the dialect of the Scots' hints at a broad aspect of linguistic politics which surfaced after the Union. Along with this public matter, there was a private

---

[1] Tobias Smollett, *The Expedition of Humphry Clinker*, ed. L. M. Knapp (London: Oxford University Press, 1972), 199–201.

concern which Boswell felt as strongly as anyone, conveyed in the words 'the Scotchman who had not yet acquired the cadence of the English'. In this chapter I shall consider briefly the broader political issue as it was manifested in Boswell's adult lifetime. This is chiefly by way of background to the second part of the chapter, which will examine Boswell's own interest in the 'Scotticism' in oral or written expression.[2]

I

It was generally agreed by Scots of all persuasions at the time of the Enlightenment that the Scottish language had become, to all intents and purposes, a variant of the main linguistic stock, i.e. English. This had happened, it was felt, not because of any inherent weakness in the older tongue, but simply as a consequence of the dependence—political, economic, moral—which had been imposed by the Union. This view is most succinctly expressed by William Robertson, in book VIII of his *History of Scotland* (1759). If the Union had not taken place, Robertson argues, two distinct nations could have continued to support two distinct languages, or at least dialects of comparable standing. 'But, by the accession,' he proceeds, 'the English naturally became the sole judges and lawgivers in Language, and rejected, as solecisms, every form of speech to which their ear was not accustomed.'[3]

The two best-known responses to this situation are the list of banned Scots idioms compiled by David Hume, and the efforts of the Select Society in the early 1760s to improve native usage in the

[2] In addition to general studies of the English Enlightenment, a valuable background to the issues considered in this chapter is provided in particular by two essays in N. T. Phillipson and Rosalind Mitchison (eds.), *Scotland in the Age of Improvement* (Edinburgh: Edinburgh University Press, 1970), namely Janet Adam Smith, 'Some Eighteenth-Century Ideas of Scotland', 107–24, and John Clive, 'The Social Background of the Scottish Renaissance', 225–44. A recent study which treats similar issues to those explored in this chapter, but from a different perspective, is James Basker, 'Scotticisms and the Problem of Cultural Identity in Eighteenth-Century Britain', *Eighteenth-Century Life*, 15 (1991), 81–95.

[3] Quoted by Smith, 'Eighteenth-Century Ideas of Scotland', 112; see also p. 110 for Hume's letter to Gilbert Elliot in 1757 on the 'very corrupt Dialect' heard in both 'Accent & Pronunciation' of the Scottish ruling class—paradoxically, when the Scottish people were 'the most distinguish'd for Literature in Europe'. John Wilkes made political capital of the prejudice in favour of English when he promised to avoid Scotticisms in the *North Briton*: see Linda Colley, *Britons: Forging the Nation, 1707–1837* (New Haven, Conn.: Yale University Press, 1992), 116.

English language. One could suggest that, at a deeper level, the efforts of creative writers to reclaim a living Scots idiom, displayed most prominently in the work of Robert Fergusson and Robert Burns, reflect a parallel effort to undo the damage of the Union; but this was a less conscious process, impelled partly by the imaginative drives of highly gifted poets.

The simpler case to analyse is the strong programmatic campaign of the Select Society.[4] The purpose in view was 'the correction of Scottish pronunciation', following a remark by the English politician Charles Townshend: 'Why can't you learn to speak the English language as you have already learnt to write it?' Despite public lectures and various publicity devices, not to mention the advocacy of men like Robertson and Hugh Blair, the campaign excited derision in Edinburgh. This was at a juncture when anti-Scottish mania, already visible at the time of John Home's *Douglas* in 1757, was about to attain new fervour in England with the rising unpopularity of Bute's ministry.[5] The activities of the Select Society reflect an awareness that anti-Scottish sentiment could be whipped up simply on the basis of their peculiar, or at least readily identifiable, manner of speech.

That a course of public lectures should have been undertaken is in itself significant. The outstanding figure in this growing profession was undoubtedly Thomas Sheridan the younger, son of Swift's friend and father of Richard Brinsley. In 1761 Sheridan lectured in Edinburgh to an impressive audience of 'three hundred nobles, judges, divines, advocates, and men of fashion.'[6] Sheridan

---

[4] Information on the Select Society is available in many standard sources, but the best general account is Davis D. McElroy, *Scotland's Age of Improvement* (n.p.: Washington State University Press, 1969), 48–67. Material particularly relevant to the present discussion can be found in E. C. Mossner, *The Life of David Hume*, 2nd edn. (Oxford: Clarendon Press, 1980), 372–3 (noting the subscriptions mounted to pay for English tutors); Ian Ross, *Lord Kames and the Scotland of his Day* (Oxford: Clarendon Press, 1972), 177–81; and Alastair Smart, *The Life and Art of Allan Ramsay* (London: Routledge, 1952), 77. A good overview of the Society is given by John Robertson, *The Scottish Enlightenment and the Militia Issue* (Edinburgh: John Donald, 1985), 85–6. For the story about Hume, see E. L. Cloyd, *James Burnett, Lord Monboddo* (Oxford: Clarendon Press, 1972), 17.

[5] See Ch. 8, below. For some Scottish reactions to this hostility, see Doreen Yarwood, *Robert Adam* (London: Dent, 1970), 97–8. Yarwood mentions Boswell's difficulty in making friends at this time.

[6] Clive, 'Scottish Renaissance', 239. For fuller details on the course of lectures, see F. A. Pottle, *James Boswell: The Earlier Years, 1740–1769* (London: Heinemann, 1966), 64–5, 473.

was notorious for speaking in a strong Irish brogue of his own, and
it can be seen as either fitting or ironic that he advocated a
standardization of the four British languages. There is an obvious
link here with Boswell, who attended Sheridan's Edinburgh lectures
and soon made Sheridan (as F. A. Pottle has put it) his 'guide,
philosopher, and friend'.[7] The details of this relationship cannot be
considered fully here: it is enough to note that the young Boswell
became a member of the Select Society at the end of 1761, and that
his own awareness of the issues surrounding what might be called
Scottish English grew up in the context of this wider national
concern.

As for Hume, there is much that could be said. His list of
solecisms has often been ridiculed, as though he ought to have
realized that this was an insult to the resources of native Scots
idiom. In fact, the list was originally compiled for private use,
though it was printed in some copies of the *Political Discourses*
(1752) and later reprinted in the *Scots Magazine* (1760). In any
case, there is no need to apologize for Hume's defensiveness on this
score; ample evidence exists that many others were ready to
criticize Scottish authors, Hume included, when they were deemed
to have departed from the norms of polite English usage. In this
sense, Townshend's confidence that Scottish people had learnt to
write English in an acceptable fashion is not borne out by the facts.[8]

Hume was by no means unique in feeling anxious on this score.
James Beattie admitted to nervousness about Scotticism in his
writing, and thanked Elizabeth Montagu for providing a model of
pure English—certainly there is a degree of flattery towards his
patron, but we need not doubt that the worry was any the less
genuinely felt.[9] (Montagu had savoured the manner of Adam
Ferguson's *Essay on Civil Society*, contending that it was

[7] *Boswell's London Journal, 1762-1763*, ed. F. A. Pottle (London: Heinemann,
1950), 9.

[8] A representative (though in this case positive) reaction of one English reader is a
comment by Gray on Adam Ferguson's *Essay on the History of Civil Society*: see his
letter to James Beattie of 12 August 1767, in *The Correspondence of Thomas Gray*,
ed. P. Toynbee and L. Whibley, rev. H. W. Starr, 3 vols. (Oxford: Clarendon Press,
1971), iii. 975. It might be added that Gray took note of Scottish words when he
made a visit to Glamis in 1765: see W. P. Jones, *Thomas Gray: Scholar* (Cambridge,
Mass.: Harvard University Press, 1937), 177.

[9] Quoted by C. B. Tinker, *The Salon and English Letters* (New York: Macmillan,
1915), 193. For Montagu's praise of Ferguson, see Mossner, *Life of David Hume*,
543.

impossible for anyone but a Scotsman to have written so.) Hume himself had advised his friendly antagonist, the clergyman and pamphleteer Robert Wallace, around 1751, to expunge Scots words such as 'expiscate' from his work.[10] As late as 1802 the historian Malcolm Laing, best known today for his enquiry into the authenticity of Ossian, sent his work to Dr Samuel Parr for the specific purpose of identifying and removing Scotticisms.[11] Very few authors were immune from this feeling of uneasiness. One exception is Adam Smith, who recorded his early conviction that someone born north of the Tweed could yet attain 'a correct and even elegant style'.[12] But Smith had received a wider cultural, educational, and social grounding than most of his countrymen by the time he came to write *The Wealth of Nations*. Stay-at-home Scots, who moved in restricted circles, naturally risked a greater appearance of provinciality or even rusticity, though in practice it was a certain pedantic formalism of language which often betrayed the Caledonian to English eyes and ears.

A well-known passage in Boswell's *Life of Samuel Johnson* records Johnson's reactions to Hume's list: 'I told him that David Hume had made a short collection of Scotticisms. "I wonder, (said Johnson), that *he* should find them" ' (*LSJ* ii. 72). Malone's gloss on this passage in the third edition of the *Life* reads: 'The first edition of Hume's *History of England* was full of Scotticisms, many of which he corrected in subsequent editions.' It is certainly true that some niggling occurred when Hume's *History* first appeared, and since Malone could still use the verb 'corrected' in this context, forty years later, it is no wonder that a Scot of Hume's generation would think it prudent to guard against such criticisms.[13] Two further glosses are possible. This first concerns Boswell's own plans for a Scottish dictionary, of which Johnson was well aware and which will be mentioned in connection with Boswell's career later

[10] Mossner, *Life of David Hume*, 263. Hume found 'only a very few Scotticisms' to complain of in a work by Kames (Ross, *Lord Kames*, 54). He later advised Kames to prune the language of the *Elements of Criticism* (Ross, *Lord Kames*, 351–2).

[11] Warren Derry, *Samuel Parr* (Oxford: Clarendon Press, 1966), 124. A curious instance, which might well have come to Boswell's attention through Johnson, is the employment of Theophilus Cibber as the nominal author of the *Lives of the Poets* (1753), to guard against both Scotticisms and possible Jacobite sentiments.

[12] Quoted by R. H. Campbell and A. S. Skinner, *Adam Smith* (New York: St Martin's Press, 1982), 37.

[13] Hume wrote to John Wilkes of the 'desperate and Irreclaimable' tongue that he inherited: cited by Mossner, *Life of David Hume*, 370.

in this chapter. The second relates to the grounds of Johnson's prejudice. In so far as his dismissive remark cannot be explained by a rooted aversion to the philosopher on account of his religious views, it may perhaps owe something to Hume's reputation in England for mixing Scottish and French idiom in his writing. Very soon after Boswell's first meeting with Johnson, he recorded the following under 20 July 1763:

The conversation now turned to Mr David Hume's style. JOHNSON. 'Why, sir, his style is not English; the structure of his sentences is French. Now the French structure and the English structure may, in the nature of things, be equally good. But if you allow that the English language is established, he is wrong.' (*LSJ* i. 439)

Most people, Scottish as well as English, had got used to the idea that the English language was the 'established' vehicle for polite communication—the great *Dictionary* may have played some part in this. It is characteristic of Johnson's more analytic approach to language that he should mention 'structure'—presumably syntax, word order, cadence—rather than simply diction, which was the usual criterion of a 'Scottish' style. Hume's friend John Peach is said to have discovered more than two hundred Scotticisms in the first edition of the *History*: this relates much more to individual words than to any broader consideration of phrasing.[14]

There is, of course, the related issue of pronunciation, which in Boswell's day was sometimes kept separate but was usually merged into the broad topic of Scotticism. Hume was not immune from criticism on this score: the most forthright statement is that of Lord Charlemont, who asserted that 'his speech in English was rendered ridiculous by the broadest and most vulgar Scottish Accent, and his French was, if possible, still more laughable.' This Irish testimony may appear tainted; equally suspect, on grounds of social prejudice, is the waspish comment by Horace Walpole: 'Mr Hume is fashion itself [in Paris], although his French is almost as unintelligible as his English.'[15] Boswell does not say much about Hume's manner of

---

[14] Ibid. 89. For a fuller discussion of Hume's alleged inability to avoid Scottish forms of words, see *LSJ* ii. 72 n. 2.

[15] Mossner, *Life of David Hume*, 214; the Yale edn. of *Horace Walpole's Correspondence*, ed. W. S. Lewis *et al.* (New Haven, Conn.: Yale University Press, 1937–83), xxxi. 49 (letter to the Countess of Suffolk, 20 Sept. 1765); see also xl. 385.

speech, though we know that as a young man he had mimicked the philosopher ('I had not only his external address, but his sentiments and mode of expression').[16]

Other notable figures of the age did not escape so lightly, especially in England. Henry Dundas, as we shall see when reviewing Boswell's relationship to the issue, was known as a broad Scots speaker who had made a virtue of this apparent defect. William Robertson, according to Alexander Carlyle, spoke with a particularly broad 'accent and tone', though he nevertheless manifested great taste in the way in which he used language.[17] An interesting case is provided by Francis Jeffrey, a generation later, who set out as a young man to eliminate his native burr: in Cockburn's words, he was 'bent on purifying himself of the national inconvenience'. The results were mixed: as John Gross has put it, 'he came back from Oxford with a queer accent which astonished his friends and delighted his enemies'.[18] Among the latter may be counted the famously demotic speaker Lord Braxfield, who said of Jeffrey: 'The laddie has clear tint his Scotch, and found nae English.'[19] It is worth adding that Boswell's own father commanded a rich Scots idiom when he chose, and the young James cannot have failed to become aware of the potentialities which a sudden leap into the vernacular could open up, in the courtroom or elsewhere. On one occasion he imitated 'the rude Scots sarcastical vivacity' when he met Jean-Jacques Rousseau at Moutiers in 1764.

The issue of pronunciation had a number of ramifications in

---

[16] See Pottle, *Earlier Years*, 93, which cites the 'Harvest Jaunt' of 1762.

[17] Alexander Carlyle, *Anecdotes and Characters*, ed. J. Kinsley (London: Oxford University Press, 1973), 253. Carlyle similarly said that Robertson's language was 'good honest natural Scotch'.

[18] John Gross, *The Rise and Fall of the Man of Letters* (London: Weidenfeld and Nicolson, 1969), 8: see also *LSJ* ii. 159 n. 6; Karl Miller, *Cockburn's Millennium* (Cambridge, Mass.: Harvard University Press, 1976), 264. Alexander Wedderburn is said to have placed himself in the hands of 'two Irish actors' to improve his accent (Ross, *Lord Kames*, 73). One of these must have been Sheridan.

[19] *Boswell on the Grand Tour: Germany and Switzerland, 1764*, ed. F. A. Pottle (London: Heinemann, 1953), 260. For the division between lawyers who strove 'to remove the least trace of any Scotticisms from their speech' and those like Braxfield who 'became almost defiantly Scottish in their language and personal habits, with the result that they came to be considered crude and illiterate by such Anglicized young advocates as James Boswell', see Cloyd, *James Burnett*, 36.

politics, too. The wholly unlikely anecdote that George III, when he came to the throne, spoke with a Scottish accent seems to be part of a scare-story directed against Bute's influence on him. (According to Lord Holland, the King, on opening his first Parliament, stressed the word *allies* on the first syllable, which is a somewhat sophisticated case to take.)[20] Sometimes the Scottish language was parodied in cartoons which identify wild Highlanders with Jacobitism, though in truth the Scottish establishment was overwhelmingly Lowland in origin and, from quite early in the century, consistently, if unenthusiastically, Hanoverian in allegiance. After the Union it was sometimes claimed that the new Scottish members of the Westminster Parliament were barely understood and, consequently, were laughed at: only with a second generation, it has been argued, did the Scottish block achieve a ready hearing, when their more Anglicized background gave them ease in speaking 'pure' English.[21]

A more direct concern for most people was a sufficient facility in spoken English to conduct business and (the crucial thing for Boswell) to advance a professional career. When Roderick Random came to London, he was told by Strap that a London schoolmaster would be ready to teach him 'the pronunciation of the English-tongue, without which (he says) you will be unfit for business in this country'.[22] Political and social prejudice reinforced this need for any aspiring Scotsman seeking to make his way in England or in a field dominated by English taste, like the profession of letters. Even if Boswell had not been split by personal conflicts, family quarrels, feudal dreams, and literary ambitions, he would have run into a whole set of disruptive ideological pressures which centred on the use of English, in print and in speech. As we have seen, most writers, from Hume downwards, were subject to intense pressure in respect of the 'correctness' of their English usage. Much less self-confident by nature than a Hume or a Smith, it is not surprising that Boswell reflects an acute form of this state of anxiety.

---

[20] *The Life and Letters of Lady Sarah Lennox, 1745–1826*, ed. the Countess of Ilchester and Lord Stavordale, 2 vols. (London: John Murray, 1901), i. 14.

[21] See Yarwood, *Robert Adam*, 33.

[22] Tobias Smollett, *The Adventures of Roderick Random*, ed. P.-G. Boucé (Oxford: Oxford University Press, 1981), 96 (from ch. 18).

II

As Scotland sought for a national identity in the era of the Enlightenment, so Boswell coveted a sense of the self which would include a proper mixture of the Scottish—proper, that is, in terms of the fulfilment of his notions of the world and of his own needs. His background might fairly be said to be multicultural. There was his upbringing amid the closes and wynds of the old city of Edinburgh; his occasional visits to the ancestral seat at Auchinleck; his studies at the ancient universities of Edinburgh and Glasgow; followed by his elopement to London, his spell at Utrecht and his grand tour, his involvement with the Scottish bar, and his hankerings after success in London. This complex heritage mirrors the divided loyalties of Scotland after the Union, with its proud indigenous culture, its close continental affinities, and its inevitable economic involvement with its larger neighbour. Some of this split makes itself apparent in linguistic areas; the mixed feelings we have seen in a number of leading figures concerning the dubious 'correctness' of Scottish usages serve to express this inheritance.

The young man began on his projected dictionary of Scottish words at least as early as January 1764, when he was at Utrecht.[23] It was one of several planned works that were never to see the light of day, though enough of a manuscript survived to be sold from his son's library in 1825. It will be best known to most readers from a passage in the *Life* under 19 October 1769;

He advised me to complete a Dictionary of words peculiar to Scotland, of which I shewed him a specimen. 'Sir, (said he,) Ray has made a collection of north-country words. By collecting those of your country, you will do a useful thing towards the history of the language.' He bade me also go on with collections I was making upon the antiquities of Scotland. 'Make a large book; a folio.' BOSWELL. 'But of what use will it be, Sir?' JOHNSON. 'Never mind the use; do it.' (*LSJ* ii. 91–2)

Boswell's motives were probably less pure than the antiquarian values suggested by Johnson would indicate. In his youth he had realized that distinctive Scottish vocabulary was a racial marker, and since he both clung to his nationality and yet resisted its

---

[23] See *Boswell in Holland, 1763–1764*, ed. F. A. Pottle (London: Heinemann, 1952), 158–64 and *passim*.

cramping effects on his career and personality, a lot depended for him personally on the state of his language.

Abundant evidence exists to show that he kept this awareness throughout his adult life. Selective quotation will demonstrate the point.[24] For example, in February 1767, back in Edinburgh after his years of travel, he received a letter from Sir John Pringle, giving high hopes for Boswell's advancement. He would shine at the bar and 'give the tone for a new eloquence'. The reason for this superiority over other candidates for fame was that 'you have the advantage of possessing the English language and the accent in a greater degree than any of your rivals, and a turn for expressing yourself in a clear and energetic manner, without those hyperbolic modes of speech that were introduced long ago, and were still kept up during my youth, and which slipped from the bar to the tea tables at Edinburgh.'[25] Pringle was more far-sighted than he knew, though Boswell's ultimate pre-eminence turns out to have lain in his biography and journals rather than in the courtroom. What Pringle said was, of course, exactly what Boswell wanted to hear. He would not have been quite so pleased if he could have known what Fanny Burney would write in her *Memoirs of Dr Burney*, long after his death: 'He spoke the Scotch accent strongly, though by no means so as to affect, even slightly, his intelligibility to an English ear.'[26] Boswell was proud of his own 'ear', and, according to G. M. Young, this enabled him to pass for an authentic English writer, unlike Hume: Boswell could 'detect provincialisms in the speech of Garrick and Johnson himself, and very rarely will a phrase be found to show that the writer was not born on Attic soil. Hume to the end had to keep by him a list of things that are not said . . .'[27] This is a peculiar way of putting it, not least because one may well feel that Attic soil lay closer to the Athens of the north than to the purlieus of Fleet Street.

The most striking single glimpse of Boswell's attitudes occurs in a brief phrase, found in his journal for 24 March 1775. He is

[24] Some further examples are provided by Smith, 'Eighteenth-Century Ideas of Scotland', 113.

[25] *Boswell in Search of a Wife, 1766–1769*, ed. F. Brady and F. A. Pottle (London: Heinemann, 1957), 31.

[26] Frances Burney, *Memoirs of Dr Burney*, 3 vols. (London: Moxon, 1832), ii. 191. For Johnson's opinion of Boswell's accent, see *LSJ* iii. 105–6.

[27] G. M. Young, 'Boswell—and Unashamed', in *Daylight and Champaign* (London: Cape, 1937), 227.

describing a meeting at the Club; naturally, the section was excised
when he wrote up the passage for the *Life*: 'I was disgusted by
[Dr George] Fordyce, who was coarse and noisy: and, as he had the
Scotch accent strong, he shocked me as a kind of representative of
myself. He was to me as the slaves of the Spartans, when shown
drunk to make that vice odious. His being a member lessened the
value of The Club'.[28] Admittedly, Boswell was so displeased with
the election of Adam Smith a year later ('Smith too is now of our
Club. It has lost its select merit') that he actually had thoughts of
seceding to form a new club.[29] But the hostility against Fordyce is
also a gesture of self-hatred, and the fear of exposure as a coarse
drunkard is closely allied to fear of exposure as a raw Scot. A
couple of weeks later Boswell reverted to his obsession in
conversation with Burke:

I maintained a strange proposition to Burke: that it was better for a
Scotsman and an Irishman to preserve so much of their native accent and
not to be quite perfect in English, because it was unnatural. I would have
all the birds of the air to retain somewhat of their own notes: a blackbird to
sing like a blackbird, and thrush like a thrush, and not a blackbird and
other birds to sing all like some other bird. Burke agreed with me . . . I said
it was unnatural to hear a Scotsman speaking perfect English. He appeared
a machine. I instanced Wedderburn . . . Lord Lisburne and I had
afterwards a discussion on this subject. My metaphor of the birds he
opposed by saying, 'A Scotsman may do very well with his own tone in
Coll; but if he comes into the House of Commons, it will be better if he
speaks English. A bagpipe may do very well in the Highlands, but I would
not introduce it into [Johann Christian] Bach's concert.' 'This,' said I,
'shows what it is to argue in metaphors. One is just as good as another'.
But I maintained to my Lord that it put me in a passion to hear a Scotsman
speaking in a perfect English tone. It was a false voice. He speaks as if he
had some pipe or speaking instrument in his mouth. And I thought always,
'Can't he take his confounded pipe out, and let us hear him speak with his
own organs?' I do still think I am right.

The exchange with Burke proceeds after this prolonged metaphoric
contest:

[28] *Boswell: The Ominous Years, 1774–1776*, ed. Charles Ryskamp and F. A.
Pottle (London: Heinemann, 1963), 94.

[29] Boswell to W. J. Temple, 28 Apr. 1776, in *The Letters of James Boswell*, ed.
C. B. Tinker, 2 vols. (Oxford: Clarendon Press, 1924), i. 250. See also the rough
notes for 10 May 1776, cited by D. M. Low, *Edward Gibbon, 1737–1794* (London:
Chatto and Windus, 1937), 229.

I said to Burke, 'You would not have a man use Scotch words, as to say a *trance* for a *passage* in a house.' 'No,' said he, 'that is a different language.' 'But,' said I, 'is it not better, too, to try to pronounce not in the broad Scotch way and to say *passage* and not *pawssage*.' 'Yes,' said Burke, 'when once you're *taught* how they pronounce it in England; but don't *try* at English pronunciation.' Said Richard Burke, 'Better say *pawssage* than *pissage*.' And indeed some Scotsmen, such as Rae, the advocate, make blunders as bad as this.[30]

One may wonder whether Boswell's dislike of a truly perfect English accent may derive from a recognition that he himself had not quite achieved this, or indeed quite *wanted* it consistently. It is also noteworthy that the subject crops up in the company of the Irish immigrants Edmund and Richard Burke; Lisburne, though he held an Irish peerage, was actually Welsh. Boswell had been shocked earlier in the same day, at a Commons committee reviewing the Clackmannan election, by Rae's 'barbarous Bath-metal English'. He alternates between the view that it is unnatural for a Scot to acquire an English indistinguishable from that of a southerner, and acute embarrassment when he hears broad Scots in an English forum.

Just a few months later the topic recurs:

I began today a curious bargain which I made with the Hon. Henry Erskine in order to acquire correctness in writing. We were to give to each other a copy of every one of our printed [legal] papers, and each was to be censor on the other. For every ungrammatical expression and every Scotticism except technical phrases, a shilling was to be incurred.[31]

This was when Boswell was no beginner: he was 35 at the time, ten years older than the future Lord Advocate Erskine. His prolonged tutelage in English expression went on almost to the end of his life. And the whole issue is seldom out of his head for long. In 1769 he quotes Thomas Sheridan on Thomas Reid's *Inquiry into the Human Mind* (1764): 'Sheridan said that Reid's book was the most correct of any that North Britain had produced, for he had not found one Scotticism in it.' Two weeks later he cites Dr John Armstrong, 'whom I found as worthy, as lively in his way, and as splenetic as ever. He is a violent Scotsman. He said the only advantage the English had over us was the *recitativo*, the tone of

[30] *Ominous Years*, 124–5.   [31] Ibid. 128–9.

speaking.[32] Nine years later Boswell noted that one 'Logic' Bayne
(according to Lord Kames) prospered despite failure at the bar and
knowing 'very little law', such were the effects of 'a slow, formal
manner, a neatness of expression and the English accent'.[33] Thus
Bayne became Professor of Scots Law at Edinburgh. We might
remind ourselves here that the Master of Edinburgh Academy was
required as late as 1823 to have 'a pure English accent'—merely to
have been born in England was not enough to guarantee this
desirable asset.[34]

The fullest single examination of the issues under review occurs
in a passage which does find a place in the published *Life*. The topic
surfaces on 28 March 1772, in the company of Sir Alexander
Macdonald (later the object of a bitter quarrel) as well as Johnson.
Macdonald remarks: 'I have been correcting several Scotch accents
in my friend Boswell,' adding, for Johnson's consideration, the
generalized reflection: 'I doubt, Sir, if any Scotchman ever attains to
a perfect English pronunciation.' This provokes Johnson into his
most sustained treatment of these matters: the gist of his comments
is that Scotsmen may attain perfect English pronunciation, but
usually relax after getting near to perfection. Johnson knows that
people are able to discover his own local origins from his speech:
'So most Scotchmen may be found out. But, Sir, little aberrations
are of no disadvantage. I never catched Mallet in a Scotch accent;
and yet Mallet, I suppose, was past five-and-twenty before he came
to London.' The editors of the *Life* quote Johnson's later biography
of Mallet, from the prefaces to the English poets, where he describes
Mallet's efforts to distance himself from his Scottish origins (in
terms of name as well as accent) and the unpopularity he thus
incurred with other Scots—'he was the only Scot whom Scotchmen
did not commend' (*LSJ* ii. 158–9). Boswell, reading this, can
scarcely have been unaware of the possible applicability to his own
case. He too worried about having alienated his fellow-countrymen,
especially after his ill-advised move to the English bar. In 1788 he
wrote in the pages of his journal: 'Perhaps it is not wise in me to

[32] *In Search of a Wife*, 312, 323. Hume sent Reid a detailed commentary on the
latter's *Inquiry*, with a lapse from 'good English' noted—in fact, a Scotticism: see
The Letters of David Hume, ed. J. Y. T. Greig, 2 vols. (Oxford: Clarendon Press,
1932), i. 375–6.
[33] *Boswell in Extremes, 1776–1778*, ed. C. M. Weiss and F. A. Pottle (London:
Heinemann, 1970), 213.
[34] Miller, *Cockburn's Millennium*, 47.

keep myself so much abstracted as I do from Scotchmen of all ranks'[35] (though at the same time he was still put off by any 'vulgar Scotch' speech he encountered). It should be added that independent testimony confirms Johnson's assessment of Mallet: 'Mallet wrote good English,' wrote Giuseppe Baretti, 'and I remember that Richardson, author of the famous *Pamela*, used to say that Mallet was the only Scotchman who never confused "shall" and "will" in the future tense.'[36]

The conversation in 1772 prompted a further section in Boswell's narrative, revealing Johnson's wider views to us. Quotation at length is necessary for the full point to emerge:

> Upon another occasion I talked to him on this subject, having myself taken some pains to improve my pronunciation, by the aid of the late Mr Love, of the Drury-lane theatre, when he was a player at Edinburgh, and also of old Mrs Sheridan. Johnson said to me, 'Sir, your pronunciation is not offensive.' With this concession I was pretty well satisfied; and let me give my countrymen of North-Britain an advice not to aim at absolute perfection in this respect; not to speak *High English*, as we are apt to call what is far removed from the *Scotch*, but which is by no means *good English*, and makes 'the fools who use it,' truly ridiculous. Good English is plain, easy, smooth in the mouth of an unaffected English Gentleman. A studied and factitious pronunciation, which requires perpetual attention, and imposes personal constraint, is exceedingly disgusting. A small intermixture of provincial peculiarities may, perhaps, have an agreeable effect, as the notes of different birds concur in the harmony of the grove, and please more than if they were exactly alike.

This is plainly a more considered version of the views set forth in the exchange with Burke, cited above. And maybe Boswell has Burke, amongst others, in mind when he proceeds:

> I could name some gentleman of Ireland, to whom a slight proportion of the accent and recitative of that country is an advantage. The same observation will apply to the gentlemen of Scotland. I do not mean that we should speak as broad as a certain prosperous member of Parliament from that country [Henry Dundas]; though it has been well observed, that 'it has been of no small use to him; as it rouses the attention of the House by its

[35] *Boswell: The English Experiment, 1785–1789*, ed. Irma Lustig and F. A. Pottle (London: Heinemann, 1986), 204.

[36] Quoted by L. Collison-Morley, *Giuseppe Baretti* (London: John Murray, 1909), 164, from *La frustra letteraria*, no. 9. See also p. 163 on Hume, 'whose history is a pleasant reading, in spite of his frequent Scotticisms'.

uncommonness; and is equal to tropes and figures in a good English speaker.'

After this dig at his *bête noire* Dundas, Boswell goes on to commend his erstwhile friend the late Sir Gilbert Elliot, whom Lord Lisburne would also mention during the conversation in April 1775. The discussion then merges into consideration of the need for a dictionary to fix English pronunciations; this in turn leads to the merits of Sheridan's dictionary, and to what Johnson calls the 'disadvantage of being an Irishman' in this context—'what entitles Sheridan to fix the pronunciation of English?' (*LSJ* ii. 159–61).

This last remark has two barbs from Boswell's point of view: it challenges his own competence as a Scot to pontificate on matters of English usage; and it casts doubt on the wisdom of his period of tutelage under Sheridan. Nevertheless, the exchange ends amicably, and for the most part the two men maintained a fairly comfortable relationship with regard to national differences. By the end of Johnson's life Boswell was approaching the stage that he had reached when John Courtenay's poem (quoted in the *Life*) described him as 'scarce by North Britons now esteem'd a Scot' (*LSJ* i. 223). Years before, Johnson had paid Boswell a cheerfully back-handed compliment: the passage in the *Life* is dated 1 May 1773:

He observed that 'The Irish mix better with the English than the Scotch do; their language is nearer to English; as a proof of which, they succeed very well as players, which Scotchmen do not. Then, Sir, they have not that extreme nationality which we find in the Scotch. I will do you, Boswell, the justice to say, that you are the most *unscottified* of your countrymen. You are almost the only instance of a Scotchman that I have known, who did not at every other sentence bring in some other Scotchman.' (*LSJ* ii. 242)

The verdict that Boswell was 'unscottified' is true in one way, but it neglects the passionate, if romantic, attachment to Scottish history which marks Boswell's general view on life. He could indeed be said to manifest 'extreme nationality' in certain of his affinities. As Janet Adam Smith has finely said, Boswell's Scotland 'is the past as well as the present, a virtue to be practised, a source of feeling, with which sober rationality has little to do'.[37] It was thus a concept of

---

[37] Smith, 'Eighteenth-Century Ideas of Scotland', 115. This is part of a judicious survey of Boswell's feelings about Scotland.

the nation that had little to do with wealth and virtue in the Enlightenment sense, that is with the concept which belonged to political economists and philosophers, social thinkers and lawyers, who were shaping the real world of eighteenth-century Scotland. It is not very much of a simplification to say that the 'unscottified' Boswell lived in the prose world of London, while the 'scottified' Boswell clung on to the poetic world of Auchinleck.

This state of affairs can be sensed behind any number of short moments of by-play in the *Life*. To take a single example, the entry for 12 May 1778, when Johnson is asked by Boswell whether he values his friend for being a Scotchman: 'Nay, Sir,' replies Johnson, 'I do value you more for being a Scotchman. You are a Scotchman without the faults of a Scotchman. You would not have been so valuable as you are, had you not been a Scotchman' (*LSJ* iii. 347). Here Johnson does recognize Boswell's otherness, the quality of an 'unscottified' individual who was able to provide insights and experience not available to Johnson himself. It follows that the situation underlines a much greater enterprise, the tour of the Hebrides. Boswell, for his part, owed his anxiety to get Johnson to Scotland in some measure to a desire to redeem and validate his own Scottish identity. And, from Johnson's point of view, Boswell was valuable as a mediator and interpreter. Though Boswell did not have the Gaelic, this must surely have extended on many occasions to a role as a literal interpreter, when Johnson found difficulty with local speech—perhaps more often in Edinburgh and the Lowlands than in the remote stages of the journey.

Boswell's joking insistence on *scottifying* Johnson's palate, mentioned early on in the tour, on 18 August 1773, is another comic extension of the metaphor (*LSJ* v. 55). The more serious side of the issue turns up in Boswell's admission in footnotes to certain Scotticisms when he published his account. Even as late as the *Life* itself, Boswell referred to criticisms that he had received on this score, and inserted a small riposte in the text of his biography (*LSJ* v. 425). It is a final indication that, first and last, Boswell was open to the impress of the age and could not escape a strong awareness of his nationality, expressed most commonly in the identifiable use of English, both written and spoken, which almost all Scottish men and women displayed whatever they went.

III

Not all contemporaries would have agreed with Thomas Blacklock when he wrote of the difficulties which Scottish men had to endure before they could write 'with that facility & Chastness which occur naturally to an Englishman'.[38] As far as the written language was concerned, Alexander Carlyle believed that English was to some degree 'a foreign tongue', which, had to be learnt as a special exercise, and which tended to abound in circumlocutions or 'additional epithets' when used by writers such as Hume and Robertson.[39] Other commentators took different views; but no one doubted the visibility, or rather audibility, of the Scotticism. Response to this awareness could take the form of guilt, or defensiveness, or aggressive counter-claims, or fierce national pride: Boswell exemplifies many of these attitudes at one time or another. As John Clive has written: 'The sense of inferiority that expressed itself in imitation of English ways, and a sense of guilt regarding local mannerisms, was ... only one aspect of the complex meaning of provincialism.'[40] The link with the continent of Europe expressed itself in education, law, and medicine, but this distinctly anti-provincial force could not operate effectively in the area of language. Hence many stern patriots could be shamefaced about their 'incorrect' English usage. David Hume, the favourite of Paris, the luminary of half of the civilized world, could seek the advice of undistinguished English scribblers. So James Beattie, taken up by fashionable London, could write in 1775: 'I become every day more and more doubtful of the propriety of publishing Scotticisms. Our language (I mean English) is degenerating very fast; and many phrases, which I know to be Scottish idioms, have got into it of late years.'[41] Beattie was one who believed that the Scots learnt English as a dead language. Such views did not promote a living engagement with current English.

[38] *The Correspondence of Robert Dodsley*, ed. J. E. Tierney (Cambridge: Cambridge University Press, 1988), 283.

[39] Quoted by Smith, 'Eighteenth-Century Ideas of Scotland', 110.

[40] Clive, 'Scottish Renaissance', 239.

[41] William Forbes, *An Account of the Life and Writings of James Beattie, LL D* (New York: Brisban and Brannan, 1807), 399. For Beattie's 'totally preposterous scheme for the linguistic education of his son', avoiding contact with Scots, see Ross, *Lord Kames*, 73.

In these circumstances, it was almost inevitable that Boswell, with his feeble sense of a determinant self, should catch the general anxiety about the subject. He was certainly pleased to be told by Burke that he spoke 'very good English', but he was embarrassed by an implict contrast with Gibbon.[42] He was probably just as proud to be informed by his friend Andrew Erskine, 'when you was in England you spoke Scotch to Englishmen and English to Scotchmen', suggesting a kind of linguistic ambidexterity at which many Scots aimed.[43] Without doubt, it would have been the utmost mortification to him if he had read Nancy Temple's remark to her mother (the wife of Boswell's great friend): 'You cannot conceive a more unpolished girl than Miss B. is [Veronica Boswell]. She is really vulgar, speaks broad Scotch . . .' Boswell also sought to ensure that his youngest daughter Betsy retained the English accent that she had acquired at her boarding-school, and allowed her to make only brief visits to his London home lest she should be infected by the Scottish housekeeper.[44] By such standards did many English people judge matters of social acceptability. He possibly always remained as puzzled as he had been in Utrecht that 'although an Englishman often does not understand a Scot, it is rare that a Scot has trouble in understanding what an Englishman says.'[45] There were so many grounds for nervousness.

John MacQueen has recently observed that Boswell 'cannot be properly understood save in the context of the Scottish life and thought of the eighteenth century'.[46] This is nowhere more true than in that muddled area of socio-linguistics which is the home of

---

[42] *Boswell in Extremes*, 238 (another passage in the journal suppressed in the *Life*).

[43] *Boswell in Holland*, 172. On this topic, see also Marlies K. Danziger, in G. Clingham (ed.), *New Light on Boswell* (Cambridge: Cambridge University Press, 1991), 168–70.

[44] *Diaries of William John Temple*, ed. L. Bettany (Oxford: Oxford University Press, 1929), 70; *Boswell: The Great Biographer*, ed. M. K. Danziger and F. Brady (London: Heinemann, 1989), 97. However, Boswell was able to report a view more in accordance with that of Johnson (quoted at the start of this chapter); this was when Bennet Langton's daughter certified Veronica as 'quite free of the Scottish accent': *The English Experiment*, 292. On the other hand, in July 1794 Boswell told his son Jamie that the other son (Sandy) had acquired a 'broad pronunciation' which needed correction: Yale University Library, Boswell Papers, L132.

[45] *Boswell in Holland*, 172.

[46] John MacQueen, *Progress and Poetry* (Edinburgh: Scottish Academic Press, 1982), 109.

the Scotticism.[47] The dominance of Walter Scott spearheaded the efforts, which have become much more evident in recent years, to recapture a form of Scots as the medium of a living literature. Boswell, like Burns, died just to soon to witness this movement. He was still convinced that 'the Scottish language is being lost every day, and in a short time will become quite unintelligible'.[48] It is a piquant thought that when the travellers came to Auchinleck, on 2 November 1773, the 14-year-old Robert Burns was growing up near Alloway, less than twenty miles west of Boswell's home. Although Burns and Boswell were neighbours, they existed in different stations of life, and the numerous friends and acquaintances that they had in common did not lead to a meeting—just a respectful letter from the former to the latter. As for the infant Walter Scott, born in 1771, he was living in the shadow of the Old College, although when the travellers passed through Edinburgh, he had been sent to the countryside, on the edge of the Borders, for the sake of his health. We have here one of the near misses of history, rather as when Bach failed to make contact with Handel after his long walk from Cöthen to Halle. If only Boswell had known it, the poet who was to render a feeling of linguistic inferiority absurd was right on his doorstep; and the novelist who was to give Scottish culture a glamour all over the western world was already abroad in the streets of Edinburgh. If Boswell could have imagined as much, he might not have worried so much about Scotticisms; but then he might have been so secure in his national identity as to follow dutifully in his father's footsteps; he might never have broken away, to London and to Johnson. The *Tour* owes not just its central figure but its whole *raison d'être* to the fact that Boswell did break away—irresolutely—from his Scottish background.[49]

---

[47] For a primary definition in answer to the question 'What is Scots?', and useful background on the state of the language at the end of the 18th cent., see the excellent study by Graham Tulloch, *The Language of Sir Walter Scott* (London: André Deutsch, 1980), esp. pp. 167–81.

[48] *Boswell in Holland*, 161.

[49] There is much useful discussion in recent work on Boswell's Scottish inheritance: see e.g. Andrew Noble, 'James Boswell: Scotland's Prodigal Son', in T. M. Devine (ed.), *Improvement and Enlightenment* (Edinburgh: John Donald, 1989), 22–42; and Kenneth G. Simpson, *The Protean Scot: The Crisis of Identity in Eighteenth-Century Scottish Culture* (Aberdeen: Aberdeen University Press, 1988), 117–43. Boswell's attempt to integrate the 'Scottish' and 'English' elements in his nature seems to me to be only distantly related to the wider search for a British

identity explored by Linda Colley in *Britons*, or the increasingly narrow sense of nationalism which is the subject of Gerald Newman's book on *The Rise of English Nationalism* (New York: St Martin's Press, 1987). Boswell was at once too individualistic, too complex, and too cosmopolitan to fit easily into such patterns of behaviour. Newman at one point (p. 126) identifies hero-worship as one of the instruments by which 'the individual identifies himself with what he has been taught to believe is the Character of his nation'. Samuel Johnson is mentioned as one of the 'new English heroes' of the period. Unfortunately, the source that Newman quotes— Churchill's *Rosciad*—actually refers to Ben Jonson, not Samuel, as 'Johnson'. Such mistakes pervade Newman's interesting argument, rendering it less cogent because of misdated passages, misreadings of tone, and a plain inability to understand the surface meaning of a text.

Finally, it should be noted that Boswell was as unembarrassed as Johnson by his failure to understand Gaelic. The notion that *Volk* = *Sprache* was only just emerging, with Herder, and there was as yet no general sense that the social comprehension of a people rested on linguistic comprehension. For an interesting discussion of relevant issues, see Jonathan Steinberg, 'The Historian and the *Questione della Lingua*', in P. Burke and R. Porter (eds.), *The Social History of Language* (Cambridge: Cambridge University Press, 1987), 198–209.

8

Johnson, Boswell, and Anti-Scottish Sentiment

Hester Piozzi thought that Johnson's dislike for the Scottish nation was a matter of common information. Well before Boswell's *Life* had enshrined familiar stories which lend credence to this view of her friend, she remarked: 'Mr Johnson's hatred of the Scotch is so well known, and so many of his *bons mots* expressive of that hatred have been already repeated in so many books and pamphlets . . .' (*JM* i. 264–5).[1] The question arises, from where exactly did all this stock of familiar knowledge derive? And when did it originate? It can be shown that it was the *Journey* which provoked the loudest clamour against Johnson in Scotland, as one who exhibited prejudice and a narrow nationalism. However, the roots of this suspicion went back as far as the first edition of the *Dictionary*; and matters would not be improved by the disputes between Johnson and James Macpherson. But there are two further complicating factors. The first is the general climate of anti-Scottish feeling which pervaded England in the third quarter of the eighteenth century—a vein of popular sentiment affecting political alignments, professional relations, and artistic trends. Second, there was the co-presence of Boswell on the Hebridean tour, which led in due course to the younger man's candid account of the trip in 1785. Boswell's interest in what he regarded as a typical Johnsonian prejudice went along with an intense anxiety about his own Scottish identity, and together these were to create a highly coloured—and perhaps misleading—portrayal of Johnson as a hostile witness on matters Scottish. Yet the *Journey* itself is plainly deeply sympathetic to many of the people and social mores encountered by the travellers.

This is a paradox which has never been fully explored. In this chapter I aim first to give a brief review of the climate of anti-Scottish feeling which had prevailed for a number of years prior to

---

[1] Mrs Piozzi goes on to tell a story about Johnson's likening Scotland to hell after returning from the Hebrides.

the Hebridean tour. Second, I shall attempt to trace the history of Johnson's reputation, earned or unearned, for dogmatic scorn of the Scottish race. Appended to this is some brief consideration of Boswell's own psychological state on the question of nationality. If this information is applied to the text of the *Journey*, its ideology may appear more precise and coherent.

I

It is possible to explain the unprecedented wave of feeling against Scotland by a number of factors. One might, for instance, interrogate the English people themselves, and search out hidden insecurities which induced them (on their first roll to empire, after world-wide successes in the Seven Years War) to turn on their immediate neighbours. Conceivably, a psychological process was at work, whereby a nation confident of its macrocosmic role felt the need to justify itself within the fragile federation which made up the island microcosm. An argument in support of this view would be that local hostilities tended to die out as a larger threat emerged from the North American colonies: as we approach and pass the year 1776, we hear less of the dangers to be expected from a creeping Scotticization of national life. The height of anti-Caledonian sentiment coincides with the heyday of Wilkesite activity; as soon as major foreign concerns arose to relegate questions such as electoral reform to a minor position, then the panic over an alleged Scottish take-over begins to diminish.

Paul Langford has remarked that 'it is difficult to account for the extent and depth of anti-Scottish feeling in the 1760s and 1770s without reference to political circumstances.' Langford points to the capital which was made of the Stuart legacy, something which carried a potent charge in the aftermath of the Jacobite risings. Naturally, this card was most commonly played in respect of Bute, since his own family name was Stuart. Langford puts it this way:

At issue . . . was the power of Lord Bute and the patronage which he supposedly directed into the acquisitive hands of his countrymen. There was also the obvious convenience [for Wilkes and his supporters] of linking George III's allegedly authoritarian tendencies with the Scottish ancestry of the Stuarts. . . . National prejudice was strengthened by the sensitivity of London opinion to the sheer number of newcomers. In 1787 it was reckoned that a century before, there had been no more than 50 Scots and 28 Irishmen in the capital, whereas it now seemed that there were almost as many as its English inhabitants. This implausible calculation was at least significant for its assumption that there had been a huge increase in the interim.[2]

There are several points which bear attention here. Not least is the fact that the panic was very largely a London-based, rather than an English phenomenon. Just as, in 1745, we hear much of the fears and tensions felt in London as the Pretender marched southwards (and very little of the alarms which may or may not have been experienced in the rest of the nation), so the rabid anti-Scots campaign is orchestrated from the capital. The Wilkesite movement as such was essentially a London affair: it involved city politics, the concerns of Middlesex electors, metropolitan issues, the grievances of Spitalfields weavers and Clerkenwell artisans. It had comparatively little to do with the emerging proletariat of the Midlands and north, or with the wider drive for parliamentary reform in the unrepresented boroughs in the provinces. All this is understandable enough. The wave which brought Scots into positions of power may or may not have been exaggerated, but, in so far as anything of the kind did occur, it certainly happened in London. This is where the parliamentarians, placemen, doctors, lawyers, painters, and writers ended up. They were drawn by economic, cultural, and social attractions as well as by any crude political magnetism.

This brings us to a second consideration. The immigrant Scottish community in the south formed a strong nexus running across the various occupational groups. Langford recognizes this briefly:

The swarm of Scotsman offended English susceptibilities and annoyed envious English competitors. An influx of Scottish doctors focused resentment on peculiarly sensitive relationships, commercial, medical, personal. It was believed that Bute's patronage was merely the most prominent expression of a national tendency: Scotsmen always favoured their own, to the detriment of native-born Englishmen. . . . The truth was that almost nothing the Scots did . . . would satisfy their hosts. Under the English Poor Law Scots who had not gained a legal settlement had no entitlement to relief. Hence the need of Scottish (like other alien) communities to provide for themselves. Yet when they did so they were criticized for encouraging national prejudices. No doubt for this reason,

---

[2] Paul Langford, *A Polite and Commercial People: England, 1727–1783* (Oxford: Clarendon Press, 1989), 327; see also pp. 214–18, 568, 589, 608.

the celebrated Scots Society at Norwich renamed itself the Society of Universal Goodwill in 1787.[3]

Undoubtedly, the Scots did stick together. As early as the 1720s, when the poet James Thomson moved down from Edinburgh, he was able to join a cohesive group of London Scots, and enter a community of artists and intellectuals who enjoyed the sponsorship of Duncan Forbes, Walpole's 'fixer' for Scottish affairs—very much in the role occupied later by Henry Dundas. By the middle of the century there were well-known Caledonian haunts in the English capital. The most important of these meeting-places was probably the British Coffee House opposite the royal mews at Charing Cross—'British' at this time was a code-word for Anglo-Scottish, whether in a serious or a mocking sense. This was a haunt of the North British community from its establishment in Queen Anne's time. It was rebuilt in 1770, to a design by none other than Robert Adam. Alexander Carlyle describes several visits in his auto-biography: at one time it was kept by Mrs Anderson, the sister of John Douglas, bishop, book-collector, and member of Johnson's Club, who came from Fife. In January 1774 Gibbon dined 'at the Breetish Coffee house *with Garrick, Coleman, Goldsmith, Macpherson, John* Hume &c.' (the spelling is designed to illustrate the Scots pronunciation of 'British' and 'Home'). Four years later John Wilkes dined there with Lord Kelly—that is, the Scottish composer the Earl of Kellie—who was well known to Boswell. Another meeting-place for the exiles was in Half Moon Street, frequented by Robert Adam. There was a dining-club in Sackville Row, attended by Carlyle, Home, Adam Ferguson, Robertson, and Wedderburn. More subversive perhaps was the home of the Glasgow-born modeller James Tassie, which stood in Leicester Fields. Among those who congregated here were members of the Highland Society of London, headed by Boswell's friend George Dempster.[4]

---

[3] Ibid. 327–8.

[4] Information on this paragraph is drawn from a wide range of scattered sources, but see in particular Alexander Carlyle, *Anecdotes and Characters of the Times*, ed. J. Kinsley (London: Oxford University Press, 1973), 175–6 and *passim*; *The Letters of Edward Gibbon*, ed. J. E. Norton, 3 vols. (London: Cassell, 1956), ii. 2; Doreen Yarwood, *Robert Adam* (London, Dent, 1970), 97–8; John Fleming, *Robert Adam and his Circle*, 2nd edn. (London: 1978), 248–50; John Carswell, *The Prospector* (London: Cresset, 1950), 211; E. C. Mossner, *The Life of David Hume* (Oxford: Clarendon Press, 1980), 394; Bryant Lillywhite, *London Coffee Houses* (London:

Through such associations, mostly loose and informal, the Scottish community made its presence felt in London. Visiting luminaries like Adam Smith or Hume could be entertained by a network of permanent London residents: their books could be promoted, and their paintings exhibited. It was this capacity for self-support and solidarity which provoked much of the English fear—and also, no doubt, the envy to which Langford refers. Johnson himself refers to 'a national combination so invidious, that their friends cannot defend it', but this is matched by a 'spirit of enterprise' which enabled the Scots 'to make their way to employment, riches, and distinction (*JWI* 160–1). The expression of this manic dislike of all things Scottish came in various forms. Two of the most notable means for ventilating hostility were the literary campaign surrounding the *North Briton*, and the explosion of graphic satires. The onset of this latter phenomenon has been picturesquely described by Michael Duffy, who implicitly aligns it with wider xenophobic trends of the age:

Hostility rose to a peak when the Scottish Earl of Bute, a political outsider and royal favourite, became Prime Minister . . . at the expense of the patriot hero William Pitt and of the old Whig hierarchy headed by the Duke of Newcastle. The result was not just a peak of Scotophobia but a veritable volcanic eruption whose lava flowed on into subsequent decades. More prints assailed the 'Jack-boot' than any other politician of the eighteenth century. Scotsmen were both ridiculed on stage and also hooted out of the audience at theatres. The prints recited and elaborated on all the prejudices built up against the 'beggarly Scotch' from their lousiness to their maladroit English pronunciation. At the root of it all was the fear that, in their clannishness, Scots in high places would give the pickings of English jobs and honours to their barbarous, impoverished fellow-countrymen, and each time a Scot reached such a position the printmakers portrayed him inviting hordes of his beggarly cronies to walk down to London . . . to enjoy the perks of 'moneyland'.[5]

Two comments are in order here. First, we should not exaggerate the extent and regularity of what might be termed 'real-life'

Allen and Unwin, 1963), 132–4. Carlyle in particular indicates the wide range of informal contacts between the Scots community, involving men like 'Doctor's Pitcairn, Armstrong, Home and myself' (p. 176).

[5] Michael Duffy, *The English Satirical Print: The Englishman and the Foreigner* (Cambridge: Chadwyck-Healey, 1986), 20.

offensiveness towards the Scots in London. It is true that in his earliest days in London Boswell witnessed an outcry against Highland officers, with shouts of 'No Scots', an episode which he described in the *London Journal*:[6] but on other occasions he tended to lead the theatrical riots, and certainly nothing took place which could deter him from going back to the playhouse. Most of the hostility was expressed in the mediate forms of writing and engraving, rather than in openly offensive behaviour. Second, if people thought that the Scots would act 'clannishly' because of their social traditions, they were making an elementary error. The clans were essentially a Highland institution, whereas the Scots who came south and prospered in the capital were overwhelmingly Lowlanders—mostly Protestants, Hanoverians, and at least fellow-travellers with the Union. Few of them doubted that the Union, whatever its iniquities or injustices, created a *carrière ouverte aux talents* for the Scotsman who arrived in London.

What, then, was the reality underlying the garish caricature in the press of 'a flight of Highlanders, kilts spread like parachutes, descending on the capital'?[7] Was there anything in the recurrent charge of a continuing rump of disloyal Scots, the abundance of 'Papists and Plaids'[8] whom the Bishop of Worcester detected in Bristol in the later 1740s? Clearly, this was an exaggeration, and one that hostile commentators developed for their own tactical ends. It is significant that the charge of disloyalty reached a crescendo not in the immediate aftermath of the Jacobite risings, but almost twenty years later, when the unpopular Bute provided a focus for lingering anti-Scottish resentments. The talent for abuse shared by Wilkes and Churchill permitted a campaign of damaging point and particularity. Also, this political furore arose at almost the same time as the controversy surrounding Macpherson's Ossian, so that wider literary and cultural issues were drawn into the same intellectual matrix. Moreover, a third factor supervened in 1761, with the publication of the last two volumes of Hume's *History*, widely regarded as representing special pleading for the

---

[6] *Boswell's London Journal, 1762–1763*, ed. F. A. Pottle (London: Heinemann, 1950), 71–2.

[7] Quoted by Alastair Smart, *The Life and Art of Allan Ramsay* (London: Routledge, 1952), 103.

[8] Maud Wyndham, *Chronicles of the Eighteenth Century* (London: Hodder and Stoughton, 1924), 123.

Tory ideology, and thus an implicit dismissal of the Hanoverian dispensation which had overlooked affairs since 1714—if not, indeed, of the Whig view of the state which had largely prevailed since 1688. In combination, these factors provided an easy handle for the anti-Scottish campaigners to grasp. For instance, Churchill's poem 'The Journey' (written *c.*1763, published posthumously 1765) contains digs at Ossian and Hume along with Bute (Macpherson's choice of Bute as a patron served to unite two prongs of anti-Scottish attack). Small wonder that the poet John Armstrong, also satirized in the poem, complained that Wilkes was bent on 'abusing my country'.[9] The targets had become so various that many Scots understandably felt that a generalized form of racist propaganda was in full sway.

Of course, there were some objective historical circumstances which underlay this onset of prejudice. So far we have worked from the other end—that is to say we have considered the pathology of the English response. But the tide of anti-Scottish sentiment needs to be regarded from the Scottish end also. What induced people from the north to go on braving hostility and ridicule as they made their way south? First of all, there was the simple matter of business. Since Scotland no longer had its own parliament, it followed that local representative peers kept their own court. Secondly, a good deal of important 'Scottish' legal business was done in London. So it was with the famous Douglas case, in which Boswell took such an active interest. This was originally heard in Edinburgh, by Auchinleck, Kames, and Monboddo amongst others (see below, p. 227)—but it was settled in the House of Lords in February 1769; a leading part in the proceedings was played by Lord Mansfield, whom many Englishmen had long regarded as a crypto-Jacobite merely on the basis of family connections. Alexander Carlyle attended the proceedings, and reported that 'the Rejoicings in Scotland were very Great on this Occasion'. (It might be added that only a few days earlier Carlyle had been at the first night of John Home's tragedy *The Fatal Discovery* and had noted: 'Garrick had been Justly allarm'd at the jealousy and Dislike which prevailed at that time against Ld Bute and the Scotch, and had advised him to change the Title of Rivine into That of The Fatal

[9] *The Poetical Works of Charles Churchill*, ed. D. Grant (Oxford: Clarendon Press, 1956), 442, 560.

Discovery, and had provided a Student of Oxford who had appear'd at the Rehearsals as the Author, and wishd Home of all things to Remain Conceald till the Play had its Run.'[10]) In short, many putatively—as well as genuinely—Scottish controversies were fought out in the south. London was the locus of many such debates in the years after the Union.

However, things went a little deeper than that. It was not just that forty-five seats in the House of Commons were allotted to Scottish constituencies. Increasingly, men of Scottish origin took over in English seats. Between 1734 and 1832, as G. P. Judd describes it, they 'invaded every species of constituency. Seven Scots sat for English counties, 171 for English rotten boroughs, and 99 for English open boroughs,' others represented Welsh seats. By contrast, few Englishmen were elected to Scottish constituencies. As Judd comments: 'The appearance of Scots in increasing numbers aggravated the traditional resentment which the English bore them. . . . Also, particularly in the first half of the eighteenth century, the unmistakable burr of the Scottish accent made them unduly conspicuous in the House, to the point that the Scottish dreaded the open ridicule which their participation in debate often provoked.' The words of Henry Fox, cited by Judd, have an ominous ring of truth: 'Every man has at some time or other found a Scotchman in his way, and everybody has therefore damned the Scotch: and this hatred their excessive nationality has continually inflamed.' Fox was pointing to the tendency of the Scottish members to form a 'solid phalanx' on parliamentary questions. We should reflect that the famous '45' in the *North Briton* was a signifier not just of the 1745 rebellion, but also of the forty-five Scottish MPs.[11]

Along with the members themselves, came a whole retinue of lawyers, clients, place-seekers, men of business. It was Scottish success at the bar, partly based on the long tradition of excellent legal training in the northern universities, which did much to fuel national unpopularity. A Scottish lawyer of a later generation, John Buchan, recognized this fact, although he presented a somewhat unflattering picture of his countrymen as they made their bid for success in the courts:

---

[10] Carlyle, *Anecdotes and Characters*, 261–3.
[11] This paragraph is based chiefly on G. P. Judd, *Members of Parliament, 1734–1832* (New Haven, Conn.: 1955; repr. Hamden, Conn.: Archon, 1972), 12–14.

They strove without much success to acquire an English accent, and Mr Adam Smith was envied because Balliol had trimmed the roughness of his Fife tongue. They cultivated a thing called rhetoric, which was supposed to be canonical use of language freed from local vulgarities, and in the shabby old College [Edinburgh] Mr Hugh Blair lectured on that dismal science with much acceptance. In their writings they laboriously assisted each other to correct the solecisms of the northern idiom, and a year or two later, when David Hume lay on his death-bed, it was the jest of a caustic Lord of Session that the philosopher confessed not his sins but his Scotticisms.[12]

There may be a level of condescension here, born of Buchan's own successful transition from a lad born in Perth of Lowland farming stock, via Brasenose, to a distinguished public servant with a manor-house outside Oxford. The truth seems to. be that the Scottish legal profession prospered because its members took more care over matters of courtroom presentation and delivery. As noted elsewhere, some individuals like Wedderburn made a virtue of their apparent deficiencies, and (much to Boswell's horrified amazement) achieved extra declamatory power in their pleadings by reason of their Scottish tang. By one means or another, the Scottish made their way at the bar or in Parliament. This rendered it peculiarly vexatious to Boswell that he succeeded as an advocate neither on the Scottish nor the English circuit; and that he failed in his efforts to achieve a seat in the Commons.

Even more prominent than the lawyers was the corps of affluent Scottish physicians. This phenomenon was apparent early in the century. When he first came down to London, James Thomson wrote to a friend back home (the date is July 1725): 'Scotland is really fruitful of Surgeons; they come here like flocks of Vultures every day, and by a mercifull providential kind of instinct transport themselves to foreign Countries.'[13] But many others stayed in the capital, and no one could miss them. Alexander Carlyle found more than one club of physicians in London which welcomed him to their convivial meetings. A string of well-known and, indeed, fashionable London doctors made no secret of their Scottish roots. There was no need for them to do so, because the medical training available in Scottish universities, especially at Edinburgh, contrasted

[12] John Buchan, *Sir Walter Scott* (1932; repr. London: Cassell, 1987), 13.
[13] *James Thomson: Letters and Documents*, ed. A. D. McKillop (Lawrence, Kan.: University of Kansas, 1958), 12–13.

sharply with the lack of anything worthy of the name in the English universities. So we find a succession of men like George Cheyne, Sir John Pringle, William and John Hunter, and George Fordyce, active in English medical circles—quite apart from those who remained at home, like William Cullen and Robert Whytt, but who exercised great influence through their theories and writings. Not all the Scots who came to practise in London made their fortune: Tobias Smollett was one who failed in this quest, and he took it out on rivals who tended to be more successful and, often, fellow-Scots. As medicine slowly evolved from primitive physic to a quasi-scientific discipline, the contribution of Scots was immense. Some had taken advantage of the long-established links with the Netherlands to pursue their studies at Leiden or Utrecht, where Boerhaave's men continued to advance the subject.[14] It was at Edinburgh that the medical Enlightenment took root as far as Britain was concerned, and Boerhaave's system influenced medical practice throughout the three kingdoms, trickling down gradually to the most remote corners and backward areas of clinical treatment. As is well known, medicine at this time was politicized to a remarkable degree, and one of the threads in the complex tapestry of these ideological disputes was the issue of nationality. Certainly, the fact that so many successful doctors were recognizably, often proudly, Scottish can have done nothing to abate English fears.

Finally, it is crucial to understand that the Union had not really turned Scotland into an integral part of a single nation-state. As we have been reminded recently, no reigning monarch visited Scotland throughout the entire eighteenth century (the most memorable royal presence had been that of 'Butcher' Cumberland in 1746). Indeed, for most people in the larger nation, 'Scotland was an alien country'.[15] This made it possible for prejudices to flourish; and it underlay the attitudes of Samuel Johnson, a representative member of the English community in this respect, as he was in many others.

[14] See Andrew Cunningham, 'Medicine to Calm the Mind: Boerhaave's Medical System, and Why it was Adopted in Edinburgh', in A. Cunningham and R. French (eds.), *The Medical Enlightenment of the Eighteenth Century* (Cambridge: Cambridge University Press, 1990), 40–66.

[15] Daniel Szecki and David Hayman, 'John Bull's Other Kingdoms', in C. Jones (ed.), *Britain in the First Age of Party* (London: Hambledon, 1987), 241, 243.

II

As we noted at the start, Hester Piozzi's *Anecdotes of the late Samuel Johnson* drew attention to the vein of anti-Scottish feeling in Johnson. The ultimate source for this information can be found in *Thraliana*, where the diarist had similarly made it clear that Johnson was already notorious on this score: 'We all know how well he loved to abuse the Scotch, & indeed to be abused by them in return.'[16] A number of stories are told to reinforce the point. But how did Johnson acquire this reputation? Few of his famous salvoes against the Caledonian race were published in his lifetime. Until the time of Piozzi's *Anecdotes* (1786) and, especially, Boswell's *Life* (1791), there were few biographic records which went into the necessary detail. Hawkins's *Life of Samuel Johnson* (1787) remarks that his prejudices 'were so strong and deeply rooted, more especially against Scotchmen and Whigs',[17] as well as relating the history of the Ossian dispute. But this was, of course, when Johnson was safely in his grave. What does not seem to have been fully explained is the way in which Johnson early acquired this name for hostility towards the Scottish nation. The furore which arose over the *Journey* had its origins in events spread over many years, and can only be properly understood if we consider the entire thrust of Johnson's intellectual career.[18]

As good a lead as any is provided by Arthur Murphy, in his *Essay on the Life and Genius of Dr Johnson* (1792). When Murphy reaches the publication of the *Journey* in 1775, he seeks to account for the fact that the book received a mixed reception. Along with warm praise, it met condemnation 'as a work of hostility to the Scottish nation'. Accordingly Murphy sets out to explore this aspect of his subject. He narrates a firsthand story in which

[16] Hester Lynch Piozzi, *Thraliana*, ed. K. C. Balderston, 2nd edn., 2 vols. (Oxford: Clarendon Press, 1951), i. 165.

[17] Sir John Hawkins, *The Life of Samuel Johnson, LL D* (London, 1787), 71.

[18] Giuseppe Baretti noted in the margin of his copy of the Johnson–Thrale correspondence (as published by Mrs Piozzi in 1788) that Johnson was a '*true-born Englishman*' who hated the Scots along with the French, Dutch, and Hanoverians. See Donald C. Gallup, 'Baretti's Reputation in England', in F. W. Hilles (ed.), *The Age of Johnson* (New Haven, Conn.: Yale University Press, 1949), 375. Baretti cannot be regarded as a wholly reliable witness, but he had known Johnson for many years and was in a good position to assess this matter.

Johnson describes to Murphy the difference between the Scots and the Irish; and he gives a variant of the immortal scene in which Boswell first met Johnson at Tom Davies's bookshop (Murphy has 'Davis'). It is worth setting down Murphy's version as a foil to the better-known form the exchange takes in Boswell: ' "I find," said Mr Boswell, "that I am come to London at a bad time, when great popular prejudice has gone forth against us North Britons; but when I am talking to you, I am talking to a large and liberal mind, and you know that I cannot *help coming from Scotland*." "Sir," said Johnson, "no more can the rest of your countrymen." ' Underlying this verbal repartee may be a proverb, quoted for instance by the Highland traveller Edward Burt: 'There never came a fool out of Scotland.'[19] (There was a nineteenth-century maxim cited by Archbishop Whately: 'An Englishman is never happy but when he is miserable, a Scotchman never at home but when he is abroad, and an Irishman never at peace but when he is fighting'— but I have not been able to trace this back to Johnson's era.) The suggestion is that the Scots knew which side their bread was buttered on when they made for the English capital.

Murphy proceeds with quite a thoughtful analysis of the grounds of Johnson's supposed prejudice:

He had other reasons that helped to alienate him from the natives of Scotland. Being a cordial well-wisher to the constitution in Church and State, he did not think that Calvin and John Knox were proper founders of a national religion. . . . It is probable that his dislike of Calvinism mingled sometimes with his reflections on the natives of the country. The association of ideas could not be easily broken; but it is well known that he loved and respected many gentlemen from that part of the island. Dr Robertson's History of Scotland, and Dr Beattie's Essays, were subjects of his constant praise. . . . He scorned to enter Scotland as a spy. . . . He went into Scotland to survey men and manners.

Some modern commentators might wish to attenuate the degree of Johnson's respect for orthodoxy in matters of Church and state; but Murphy was writing from close firsthand knowledge, and with the relative objectivity of an Irishman. As he observes: 'Mr Boswell, Dr Rose of Chiswick, Andrew Millar, Mr Hamilton the printer, and the late Mr Strahan, were among [Johnson's] most intimate

---

[19] See *Beyond the Highland Line*, ed. A. J. Youngson (London: Collins, 1974), 157.

friends': it is clear that the Scots who were admitted into Johnson's circle of friends tended to be those with less radical or revolutionary principles. What emerges from the discussion in Murphy (which leads into a brief passage on the Ossian controversy) is the fact that those intimate with Johnson plainly recognized that he had an inherent problem when it came to Scottish affairs, though they usually believed—like Murphy—that he had done his best to restrain his prejudices in the *Journey* and had managed to produce a balanced survey of Scottish men and manners in the book.[20]

In his *Life* Boswell points to a slender thread of prejudice as early as the poem *London* (1738), although the content is sometimes more favourable towards Scotland than the overall tone might suggest:

> For who would leave, unbribed, Hibernia's land,
> Or change the rocks of Scotland for the Strand?
> There none are swept by sudden fate away,
> But all whom hunger spares, with age decay:
> Here malice, rapine, accident, conspire,
> And now a rabble rages, now a fire.

In any case, the apparent slurs on the Scottish race in the poem are casual flicks of the satirist, echoing Juvenal's thrusts without any strong animus against the Scots as such. Nothing very relevant appears in the *Miscellaneous Observations on the Tragedy of Macbeth* (1745) or in the *Rambler* (1750–2). Unquestionably, it was a few playful entries in the *Dictionary* (1755) which first spread abroad the idea of Johnson's implacable hostility towards the Scots. Years later these comments were still recalled to form the basis of most Scottish assaults on his character. Above all, it was the unlucky definition of 'oats' which caused outrage: some commentators have suggested that the entry was not intended as a joke against the Scots, but simply as a statement of fact—a view which seems not to allow for Johnson's unquenchable humour. At all events, Johnson was never able to live down the effect of these words. From 1755 onwards he was regarded by the people of the north—and probably by others—as an inveterate opponent of Scotland, always ready to cast an aspersion or to throw a flippant aside.

---

[20] For this passage in Murphy, see *JM* i. 428–32.

Once Johnson had met Boswell, it is likely that the younger man's loquacity—allied to a natural pride in his new acquaintance—permitted the circulation of stories which encouraged the prevailing beliefs about Johnson. Thus, even if the world at large had to wait until 1791 to learn of a particular exchange which took place in 1763 (within a few days of the initial encounter at Tom Davies's shop), it may be that men and women about town learnt straight away of Johnson's reasons for quitting the company of Dr John Campbell—'I used to go pretty often to Campbell's on a Sunday evening, till I began to consider that the Shoals of Scotchmen who flocked about him might probably say, when any thing of mine was well done, "Ay, ay, he has learnt this of CAWMELL!" ' (*LSJ* i. 418).

The key issue was plainly Ossian. At the outset of his nodal discussion in the *Journey* Johnson states: 'I suppose my opinion of the poems of Ossian is already discovered' (*JWI* 118). It is not exactly clear how this scepticism could have become public knowledge, since I can find no evidence that Johnson had committed himself in print prior to the *Journey*. No doubt he had been free enough in asserting in private conversation that the 'poem of Fingal was a mere unconnected rhapsody' (a remark passed on to Boswell by Dr Maxwell, and entered in the *Life* arbitrarily under the year 1770: *LSJ*, ii. 126). But Macpherson made no move until after the *Journey* had been published, though according to Boswell's letter to Johnson of 2 February 1775, it was 'confidently' told in Edinburgh that 'before your book came out he sent to you, to let you know that he understood you meant to deny the authenticity of Ossian's poems' (*LSJ* ii. 295). It is possible that the publisher, William Strahan, showed Macpherson the offending passage in advance of publication. Around 15 January 1775 Macpherson sent Strahan an 'ostensible letter' addressed to Johnson, requesting the deletion of 'injurious expressions' from the text of the *Journey*. Soon afterwards Macpherson drafted an 'advertisement'—in effect a withdrawal and apology—to be inserted in copies of the book. Johnson, unsurprisingly, refused, and it was this which elicited from Macpherson his final threatening letter. No copy of that letter has survived, and we can only infer its contents. But it was this same communication which inspired Johnson's immortal letter of defiance, beginning 'I received your foolish and impudent letter.' This eventually found its way into the press and, as Boswell stated in the *Life*, it was afterwards 'frequently re-published' (*LSJ* ii. 297). From this time on (i.e. from 20 January 1775), anyone taking sides on the question of Johnson's alleged anti-Scottish bias would have to take account of this famous episode.[21]

According to Thomas Percy, the two protagonists had met once, some time prior to July 1764, when they had engaged in discussion of the authenticity of Ossian (*LSJ* ii. 513). But it scarcely needs to be said that the matter was much more than a private quarrel between two strong-minded individuals. The contest enacted a large eighteenth-century *Kulturkampf*, with the debate over alleged forgery (as in the case of Chatterton) shadowing a broader discussion of the meaning of creativity, not to add the relation of 'authenticity' to literary property in the legal sense.[22] More relevantly to this book, the controversy hinged on warring concepts of the age—primitivism and civilization, oral and written culture, ancient and modern versions of epic. More particularly, it was a battle about the survival of an indigenous Scottish literature, and about the endurance of a body of customs and beliefs in the Highlands, unaffected by the English take-over of the Scottish nation in terms of its institutions and political system. Modern scholars have shown how the Ossian controversy fed on lasting resentments among the Scottish people. To be anti-Ossian was therefore to do more than to take sides on a matter of narrow palaeographic scholarship. It could be interpreted as being anti-Scots.

Up to a point, Johnson may have been unfairly treated. Unlike most of the participants in the long-running Ossian affair, he actually *was* interested in strict palaeographic matters: his concern with literary forgery went back as far as the affair of William Lauder—yet another Scot—in 1751. And, as we have seen (Chapter 4, above), his very decision to take a trip into the Highlands expressed a more open-minded attitude towards the primitive than most educated Englishmen of his time would have been likely to display. Broadly speaking, too, he was right about the Ossian manuscripts, at least in the sense that nobody has ever managed to

---

[21] For an account of the quarrel with Macpherson, see *LSJ* ii. 510–13.

[22] This is a topic much discussed in recent scholarship: see e.g. Ian Haywood, *The Making of History* (London: Associated University Presses, 1986).

come up with unimpeachable 'originals' for the Gaelic text. But there is a certain blunt finality about his judgements in the *Journey* which understandably riled his opponents. He might have done better to compose a detailed pamphlet, along the lines of his political writings of the 1770s: no one was more capable of marshalling a coherent case on complicated matters of this kind, especially where issues of a broad historical character were at stake. He could then have set out his view of Ossian in a more closely argued and documented fashion. More to the point here, he could have separated the issue from his general survey of Highland lore. As it was, his position on the Fingal question deflected attention from his positive comments on life in remote Scotland, so that it was many years before the warmth and sympathy of his human insights gained wide recognition. The reputation of a remarkably acute general survey suffered because Johnson had implicated himself in a more localized area of ideological strife. If he had kept Ossian for another occasion, his *Journey* would have seemed less offensive to the Scots. As it was, the book simply confirmed the impression that they had already formed of his bigoted outlook.

As soon as word got round that Johnson was to make his tour of Scotland, newspapers (no doubt alerted by Boswell) began to comment on the approaching event. Numerous versions of what was in store, both serious and facetious, were presented to the public in the summer of 1773. Those writers politically hostile to Johnson intimated that the outcome would be a work of Jacobite propaganda. Then, while the tour was actually in progress, stories continued to appear in the press, conveying both true and false information indiscriminatingly. One paragraph, reprinted in the *Caledonian Mercury* of 20 October, passed on the intelligence that Johnson had travelled north in order to propagate the growth of potatoes in Scotland. Another item in the London press reported the Scots' belief that Johnson was being punished for his *Dictionary* definition of 'oats' by having to eat oatmeal cake while confined on Skye. It would be going too far to describe this as an orchestrated press campaign, but there is no doubt that both London and Scottish newspapers took advantage of the occasion to unload some of their long-held resentments against Johnson.[23]

---

[23] Newspaper stories are cited from Helen L. McGuffie, *Johnson in the London Press* (New York: Garland, 1976).

When the *Journey* was published in 1775, journalists in both London and Edinburgh launched into a more sustained attack on Johnson. The principal objects of their criticism were his attack on James Macpherson, the 'author' of Ossian's works, and his ingratitude in abusing Scottish hospitality. The first accusation is obviously charged with greater historic significance, and of greater moment for the themes of this book. The story even got about that Johnson had challenged Macpherson to a duel with pistols. Echoes rumbled on through 1775, with evidence of widespread Scottish pique against Johnson for his unkind portrait of the nation in the *Journey*. There were occasional witty parodies of his style; but often the method was simple abuse, as when the *Caledonian Mercury* reported that Johnson had 'caught the Scottish fiddle [pox], in the embraces of a female mountaineer'. Another Edinburgh journal claimed that the Highlanders had made Johnson merry 'with the jovial glass of sparkling wine and good whisky', a comment which might have been better directed at Boswell. More seriously, Johnson's attitude towards the Scottish universities and the reformed Church came in for extensive criticism. It took some years before a more balanced view became possible, and Johnson's strictures could be assessed in a more judicious vein of debate.

If the word 'campaign' was inappropriate in connection with the earlier press onslaughts on Johnson, this cannot be said the fracas over Ossian. That much can be asserted on the evidence of a single document, a letter from William Woodfall, the bookseller and writer for the *Morning Chronicle*. A few days after the famous letter from Johnson to Macpherson, on 24 January 1775, Woodfall addressed a letter to Caleb Whitefoord, who was a friend of Benjamin Franklin's and (though born in Edinburgh) a London merchant. Johnson had conceived a strong respect for Whitefoord's talents, but by this time the latter was dominated by an urge to redress the anti-Scottish bias which he saw everywhere in England. He had written a series of articles intended to disabuse the public of the view propagated by the *North Briton* that 'most places of trust and profit in England were engross'd by Scotchmen'. Hence his desire to co-operate with William Woodfall and his brother Henry Sampson (the journalist best known for his links with Junius) in rebutting the negative implications of the *Journey*.

William Woodfall's letter has been in print since 1898, but it is not well known and merits quotation at length:

Before my Brother had intimated to me your wish that I would fall foul of Dr Johnson for the objectionable passages in his dogmatical account of his *Journey to the Western Islands of Scotland*, I had resolved to give him a bite or two, in return for his biting off Macpherson's head and opening so frequently on a false Scent. You know I have been north of the Tweed, and that I am one of those ridiculous Englishmen who entertain an opinion of the Country and its Inhabitants, widely different from that of Dr Johnson, and men who have imbibed early and unjust prejudices against Scotland. I mean, as often as opportunity will admit, to say a word or two respecting the literary Dictator's Tour; and I think the attack would gain strength if . . . Mr M. was one of the Crew.

Woodfall goes on to refer to some mysterious measures to be taken, a 'small gun' to be fired in the morning, and concludes: 'As the fire on the other side is managed by a skillfull engineer it will doubtless be brisk. The nature of the case . . . demands immediate aid. 'Till I am relieved my feeble efforts shall not be wanting.'[24] All this shows that a concerted effort was deemed necessary to combat Johnson's dangerous and influential anti-Scottish publicity. It is unlikely that Johnson himself had regarded the *Journey* as so polemical a work, at last in terms of day-to-day politics, but in such a fiercely partisan climate almost anything written about Scotland could be interpreted in this way.

There is a final consideration here. The presence of Boswell as Johnson's bear-leader complicated matters in several ways. He was a Scot, but a Lowlander; one who flirted with a sentimental Jacobitism whilst seeking favour and advancement in the public world, dominated as it was by pragmatic Hanoverians; and he was a blatant self-publicist who had his own agenda for the tour. He had friends and enemies in both Edinburgh and London. Deeply split in his own nature, he looked on his native land with a mixture of affection and disdain (see Chapter 7, above). He wished to gain credit by association with Johnson; his motive in introducing his friend to the Edinburgh illuminati was not untouched by a sliver of self-interest. To many Scots, it made things worse that the notorious Sassenach should be brought into their country by the

---

[24] Quoted from *The Whitefoord Papers*, ed. W. A. S. Hewins (Oxford: Clarendon Press: 1898), 161.

upstart Boswell, a man whose own commitment to pure ideas of Scottish nationhood they had reason to doubt. He could even be viewed as a cunning Ulysses who had infiltrated a wooden horse within their walls, out of which then stepped the towering champion of their adversaries.

As time went on, Boswell became increasingly suspect to many of his own people. His unsuccessful foray at the English bar and his growing intimacy with the London intelligentsia (not to mention his close association with the name of Johnson, especially when the *Life* appeared) gave some credit to the view expressed by John Courtenay that he was 'scarce esteemed a Scot'.[25] He had always been anxious about the popular impression of his character which circulated in the press: as early as 1772 he had worried that Grub Street might say that General Paoli kept Scotsmen gratis in his house.[26] Doubts continued to plague him about his own national identity: once in his courting days he had resolved to avoid young women from his own country—'After this, I shall be on my guard against ever indulging the least fondness for a *Scots lass*. I am a soul of a more southern frame'[27] (two years later he married his cousin and near-neighbour in Ayrshire, Margaret Montgomerie). Throughout the *Life* we see Johnson goading his friend on the subject of Scotland, but also Boswell under a compulsion to provoke such outbursts. He was plainly flattered to be told by Johnson, 'I will do you, Boswell, the justice to say that you are the most *unscottified* of your countrymen' (*LSJ* ii. 242). He resolutely declined to intervene on most of the occasions when Johnson expressed critical views on his homeland—when Mrs Thrale expressed a desire to visit Scotland for instance: 'Seeing Scotland, Madam, is only seeing a worse England' (*LSJ* iii. 248).

---

[25] John Courtenay, *A Political View of the Literary and Moral Character of the Late Samuel Johnson, LL D* (London: Dilly, 1786), 25. Courtenay was a member of the Anglo-Irish 'Gang' in London, which meant more to Boswell in his later years than any Scottish friendship.

[26] *Boswell for the Defence, 1769–1774*, ed. W. K. Wimsatt and F. A. Pottle (London: Heinemann, 1960), 36.

[27] *Boswell in Search of a Wife, 1766–1769*, ed. F. Brady and F. A. Pottle (London: Heinemann, 1757), 109. A few months later, in Feb. 1768, Boswell writes: 'The Heiress is a good Scots lass. But I must have an Englishwoman. My mind is now twice as large as it has been for some months' (p. 137). The association of an English bride with 'enlarged' notions is suggestive.

In this context, Boswell's treatment of his own tourist material in the *Tour* is of some interest. When he revised the private memoranda for publication in 1785, he went to some trouble to suppress the 'Scottish' content. He eliminated those passages which drew attention to specifically Scottish concerns, and reduced his own self-awareness as a Scot travelling in company with an Englishman.[28] The result was what he wanted. The *Tour* was praised and blamed on a number of grounds, but mainly for what Johnson did or did not say. Boswell's own tremulous feelings of national identity were largely overlooked. Instead, the Scots wanted Mrs Piozzi to make her own journey to contradict Johnson.[29] This was in 1789: she did make a protracted visit later that year, but her journals have only been published (in part) in recent years.[30] On literary grounds this is a pity, because there are signs that she saw her account as a complement to that of her friend: 'Were you ever much a Reader of Johnson's tour to Hebrides? its one of his first Rate Performances—I look it over now every day with double Delight—Oh how the Scotch do detest him!'[31] In the event, neither Boswell's published volume nor Mrs Piozzi's unpublished journal undid the damage of the original *Journey*. For generations, Johnson was firmly fixed in the Scottish imagination as an uncritical opponent of all things Caledonian. It was something of a travesty, but in the cultural context of the age not an inexplicable misreading.

III

It is time to set out some brief conclusions. In an age when the Scottish issue was so heavily politicized, it was inevitable that a work so rich, so opinionated, and so personal as the *Journey* should

---

[28] See the important discussion of these issues in an unpublished dissertation by Barbara Looney, 'The Suppressed Agenda of Boswell's *Tour*' (University of South Florida, 1992).

[29] P. W. Clayden, *The Earlier Life of Samuel Rogers* (London: Smith Elder, 1887), 92.

[30] See Richard R. Reynolds, 'Mrs Piozzi's "Scotch Journey", 1789', *Bulletin of the John Rylands Library*, 60 (1977), 114–34.

[31] Hester Piozzi to Sophia Byron, 11 July 1789 (from Edinburgh): *The Piozzi Letters*, in progress: vols. i–iii published, ed. E. A. Bloom and L. D. Bloom (Newark, Del.: University of Delware Press, 1989), i. 304.

excite complicated reactions. Ever since the accession of George III and the rise of Bute, people on both sides of the political and national fence had been on the look-out for slurs and innuendoes. When Bute engineered the insertion of the phrase 'I glory in the name of Britain' in the King's speech at the opening of Parliament in 1760, the Duke of Newcastle had seen this as a covert strike on behalf of the Scots.[32]

Whatever the truth in political and economic terms, the Union of 1707 had not forged much in the way of cultural unity. It is an old observation that the Scots, thrown back on themselves by the loss of political institutions, had tended to become distinctively Scottish in their social practice. Visitors to Edinburgh were struck by its radically un-English tone: when the Club member William Windham dined with Adam Smith there in 1785, he noted in his diary: 'Felt strongly the impression of a company completely Scottish.'[33] Boswell was anxious that when Johnson got to the Scottish capital, he should meet men like Robertson and Ferguson, figures greater than 'mere *oaten* Professeurs'[34]—what others saw as proudly independent, Boswell construed as seeming provincial to his illustrious guest. There was no social occasion so innocent that these charged issues of national independence might not surface.

Of course, routine anti-Scottish prejudice did exist in England: it was not a paranoid invention of men like David Hume, who constantly complained of the treatment that he received simply because of his race. There was, for example, the well-known gadfly John Shebbeare (seen by many as a coarser version of Johnson), whom Fanny Burney heard mouthing racist inanities in 1774: 'And as to the Scotch!—there is but one thing in which they are clever, and can excell the English;—and that is, they can use both Hands at once to scratch themselves—the English never think of using more than one.'[35] It is hardly surprising that Johnson was not able to get

---

[32] Lewis Namier, *England in the Age of the American Revolution*, 2nd edn. (London: Macmillan, 1961), 128.

[33] William Windham, *Diary*, ed. Mrs H. Baring (London: Longman, 1866), 64.

[34] A previously unpublished letter to Lord Elibank of 16 Aug. 1773, printed in M. J. C. Hodgart, *Samuel Johnson and his Times* (London: Batsford, 1962), 81–2.

[35] *The Early Journals and Letters of Fanny Burney*, ed. L. Troide, in progress, 2 vols. published (Oxford: Clarendon Press, 1990), ii. 6. The Gordon riots in 1780 prompted new bursts of anti-Scots feeling, based on Lord George Gordon's origins: 'If the nation . . . will submit to being led by Scottish fanatics, and to the tune of the bagpipe . . . such a nation *cannot* be saved' (the Duke of Richmond to Lord Rockingham, 1780).

inclined to find men more wicked and miserable the more civilised they are. B—Without enumerating all the countries in the world, let me just remark that nowhere but in Tahiti will you find the condition a happy one, nor is it elsewhere even tolerable, apart from in a little backwater of Europe [Venice].'[1] These are the views underlying Johnson's verbal battles with Boswell over the blessings of savage life, such as the debates about Omai, recorded in the *Life* and quoted above (pp. 83–4). But, equally, the attitudes implicit in Diderot's dialogue provide a hidden agenda for the entire *Journey*, as Johnson sets out to explore a region which could scarcely have been further, morally, from the civilized domain of Edinburgh: 'To the southern inhabitants of Scotland, the state of the mountains and the islands is equally unknown with that of Borneo or Sumatra' (*JWI* 88). Moreover, Johnson's comments on feudal tenure in the Highlands and on the economy of Skye could be seen as a proleptic response to the work of his fellow Club member Adam Smith in *The Wealth of Nations* (1776). And, as a final example, is not his study of a culture in decline, as he sees it in Gaelic Scotland, something of a parallel to the survey of the fall of Rome which Edward Gibbon would bring out, also in 1776?

Again and again the travellers were thrust up against the big debates of their age. When Johnson quarrelled with Lord Monboddo, he knew that he was engaging with a man who had set the polite world agog with his unorthodox views on language, society, and what we should call anthropology (see Appendix, pp. 226–31). Monboddo had once written to James Harris, a philosopher on the fringe of Johnson's circle: 'There is a progression of our species from a state little better than mere brutality to that most perfect state you describe in ancient Greece, which is really amazing and peculiar to our species.'[2] Monboddo would have extended the definition of the species lower down the chain of primates than most of his contemporaries would have done: but he was not alone in detecting a graduated series of planes of living, from the barbarous to the most civilized. In the theories of Adam Smith and Adam Ferguson this series could be developed into a historical or sociological system. (As a matter of fact, Ferguson directly

---

[1] Denis Diderot, *Political Writings*, trans. and ed. J. H. Mason and R. Wokler (Cambridge: Cambridge University Press, 1992), 32–3, 72–3.

[2] Quoted by Henry Steele Commager, *The Empire of Reason* (London: Weidenfeld and Nicholson, 1978), 47.

contrasted the 'citizen' and the 'savage' in part III of his *Essay on the History of Civil Society*, thus setting up the terms of the dispute between Johnson and Monboddo.) It must have been a conscious decision by Johnson to make his way into the remotest part of Britain, undertaking what I have called his grand detour in the wake of the accounts of Pacific travellers and at the very moment of Omai, that brief window of history which gave the Tahitian his fifteen minutes of fame. Perhaps it was a kind of defiant joke which led Johnson to set out from Edinburgh, the crucible of that Enlightenment which had brought such matters to public attention.

One recent work—published, indeed, just seven years before the Hebridean trip was made—which underlies much of the *Journey* is Adam Ferguson's *Essay on the History of Civil Society*. Few works are more expressive of the high Scottish Enlightenment, and few discussions of enlightened knowledge are more pertinent to what the travellers witnessed on their peregrinations. Ferguson considers the standard topics of that age—wealth, commerce, luxury, liberty, manners, politeness, and so on. But his approach is not that of political economy, as in Adam Smith, or morality, as in Hume, so much as that of sociology. The entire book bears on the concerns of Johnson's own work, but it is especially in part II, 'Of the History of Rude Nations', that we are made most aware of the link. It could be said that Johnson's prolonged meditation on Skye (*JWI* 78–120) constitutes a set of variations on Ferguson's theme, by way of response to the treatment of such issues as the importance of traditional myth and fable; the effect of climate; superstition; the nature of 'primitive' agriculture; and so on. Ferguson devotes a chapter to 'Luxury' in part VI; at Inveraray, as the travellers dined with the Duke of Argyll, 'the subject of luxury' was introduced (*LSJ* v. 357). Often the accents in Ferguson are close to those of Johnson's prose: 'We are generally at a loss to conceive how mankind can subsist under customs and manners extremely different from our own; and we are apt to exaggerate the misery of barbarous time, by an imagination of what we ourselves should suffer in a situation to which we are not accustomed.' Again, in part III of the *Essay on the History of Civil Society*, there are numerous premonitions of the *Journey*: 'To them [the southern nations of Europe] we owe the romantic tales of chivalry, as well as the subsequent models of a more rational style, by which the heart and the imagination are kindled, and the understanding informed' (cf.

JWI 77, 155). Here, too, Ferguson devotes a section to 'The History of Literature', where his comments on primitive poetry make an interesting contrast to what Johnson says about Gaelic bards: 'Every tribe of barbarians have their passionate or historic rhymes, which contain the superstition, the enthusiasm, and the admiration of glory, with which the breasts of men, in the earliest state of society, are possessed.'[3]

In the light of all this, it might seem only natural that amongst those to whom Boswell introduced Johnson in Edinburgh, at the start of the tour, was 'Dr Adam Ferguson, whose *Essay on the History of Civil Society* gives him a respectable place in the ranks of literature' (*LSJ* v. 42). But there is an irony underlying this apparent willingness on Johnson's part to appropriate the idiom of his hosts, if not another bitter joke. Ferguson's examples of 'rude nations' are taken from *partes infidelium* outside Europe:

From one to the other extremity of America: from Kamschatka westward to the river Oby, and from the Northern sea, over that length of country, to the confines of China, of India, and Persia; from the Caspian to the Red sea, with little exception, and from thence over the inland continent and the western shores of Africa; we every where meet with nations on whom we bestow the appellations of barbarous or savage.[4]

In practice, Ferguson usually applies such terms as 'savage nations' to the native peoples of America, especially North America. The 'Americans' are representatives of the childhood of mankind, who will show what the Germans and Britons were like in the infancy of their race. The irony to which I referred lies in the fact that Johnson conducted his survey of primitive manners on Scottish soil, within earshot almost of the Old College in Edinburgh, that centre of civilized eighteenth-century living. When the English sage sets out to test the theories of the Scottish Enlightenment, he does it not by a trek through the Andes or a voyage up the Ohio, but by a journey to the hidden recesses of Scotland itself.

We do not know what Johnson made of *The Wealth of Nations*, or indeed if he ever read it to the end. In March 1776 Boswell tells

---

[3] Adam Ferguson, *An Essay on the History of Civil Society*, introd. Louis Schneider (Brunswick, NJ: Transaction Publishers, 1991), 105, 114, 172.

[4] Ibid. 81. Cf. Johnson's remark to Monboddo that emigration to America would be, for 'a man of any intellectual enjoyment', tantamount to immersing 'himself and his posterity for ages in barbarism' (*LSJ* v. 78).

us that he mentioned the book 'which was just published' to Johnson, and quoted Sir John Pringle's view that 'Dr Smith, who had never been in trade, could not be expected to write well on that subject any more than a lawyer upon physick.' Johnson demurs, and takes this as an opportunity to assert his view that 'A merchant seldom thinks but of his own particular trade. To write a good book upon it, a man must have extensive views' (*LSJ* ii. 430). Of course, this is a characteristic Johnsonian emphasis; but there is no direct comment on *The Wealth of Nations*. If he did read the book, Johnson might have been amused to note this passage in book I, chapter 11:

In some parts of Lancashire it is pretended, I have been told, that bread of oatmeal is a heartier food for labouring people than wheaten bread, and I have frequently heard the same doctrine held in Scotland. I am, however, somewhat doubtful of the truth of it. The common people in Scotland, who are fed with oatmeal, are in general neither so strong nor so handsome as the same rank of people in England, who are fed on wheaten bread.[5]

More seriously, he would have observed Smith's pervasive use of Scottish examples to illustrate his general theses, with numerous points of contact with the text of the *Journey*. To cite two examples out of many, Smith reflects on poverty:

But poverty, though it does not prevent the generation, is extremely unfavourable to the rearing of children. The tender plant is produced, but in so cold a soil, and so severe a climate, soon withers and dies. It is not uncommon, I have been frequently told, in the Highlands of Scotland for a mother who has borne twenty children not to have two alive.[6]

More cautiously, Johnson remarks that poverty does not bring longevity to the population: the Highlander grows old like anyone else, and 'he escapes no other injury of time' (*JWI* 84). Secondly, Smith writes of the ancient, even pre-feudal, state of society as seen in the Highlands:

The occupiers of land were in every respect as dependent upon the great proprietor as his retainers. Even such of them as were not in a state of villanage, were tenants at will, who paid a rent in no respect equivalent to

---

[5] Adam Smith, *The Wealth of Nations*, ed. Edward Cannan (New York: the Modern Library, 1937), 160–1 (sect. I. 11).
[6] Ibid. 79 (I. 8).

the subsistence which the land afforded them. A crown, half a crown, a sheep, a lamb, was some years ago in the highlands of Scotland a common rent for lands which maintained a family. In some places it is so at this day; nor will money at present purchase a greater quantity of commodities there than in other places. In a country where the surplus produce of a large estate must be consumed upon the estate itself, it will frequently be more convenient for the proprietor, that part of it be consumed at a distance from his own house, provided they who consume it are as dependent upon him as either his retainers or his menial servants. He is thereby saved from the embarrassment of either too large a company or too large a family. A tenant at will, who possesses land sufficient to maintain his family for little more than quit-rent, is as dependent upon the proprietor as any servant or retainer whatever, and must obey him with as little reserve. Such a proprietor, as he feeds his servants and retainers at his own house, so he feeds his tenants at their houses. The subsistence of both is derived from his bounty, and its continuance depends upon his good pleasure.[7]

Johnson describes the social system of Skye in recognizably similar terms:

The name of highest dignity is laird, of which there are in the extensive Isle of Sky only three, Macdonald, Macleod, and Mackinnon. The laird is the original owner of the land, whose natural power must be very great, where no man lives but by agriculture; and where the produce of the land is not conveyed through the labyrinths of traffic, but passes directly from the hand that gathers it to the mouth that eats it. The laird has all those in his power that live upon his farms. Kings can, for the most part, only exalt or degrade. The laird at pleasure can feed or starve, can give bread or withhold it. This inherent power was yet strengthened by the kindness of consanguinity, and the reverence of patriarchal authority. The laird was the father of the clan and his tenants commonly bore his name. And to these principles of original command was added, for many ages, an exclusive right of legal jurisdiction. (*JWI* 85–6)

These brief examples constitute only a small portion of a much bigger overlap, which is not confined to passages in *The Wealth of Nations* where Scotland is explicitly mentioned. Both Smith and Johnson discuss the 'territorial jurisdictions' formerly held by local proprietors;[8] Johnson's treatment of the decay of St Andrews University may be read in conjunction with Smith's section on the

[7] Ibid. 386 (III. 4). For a good account of the clan system, especially by Stuart sympathizers, see A. J. Youngson, *The Prince and the Pretender* (London: Croom Helm, 1985), 167–70.

[8] Smith, *Wealth of Nations*, 387–9 (III. 4); *JWI* 92–5.

corruption of (mainly British) universities;[9] and Smith writes of the way in which better communications 'encourage the cultivation of the remote',[10] whilst Johnson tells us that the Highlanders, although once 'their rocks secluded them from the rest of mankind', now 'are losing their distinction, and hastening to mingle with the general community' (*JWI* 47). Smith is neutral about such changes, or approbatory on economic grounds; Johnson displays more mixed feelings. The point, naturally, is not that Smith was agreeing or disagreeing with Johnson, whose *Journey* appeared too late to have affected his thinking in any case. It is rather that both books inhabit the conceptual world of the Enlightenment.

As a final point of comparison, it is worth remarking that Smith habitually avoids directly political issues and immediate topical concerns. In part this derives from the nature of his enquiry and its generalizing function. In part it may indicate a certain caution or *pudeur* on his side. For example, almost the only mention of emigration occurs in the sentence 'The frequency of emigration from Scotland, and the rarity of it from England, sufficiently prove that the demand for labour is very different in the two countries' (and this was not in the first edition).[11] The comparison underlines still further the boldness and openness of the *Journey*. A prudent writer would have kept off emigration, along with the effects of the dissolution of the clans, the mixed results of the Union, and Ossian. Boswell, too, does not disguise the fact that the travellers were confronting a society which had been traumatized by the 1745 insurrection and its aftermath. Both accounts deal with the here and now, even though Johnson deploys a vocabulary which had evolved to describe the large forces of human history. The *Journey* and the *Tour* are at once diachronic and synchronic, which is to say that they are narratives and not, like *The Wealth of Nations*, simply anatomies.

There has been virtually no mention in this book of Lord Kames, despite the fact that his role in the Scottish Enlightenment was so pervasive, and despite the added consideration that Boswell knew

---

[9] Smith, *The Wealth of Nations*, 716–28 (V. 1); *JWI* 6–9.

[10] Ibid. 147 (I. 11).

[11] Ibid. 189 (I. 11). For the course of emigration in the 1770s, and an attempt to suppress it during the war of the American Revolution, see Bruce Lenman, *The Jacobite Clans of the Great Glen, 1650–1786* (London: Eyre Methuen, 1984), 213–16.

him extremely well and that Johnson read his works. Their are
several reasons for this omission. First, Kames hardly appears in the
text of the narratives, and was not among the notabilities
introduced to Johnson in Edinburgh. Second, the only book, among
so many, to resonate to the same cultural vibrations as the *Journey*
and the *Tour* is probably Kames's *Sketches of the History of Man*,
which was not published until a few months after the travellers
returned, in early 1774. Johnson later read this work and made
objections to it (*LSJ* iii. 352); but it is unlikely that it reached him in
time to affect the composition of the *Journey*. Third, a thorough
study of Kames has been written by Ian Ross, which considers
Boswell's relations with the older man.

Kames, of course, was more than a critic and rhetorician, the
aspect of his work best known today. He was a colleague of Lord
Auchinleck on the judicial bench; an agricultural improver; an ally
(for the most part) of David Hume, and an adversary of
Monboddo; a commissioner of forfeited estates who helped in the
task of 'civilizing and improving the Highlands of Scotland', as the
Act of 1752 put it. There is much about Kames which reminds one
of Johnson—his desire for clear principles in approaching the arts;
his absorption in the law—where Johnson actually wrote a paper
opposing his views; his practical and economically aware appraisal
of the state of society; and much else. Equally, there are marked
points of difference, including Kames's friendship with Franklin,
Hume, and Mrs Montagu (whom he entertained at his home near
Stirling), and his belief that the work of Ossian accurately reflected
an ancient Caledonian civilization in which original 'benevolence'
held sway. Kames was not a primitivist, and differed sharply from
Monboddo in alluding dismissively to wonder as 'the passion of
savages and rustics; to raise which, nothing is necessary but to
invent giants and magicians, fairy-land and inchantment', an
attitude not so far removed from that of Johnson towards popular
and chivalric folk-literature.[12]

[12] This paragraph is largely based on Ian Ross, *Lord Kames and the Scotland of
his Day* (Oxford: Clarendon Press, 1972), *passim*; see esp. pp. 247–59, on Kames
and Boswell (but also Lord Auchinleck and Johnson), and pp. 368–70, on Boswell's
aborted plans to write a life of Kames; the letter to James Lind cited in the text is
reproduced on pp. 333–5. A final point made by Ross, and bearing on the argument
of this conclusion, is that Kames and others were unaware of the notable Gaelic
poets of their own age—hence their need for Ossian. Ross writes of 'the curious
remoteness of the Edinburgh *literati* from the genuine Gaelic culture of their day'
(ibid. 341).

Kames had crossed Boswell's path on many occasions, generally in ways which are irrelevant to our concerns here. But it is worth noting that he had been a judge in the Douglas case (coming down on the side of the Douglasites) and had also been on the bench when the celebrated perpetual-copyright case involving Alexander Donaldson came before the Court of Session in 1773—he sided with all his colleagues, apart from Monboddo, in opposing the book trade's claim to a common-law right in the copy of books. It was a case with widespread implications, on which Johnson spoke forcibly, as reported by Boswell in the *Life* (*LSJ* i. 437–9). However, a more intriguing link with the argument of the present book is provided by a letter which Kames wrote to Dr James Lind just a year before the Highland jaunt was mounted. At that time Lind was planning to travel with Joseph Banks on the second of Captain Cook's voyages; when Banks defected, he went with his patron on an almost equally momentous journey to Iceland, via the Hebrides, which is when Staffa first penetrated the consciousness of Europe. Kames hoped that Lind would come back from the South Pacific with answers to some questions that puzzled him, including the state of the population of European immigrants to Batavia, and whether 'there are different species of men fitted for the different climates'. The issues are those of Montesquieu, but by the 1770s this discourse had been wrenched from the theorists and taken over by explorers—Bougainville, Cook, Banks, and, it is not perverse to add, Johnson and Boswell (see Chapter 3, above).

Finally, in this context, it is worth noting that Hugh Blair was amongst those who met the travellers on their return to Edinburgh. His *Critical Dissertation on the Poems of Ossian* (1763) had claimed that Ossian represented the earliest of the four stages of civilization, that is the world of hunters (followed by pasturage, agriculture, and commerce). Blair's remarks on how language 'advances from sterility to copiousness' over the course of civilization foreshadows Johnson's treatment of oral and written culture in his review of Highland culture. Again we can see that, although Johnson took a quite different line on Ossian as a work of literature, his historical understanding of the issues is couched in terms which belong to precisely the same discursive world as that of Blair.[13]

[13] Blair is cited from Scott Elledge (ed.), *Eighteenth-Century Critical Essays*, 2 vols. (Ithaca, NY: Cornell University Press, 1961), ii. 848–60.

Boswell, as we have seen, had his own motive for the journey. He was less fastidious than Johnson in dealing openly with another current public concern, the Jacobite legacy: indeed, as we have seen in Chapter 6, he went out of his way to augment his original journal of 1773 with a long section on Prince Charles Edward when the *Tour* appeared in 1786 (*LSJ* v. 187–205). In some obscure way, I have argued, he identified with the 'Wanderer' as he, Boswell, explored the far nooks and crannies of his native land for the first time. But his primary purpose was to reveal Johnson, to set up the conditions in which Johnson could expose his own deepest feelings about the world. Boswell was as well aware as anyone of the bad reputation that Johnson had acquired among the Scots, and he was perennially anxious about his own guilty love for his homeland. Beneath their superficial differences, the two travellers shared many human attributes, along with a common absorption in the large issues of society. They embarked on their journey partly to satisfy unappeased personal desires, but also to advance debate on the many questions which had played around Scotland and the Scottish for many years past.

Appendix
Monboddo, Johnson, and Boswell

One of the most celebrated episodes in the *Journal of a Tour to the Hebrides* concerns the travellers' visit to Lord Monboddo (*LSJ* v. 74–83). The scene makes an immediate point, and Boswell's full report compensates for Johnson's almost total silence on the encounter (see Chapter 4, above). However, few readers will be aware of all the complex personal and intellectual relations between the participants. As this book has attempted to show, there is often a subtext to both narratives, deriving from hidden Scottish issues to which their authors do not make any explicit allusion. The Monboddo episode provides a good example of this; in order to understand the dynamics of the scene, we need to explicate the surface events and dialogue to uncover deeper strata of implication.[1]

Long before 1773 Monboddo knew Boswell personally and Johnson by reputation. James Burnett was born in 1714 in a strongly Jacobite area, the Mearns; his father fought for the Old Pretender in 1715 and was captured at Sheriffmuir—the elder Burnett, after his release, was one of those who underwent conversion and remained 'skulking at home', unregenerate in his faith until his death. He sent twenty-five men from his estate to fight for Charles Edward in 1745. His son spent this crucial period in London, which can only be interpreted as a gesture of non-involvement.

When the meeting took place at Monboddo, the host was approaching 59 and, like Johnson, was a widower. He had been a judge of the Court of Session since 1767, assuming the title of Lord Monboddo. His colleagues on the bench included Lord Auchinleck, Kames, Hailes, and later Braxfield. In fact, Monboddo was generally at odds with Kames, just as he tangled regularly with David Hume, who was the keeper of the Advocates' Library at a time when Burnett (as he was then) served as one of the curators. Monboddo's opposition to the ideas of Kames and Hume should prevent us from ascribing to the group a totalized 'Scottish Enlightenment' viewpoint, necessarily suspect to the English visitor. Monboddo had been influenced by a previous keeper of the Library, Thomas Ruddiman, one of the most important Jacobite scholars of the earlier eighteenth century.

---

[1] This appendix draws chiefly on Monboddo's works and two valuable secondary sources: William Knight, *Lord Monboddo and Some of his Contemporaries* (London: John Murray, 1900); and E. L. Cloyd, *James Burnett, Lord Monboddo* (Oxford; Clarendon Press, 1972). Other scattered sources are not listed.

Like Boswell, though in a milder way, Monboddo seems to have rebelled against his father. His educational progress was also parallel: he moved from King's College, Aberdeen, to Groningen and Leiden, and then to admission to the Faculty of Advocates with a thesis on Roman law. In Holland he acquired the habit of writing regular assignments and essays, as Boswell had done there. He became a leading light of the Select Society (see Chapter 7), and as assiduous as anyone in seeking to 'purify' his language—when Sir John Pringle pointed out some suspect idioms in his published work, he replied to a friend: 'As to Scoticisms in my style, I have avoided them as much as I was able, but some have escaped me.' He developed a strong interest in drama, and was one of the managers of the Canongate Theatre in Edinburgh, when it was under the artistic control of West Digges—a few years later Boswell became obsessed with the theatre, and Digges represented his ideal of a man of fashion. After his return from the Continent, Boswell grew closer to his father's judicial colleague and adopted him as one of many surrogate parents, consulting Monboddo on the choice of a wife, for example. In later years their relations soured, but in 1773 the two men were still on excellent terms.

They had one obvious point of affinity, in spite of deep divisions in outlook on many issues. Monboddo's greatest triumph as an advocate had come in his efforts on behalf of the Douglas family against the Hamiltons, during the unrolling of the epic Douglas case in the 1760s. As Boswell's uncomfortable sojourn at the home of the Duchess of Argyll reveals, later in the *Tour*, Boswell had been one of the strongest adherents of the Douglas party. By the time the trial was held in the Court of Session, Monboddo had been promoted to the bench, and his was one of the most eloquent voices on the Douglas side. The verdict went to the Hamiltons, on the casting vote of the Lord President; but in March 1769 the House of Lords reversed this on appeal. Boswell was among the almost riotous crowd which celebrated in Edinburgh. Another festive event to mark the result was a performance of John Home's tragedy *Douglas*, a play which Monboddo rated as superior not only to the non-Aristotelian Shakespeare, but also, in its use of dramatic discovery, to the *Oedipus Tyrannus*. Since to Monboddo anything Greek was almost always better than anything modern, this was high praise indeed.

If such views were unlikely to impress Johnson, so was the circle of friends that Monboddo had acquired during his visits to London. This included David Mallet, George Lyttelton, and James Harris, men who would not have appealed to Johnson, individually or collectively. From about 1780 Monboddo began to make regular spring visits to London, and he and Boswell must sometimes have been on the Great North Road together. The trips continued well into his eighties: in 1794, at an inn in Bedfordshire, John Byng had a Smollettian encounter with a strange figure draped in 'all kind of odd coverings; and appear'd a modern Don Quixote'.

By now Monboddo had a long-established reputation for eccentricity, built up partly from his private behaviour but also from the content of his works.

His literary productions began with short essays on topics such as the North American Indians and the South Sea islands. One of the first to be published was the account of a savage girl 'caught wild in the woods of Champaign'; this was translated by his clerk and furnished with an introduction by Monboddo, appearing in Edinburgh in 1768. This is recalled in the text of the *Tour*, a few days after the visit to Monboddo:

I called on Mr Robertson, who . . . was formerly Lord Monboddo's clerk . . . and translated Condamine's Account of the Savage Girl, to which his lordship wrote a preface, containing several remarks of his own. Robertson said, he did not believe so much as his lordship did; that it was plain to him, the girl confounded what she imagined with what she remembered: that, besides, she perceived Condamine and Lord Monboddo forming her theories, and she adopted her story to them. (*LSJ* v. 110–11)

It is at this point that Boswell introduces Johnson's comments, often quoted, concerning Monboddo's pride in his own tail (see above, p. 103). The point here is that Johnson would also have known of the support that Monboddo had given to the claims of the Savage Girl, one of the many wild creatures discovered in the eighteenth century. We must take this into account in the exchanges between the two sages, in the scene at Monboddo.

When that encounter took place, Monboddo had published only the first part of his serial work, *Of the Origin and Progress of Language*, which eventually ran to six volumes (1773–92; its London publisher was Thomas Cadell). This was succeeded by another compendious work, *Ancient Metaphysics* (1779–99). The titles belie the range of materials covered, which include anthropology, history, philology, rhetoric, Newtonian physics, and much else. Some of the later volumes of the first series discuss language and rhetoric in ways which might have interested Johnson, whilst the second series includes a long analysis of history which deserves a larger place in accounts of the Scottish Enlightenment than it generally receives. If Johnson could have read the entire set of volumes in 1773, he would probably not have formed any very different view of their author; but his thinking might have been less dominated by the issue of the orang-utans, which became the notorious feature of the opening volume. Monboddo claimed not that mankind was directly related to any extant members of the ape family, but that the two species had a common ancestry. Few people bothered to find out exactly what Monboddo had said.

This first volume had been published on 23 February 1773. Boswell notes allusions to it by Johnson as early as 13 April (mankind in a state of equality 'would soon degenerate into brutes;—they would become

Monboddo's nation;—their tails would grow') and on 8 May ('He attacked Lord Monboddo's strange speculation on the primitive state of human nature': *LSJ* ii. 219, 259). On the former date he had also launched into an assault on Goldsmith's idea that the physical size of the human race was degenerating owing to luxury. Since this was a key aspect of Monboddo's beliefs, first and last, no meeting of minds could be expected on this point. More generally, Monboddo's claim that primitive societies had lived an animal-like existence, before the invention of language, would have found no echo in Johnson's breast. The fact that Monboddo's idealism involved a wholesale rejection of Locke would have put his entire theory of knowledge at a distance from Johnson's position.

So much, briefly, on the situation in 1773. Boswell arranged the meeting, having observed both likeness and unlikeness in the views of the two men. He was able to steer the conversation along reasonably harmonious lines, but there is a deceptive quality in their agreement at times. That both were able to concur in speaking highly of Homer should not blind us to the fact that this is a momentary collision of trajectories otherwise veering widely apart. Monboddo's respect for the Greek bordered on the idolatrous, and required a comparable disparagement of Roman culture. He did not regard Johnson as a competent Greek scholar, in any case. And his regular use of Milton as the touchstone of modern sublimity would have called for some degree of qualification as far as Johnson was concerned. Nevertheless, the two men certainly found some common beliefs during their discussion. Later, Monboddo went on to even more daring speculations. Before Johnson's friend and fellow Club member Sir William Jones elaborated his theories regarding historical philology, Monboddo had evolved his own ideas. He wrote to Jones in 1789, outlining his view that 'either Greek is a dialect of the Sanscrit, or they are both dialects of the same parent language'. His enquiries into the origin of language had led to such a conclusion several years earlier. He studied a number of exotic tongues, including Huron, Algonquin, Eskimo, and, most aptly, Tahitian—whilst Johnson did not even come to grips with Gaelic.

With his deliberate lack of tact, Boswell continued to goad his friends into action after the Hebridean tour was over. In a letter of August 1775 Johnson linked Monboddo's belief that there were men with tails in some remote parts of the world with Donald Macqueen's continuing support for the authenticity of Ossian: this was prompted by a supper in Edinburgh, reported by Boswell, at which the two Scots had opposed Johnson's 'proposition, that the Gaelick of the Highlands and Isles of Scotland were not written till of late'. Johnson's riposte—'If there are men with tails, catch an *homo caudatus*; if there was writing of old in the highlands or Hebrides, in the Erse language, produce the language' (*LSJ* ii. 381–3)— shows just how closely intertwined the issues of primitive culture were, as adumbrated in the narratives of the *Tour* and as identified in this book.

In 1777 Boswell was at it again. He brought a copy of the *Journey* to Monboddo and read passages aloud, on the pretext that the Scottish sage had read it 'superficially'. Boswell excited the other man's interest, and arranged for a presentation copy to be sent to him. In time there was a response and, naturally, Boswell communicated this to Johnson: 'I read to him a letter which Lord Monboddo had written to me, containing some critical remarks upon the style of his "Journey to the Western Islands of Scotland." His Lordship praised the very fine passage upon landing at Icolmkill; but his own style being exceedingly dry and hard, he disapproved of the richness of Johnson's language, and of his frequent use of metaphorical expressions' (*LSJ* iii. 173). Johnson defends himself as one would expect. The answer would not have mollified Monboddo, who continued to warn Boswell against using Johnson as a model for the scholar or polite writer. Soon after this the relations between the two Scots began to deteriorate. By 1785, when the *Tour* appeared, they had grown further apart, and Monboddo was understandably offended by some of the references to himself in the text. In January 1786 Monboddo cut Boswell at a meeting of the curators of the Advocates' Library. It must be said that Boswell's response was characteristic. He notes in his journal: 'I did not care. I considered that it would make him *fair game* in Dr Johnson's life.'

To the end of his life Monboddo continued to snipe at Johnson. The fifth volume *Of the Origin and Progress of Language* rebukes Johnson for his treatment of Milton in the *Lives of the Poets*, developing comments in a letter to Sir George Baker in 1782, where he goes on to deplore the absence of 'a proper subject' in *Paradise Lost*, almost the last thing that Johnson holds against the poem. Finally, in this connection, it is worth noting the unpublished draft of an essay 'On the Degeneracy of Man in a State of Society'. This almost Rousseauesque treatise on the harmful effects of commerce on society, the degeneracy induced by luxury, and even the depopulation caused by trade, would have trodden on many of Johnson's most sensitive spots. It is perhaps fortunate that it did not come to his notice.

In a brief appendix it is impossible to consider all the ways in which Monboddo's life and ideas intersected with matters raised during the Hebridean venture. We might cursorily note that Monboddo entertained the Abyssinian traveller Bruce, though Bruce had turned down an invitation from Boswell to meet the great theorist of wild places. Not surprisingly, Monboddo came to know Sir Joseph Banks and corresponded with him. He even entered the circle of Fanny Burney and met some of the Bluestockings—according to one story, he proposed in turn to Hannah More and Eva Maria Garrick, the actor's widow. He must have seemed almost as exotic as Omai to some of the assembled ladies. More significantly, his published work continued to outline a view of the natural history of mankind which, however individual and crochety, represented a powerful current of Enlightenment thought in general, especially in its quest for origins, its search for aboriginal purity, its condemnation of 'luxury', and its desire for a universal key to social behaviour. In this sense, Monboddo's books are genuine Enlightenment texts. Johnson and Boswell set out to test the new heresies, and Monboddo could not have been very surprised when they returned from the Highlands and Islands with negative findings—Ossian was a fraud, there were no tailed inhabitants, and civilization was a blessing to be greeted with relief.

Select Bibliography

This list is confined to the primary editions used, and to the most immediately relevant secondary materials drawn on.

EDITIONS

Johnson's Journey to the Western Islands of Scotland and Boswell's Tour to the Hebrides, ed. R. W. Chapman (London: Oxford University Press, 1924).
James Boswell, *The Life of Samuel Johnson, LL D*, ed. G. B. Hill and L. F. Powell, 6 vols. (Oxford: Clarendon Press, 1934–64); vol. v contains Boswell's *Journal of a Tour to the Hebrides*.
—— *A Journal of a Tour to the Hebrides*, ed. F. A. Pottle and C. H. Bennett (London: Heinemann, 1961).
A Journey to the Western Islands of Scotland, ed. Mary Lascelles (Yale edn. of *The Works of Samuel Johnson*, ix; New Haven, Conn.: Yale University Press, 1971).
A Journey to the Western Islands of Scotland, ed. J. D. Fleeman (Oxford: Clarendon Press, 1985).

JOHNSON AND BOSWELL

The Letters of Samuel Johnson, ed. R. W. Chapman, 3 vols. (Oxford: Clarendon Press, 1952).
The Letters of Samuel Johnson, ed. B. Redford, in progress (Princeton, NJ: Princeton University Press, 1992–). Chapman's ed. is cited in the text, since Redford's is incomplete and does not contain Mrs Thrale's letters; but I have checked the text against Redford as a safeguard.
Johnsonian Miscellanies, ed. G. B. Hill, 2 vols. (Oxford: Clarendon Press, 1897).

The Yale Edition of the Private Papers of James Boswell

Boswell's London Journal, 1762–1763, ed. F. A. Pottle (London: Heinemann, 1950).
Boswell in Holland, 1763–1764, ed. F. A. Pottle (London: Heinemann, 1952).

Boswell on the Grand Tour: Germany and Switzerland, 1764, ed. F. A. Pottle (London: Heinemann, 1953).

Boswell on the Grand Tour: Italy, Corsica and France, 1765–1766, ed. F. Brady and F. A. Pottle (London: Heinemann, 1956).

Boswell in Search of a Wife, 1766–1769, ed. F. Brady and F. A. Pottle (London: Heinemann, 1957).

Boswell for the Defence, 1769–1774, ed. W. K. Wimsatt, jun., and F. A. Pottle (London: Heinemann, 1960).

Boswell: The Ominous Years, 1774–1776, ed. C. Ryskamp and F. A. Pottle (London: Heinemann, 1963).

Boswell in Extremes, 1776–1778, ed. C. M. Weiss and F. A. Pottle (London: Heinemann, 1970).

Boswell: The English Experiment, 1785–1789, ed. I. Lustig and F. A. Pottle (London: Heinemann, 1986).

Boswell: The Great Biographer 1789–95, ed. M. K. Danziger and F. Brady (London: Heinemann, 1989).

Boswell's Correspondence with Hon. Andrew Erskine and his Journal of a Tour to Corsica, ed. G. B. Hill (London: De La Rue, 1879).

SECONDARY MATERIALS

Brady, F., *James Boswell: The Later Years, 1769–1795* (London: Heinemann, 1984).

Curley, T. M., *Samuel Johnson and the Age of Travel* (Athens, Ga.: University of Georgia Press, 1976).

Hyde, M., *The Impossible Friendship: Boswell and Mrs Thrale* (London: Chatto and Windus, 1973).

Nath, P. (ed.), *Fresh Reflections on Samuel Johnson: Essays in Criticism*, (Troy, NY: Whitston, 1987).

Pottle, F. A., *James Boswell: The Earlier Years, 1740-1769* (London: Heinemann, 1966).

BACKGROUND

Langford, P., *A Polite and Commercial People: England, 1727–1783* (Oxford: Clarendon Press, 1989).

McCormick, E. H., *Omai: Pacific Envoy* (Auckland: Auckland University Press, 1977).

Piozzi, Hester Lynch, *Thraliana*, ed. K. C. Balderston, 2nd edn., 2 vols. (Oxford: Clarendon Press, 1951).

TRAVEL AND TOURISM

Black, J., *The British and the Grand Tour* (London: Croom Helm, 1985).
Hibbert, C., *The Grand Tour* (London: Thames Methuen, 1985).
Mead, W. E., *The Grand Tour* (1914; repr. New York: Benjamin Blom, 1972).
Baretti, Joseph, *A Journey from London to Genoa* (Fontwell, Sussex: Centaur Press, 1970).
Goethe, J. W. von, *Italian Journey*, trans. W. H. Auden and E. Mayer (n.p.: Pantheon Books, 1962).
Piozzi, Hester Lynch, *Observations and Reflections Made in the Course of a Journey through France, Italy, and Germany*, ed. H. Barrows (Ann Arbor, Mich.: University of Michigan Press, 1967).

THE SCOTTISH ENLIGHTENMENT

Bryson, G., *Man and Society: The Scottish Inquiry of the Eighteenth Century* (1945; repr. New York: Kelley, 1968).
McElroy, D. D., *Scotland's Age of Improvement* (n.p.: Washington State University Press, 1969).
Phillipson, N. T., and Mitchison, R. (eds.), *Scotland in the Age of Improvement* (Edinburgh: Edinburgh University Press, 1970).
Sher, R. B., *Church and University in the Scottish Enlightenment: The Moderate Literati of Edinburgh* (Princeton, NJ: Princeton University Press, 1985).

JACOBITISM

Lenman, B., *The Jacobite Risings in Britain, 1689–1746* (London: Eyre Methuen, 1980).
Linklater, E., *The Prince in the Heather* (New York: Harcourt Brace, 1965).
McLynn, F., *Charles Edward Stuart: A Tragedy in Many Acts* (Oxford: Oxford University Press, 1991).
Youngson, A. J., *The Prince and the Pretender: A Study in the Writing of History* (London: Croom Helm, 1985).

NATIONALISM

Colley, L., *Britons: Forging the Nation, 1707–1837* (New Haven, Conn.: Yale University Press, 1992).

Crawford, R., *Devolving English Literature* (Oxford: Clarendon Press, 1992).

Newman, G., *The Rise of English Nationalism* (New York: St Martin's Press, 1987).

STUDIES OF INDIVIDUALS

Beaglehole, J. C., *The Life of Captain James Cook* (Stanford, Calif.: Stanford University Press, 1974).

Carter, H. B., *Sir Joseph Banks, 1743–1820* (London: British Museum (Natural History), 1988).

Clifford, J. L., *Hester Lynch Piozzi (Mrs Thrale)* (Oxford: Clarendon Press, 1971).

Cloyd, E. L., *James Burnett, Lord Monboddo* (Oxford: Clarendon Press, 1972).

Connell, B., *Portrait of a Whig Peer* (London: André Deutsch, 1957).

Ross, I., *Lord Kames and the Scotland of his Day* (Oxford: Clarendon Press, 1972).

Index

Club refers to members of the Literary Club or 'Johnson's Club', with the date of election. SJ = Johnson, JB = Boswell.